FIST STICK KNIFE GUN

A PERSONAL HISTORY OF VIOLENCE

G OFFREY CANADA

ADAPTED BY
JA AR NICHOLAS

BEACON PRESS, BOSTON

BEACON PRESS
25 BEACON STREET
BOSTON, MASSACHUSETTS 02108-2892
WWW.BEACON.ORG

BEACON PRESS BOOKS
ARE PUBLISHED UNDER THE AUSPICES OF
THE UNITARIAN UNIVERSALIST ASSOCIATION OF CONGREGATIONS.

LIBRARY OF CONGRESS CONTROL NUMBER: 2010908396

PRINTED IN THE UNITED STATES OF AMERICA

13 12 11 10 8 7 6 5 4 3 2 1

THIS BOOK IS PRINTED ON ACID-FREE PAPER THAT MEETS THE UNCOATED PAPER
ANSI/NISO SPECIFICATIONS FOR PERMANENCE AS REVISED IN 1992.

SOME OF THE NAMES IN THIS BOOK HAVE BEEN CHANGED.

ISBN 978-0-8070-4449-0 (PAPERBACK : ALK. PAPER)

THIS BOOK IS DEDICATED TO THE YOUNG PEOPLE OF THE HARLEM CHILDREN'S ZONE.

TABLE OF CONTENTS

1

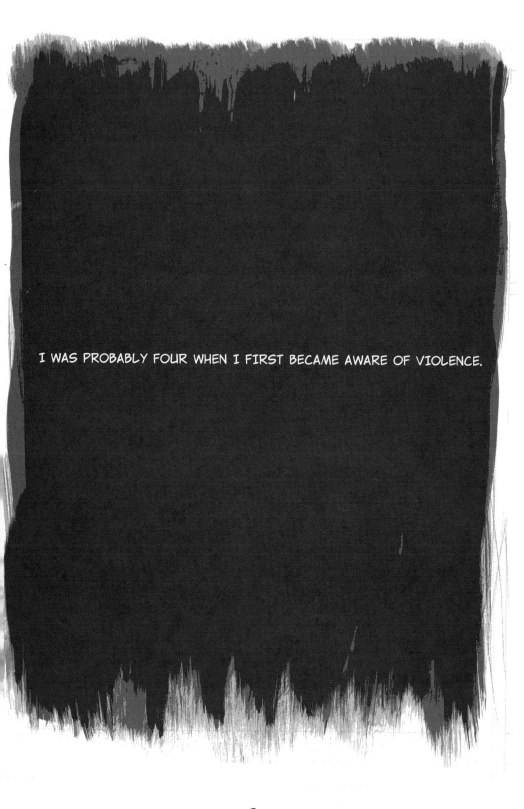

I WAS PROBABLY FOUR WHEN I FIRST BECAME AWARE OF VIOLENCE.

WE WERE LIVING IN THE BRONX ON CAULDWELL AVENUE.

MY MOTHER, MY THREE BROTHERS, AND I IN A SMALL APARTMENT.

MY FATHER LIVED THERE FOR SOME SMALL PORTION OF THAT EARLY PART OF MY LIFE BUT HE WAS NOT A STRONG PRESENCE IN OUR FAMILY.

MY MOTHER AND HE WERE ALREADY BREAKING UP.

HIS DRINKING WAS BECOMING INTOLERABLE, HIS FINANCIAL SUPPORT SPORADIC AT BEST, AS HE SEEMED INCAPABLE OF KEEPING A JOB.

THE IMAGES FROM THIS PART OF MY LIFE ARE CLOUDY TODAY, AND MEMORIES OF MY FATHER ARE NEUTRAL.

HE WAS NOT A BAD MAN; HE TREATED US WELL.

HE WAS JUST NOT MUCH OF A FATHER.

EVEN AS A VERY YOUNG CHILD I KNEW OUR SURVIVAL DEPENDED ON MY MOTHER.

THIS DIDN'T BOTHER ME AT THE TIME.

LATER THE FRAGILITY OF OUR ABILITY TO SURVIVE WOULD HAVE A PROFOUND IMPACT ON MY BROTHERS AND ME, BUT I WAS FOUR AND THE WORLD SEEMED FINE.

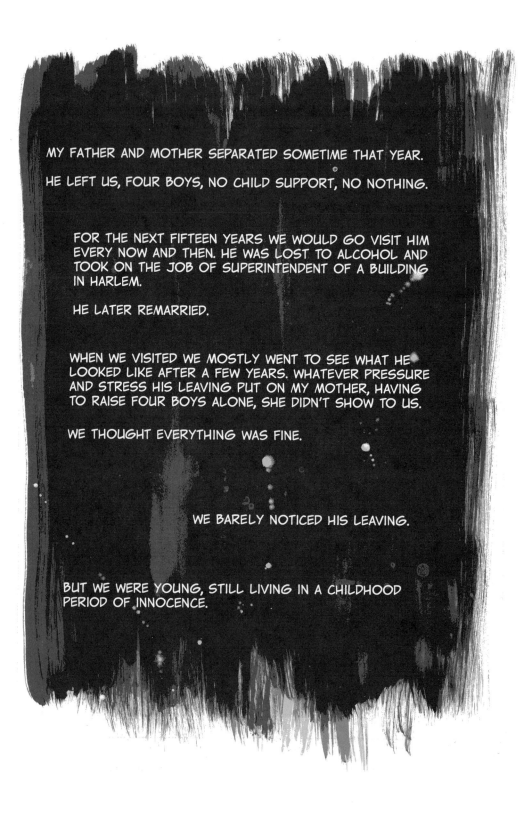

MY FATHER AND MOTHER SEPARATED SOMETIME THAT YEAR.

HE LEFT US, FOUR BOYS, NO CHILD SUPPORT, NO NOTHING.

FOR THE NEXT FIFTEEN YEARS WE WOULD GO VISIT HIM EVERY NOW AND THEN. HE WAS LOST TO ALCOHOL AND TOOK ON THE JOB OF SUPERINTENDENT OF A BUILDING IN HARLEM.

HE LATER REMARRIED.

WHEN WE VISITED WE MOSTLY WENT TO SEE WHAT HE LOOKED LIKE AFTER A FEW YEARS. WHATEVER PRESSURE AND STRESS HIS LEAVING PUT ON MY MOTHER, HAVING TO RAISE FOUR BOYS ALONE, SHE DIDN'T SHOW TO US.

WE THOUGHT EVERYTHING WAS FINE.

WE BARELY NOTICED HIS LEAVING.

BUT WE WERE YOUNG, STILL LIVING IN A CHILDHOOD PERIOD OF INNOCENCE.

4

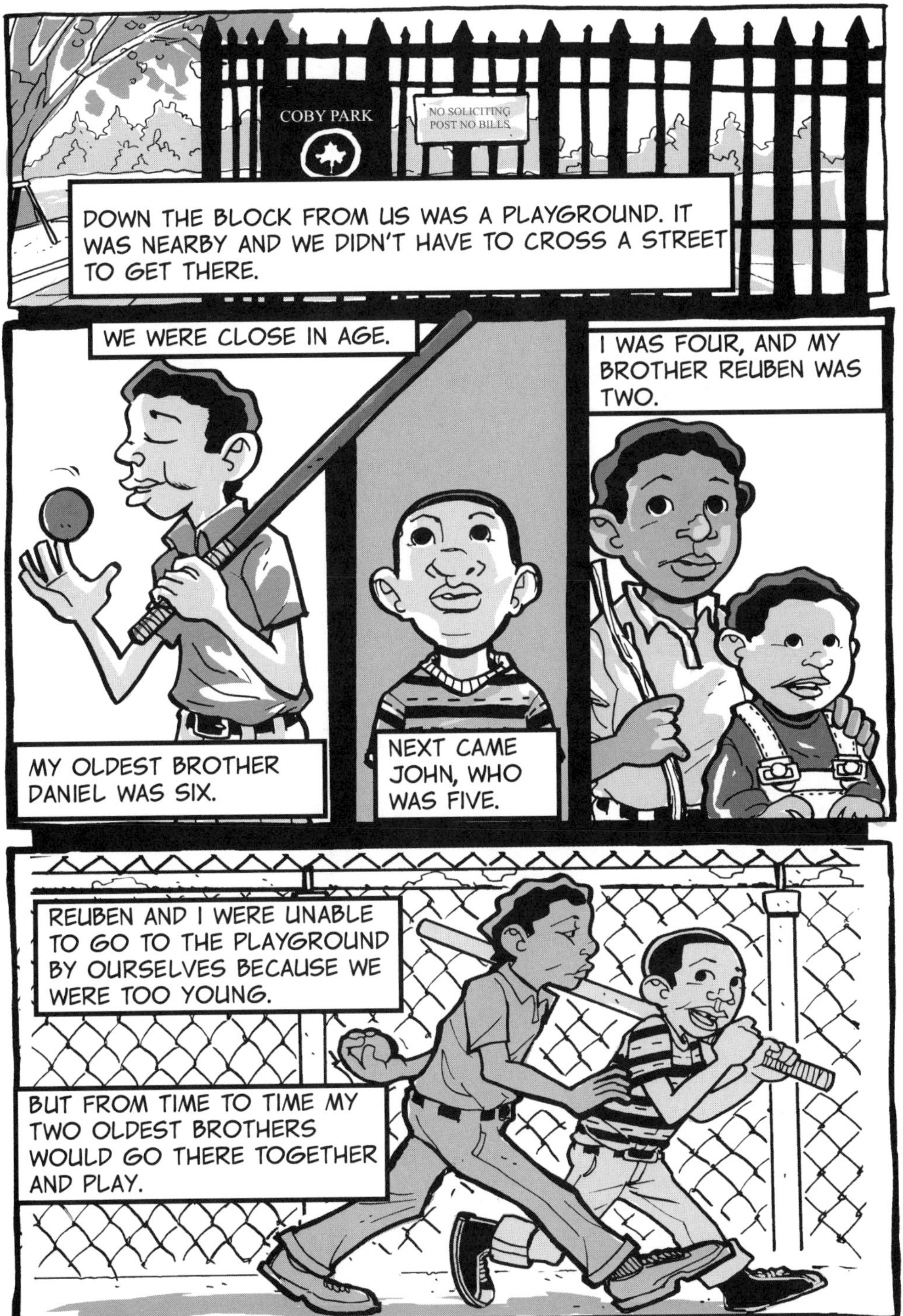
COBY PARK
NO SOLICITING POST NO BILLS
DOWN THE BLOCK FROM US WAS A PLAYGROUND. IT WAS NEARBY AND WE DIDN'T HAVE TO CROSS A STREET TO GET THERE.
WE WERE CLOSE IN AGE.
MY OLDEST BROTHER DANIEL WAS SIX.
NEXT CAME JOHN, WHO WAS FIVE.
I WAS FOUR, AND MY BROTHER REUBEN WAS TWO.
REUBEN AND I WERE UNABLE TO GO TO THE PLAYGROUND BY OURSELVES BECAUSE WE WERE TOO YOUNG.
BUT FROM TIME TO TIME MY TWO OLDEST BROTHERS WOULD GO THERE TOGETHER AND PLAY.

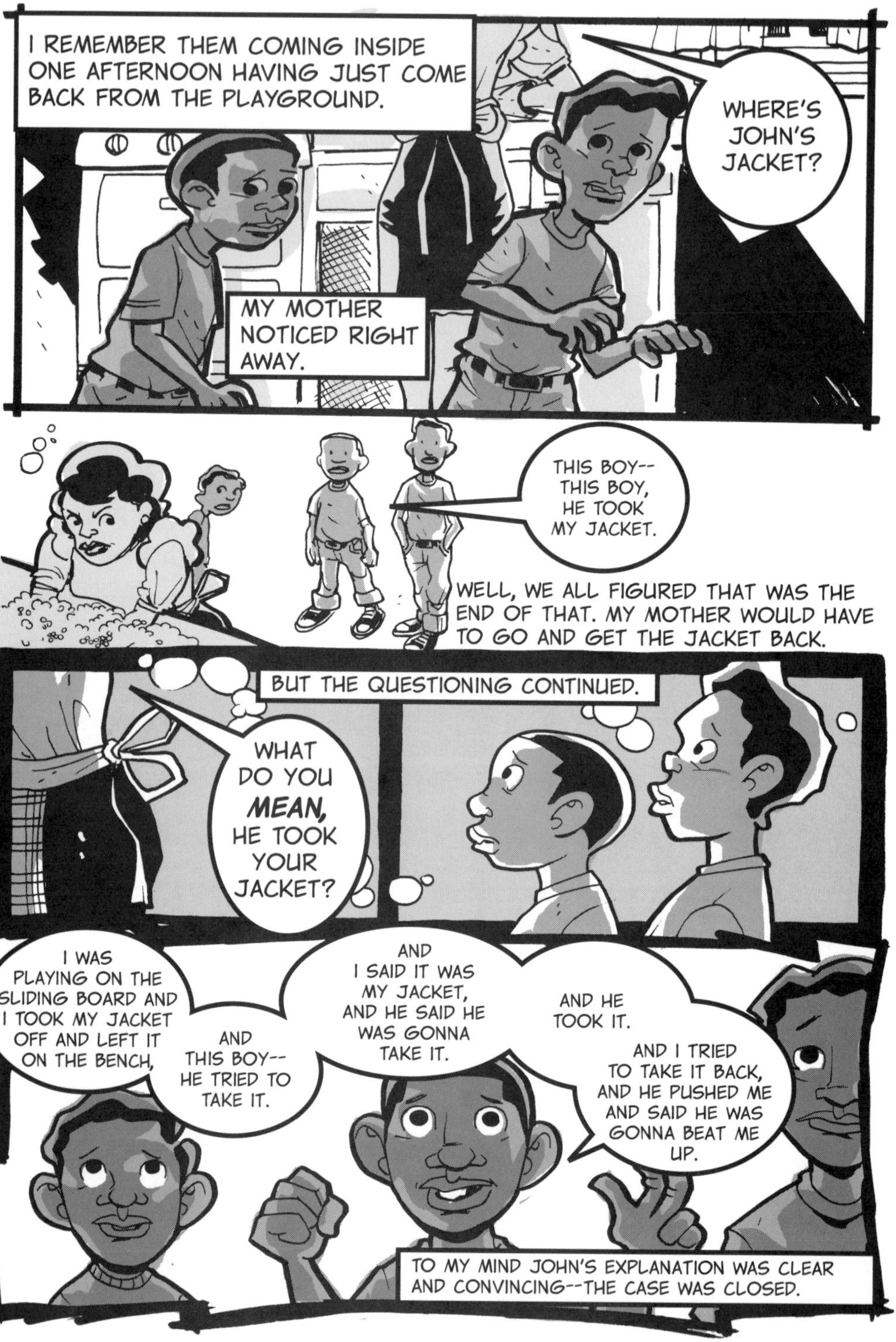
I REMEMBER THEM COMING INSIDE ONE AFTERNOON HAVING JUST COME BACK FROM THE PLAYGROUND.
WHERE'S JOHN'S JACKET?
MY MOTHER NOTICED RIGHT AWAY.
THIS BOY-- THIS BOY, HE TOOK MY JACKET.
WELL, WE ALL FIGURED THAT WAS THE END OF THAT. MY MOTHER WOULD HAVE TO GO AND GET THE JACKET BACK.
BUT THE QUESTIONING CONTINUED.
WHAT DO YOU ***MEAN,*** HE TOOK YOUR JACKET?
I WAS PLAYING ON THE SLIDING BOARD AND I TOOK MY JACKET OFF AND LEFT IT ON THE BENCH,
AND THIS BOY-- HE TRIED TO TAKE IT.
AND I SAID IT WAS MY JACKET, AND HE SAID HE WAS GONNA TAKE IT.
AND HE TOOK IT.
AND I TRIED TO TAKE IT BACK, AND HE PUSHED ME AND SAID HE WAS GONNA BEAT ME UP.
TO MY MIND JOHN'S EXPLANATION WAS CLEAR AND CONVINCING--THE CASE WAS CLOSED.

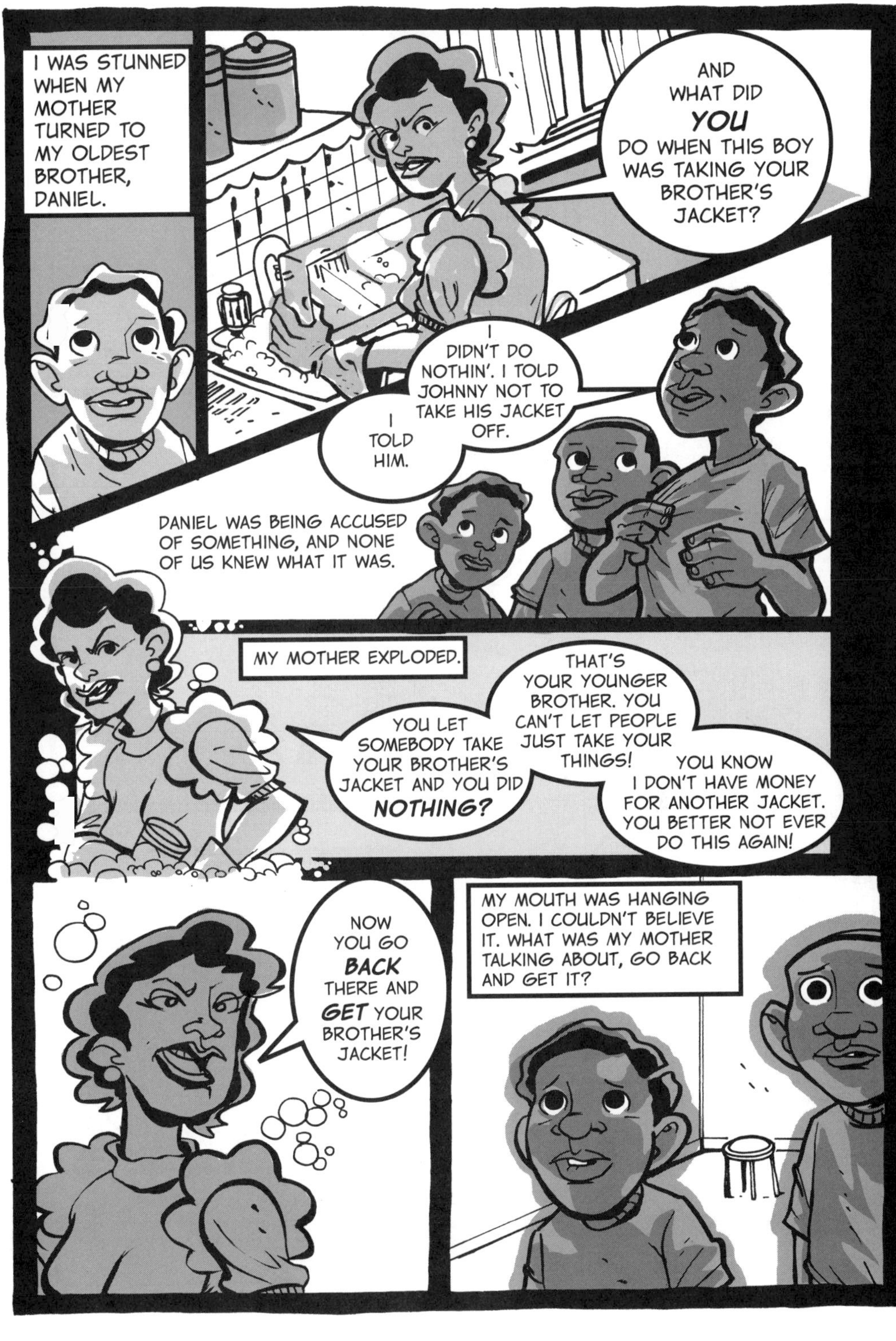
I WAS STUNNED WHEN MY MOTHER TURNED TO MY OLDEST BROTHER, DANIEL.
AND WHAT DID *YOU* DO WHEN THIS BOY WAS TAKING YOUR BROTHER'S JACKET?
I DIDN'T DO NOTHIN'. I TOLD JOHNNY NOT TO TAKE HIS JACKET OFF.
I TOLD HIM.
DANIEL WAS BEING ACCUSED OF SOMETHING, AND NONE OF US KNEW WHAT IT WAS.
MY MOTHER EXPLODED.
YOU LET SOMEBODY TAKE YOUR BROTHER'S JACKET AND YOU DID *NOTHING?*
THAT'S YOUR YOUNGER BROTHER. YOU CAN'T LET PEOPLE JUST TAKE YOUR THINGS!
YOU KNOW I DON'T HAVE MONEY FOR ANOTHER JACKET. YOU BETTER NOT EVER DO THIS AGAIN!
NOW YOU GO *BACK* THERE AND *GET* YOUR BROTHER'S JACKET!
MY MOUTH WAS HANGING OPEN. I COULDN'T BELIEVE IT. WHAT WAS MY MOTHER TALKING ABOUT, GO BACK AND GET IT?

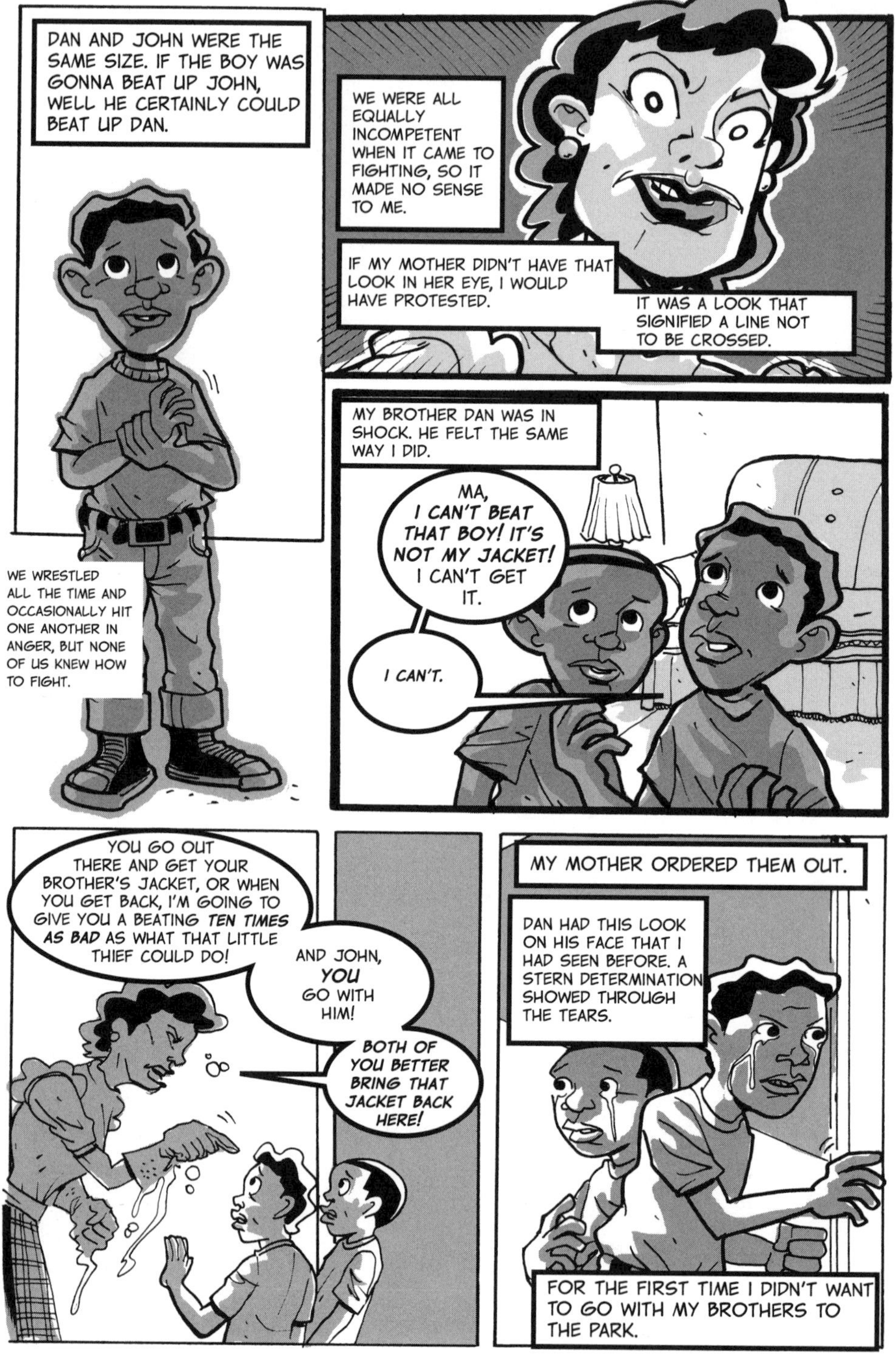
DAN AND JOHN WERE THE SAME SIZE. IF THE BOY WAS GONNA BEAT UP JOHN, WELL HE CERTAINLY COULD BEAT UP DAN.
WE WRESTLED ALL THE TIME AND OCCASIONALLY HIT ONE ANOTHER IN ANGER, BUT NONE OF US KNEW HOW TO FIGHT.
WE WERE ALL EQUALLY INCOMPETENT WHEN IT CAME TO FIGHTING, SO IT MADE NO SENSE TO ME.
IF MY MOTHER DIDN'T HAVE THAT LOOK IN HER EYE, I WOULD HAVE PROTESTED.
IT WAS A LOOK THAT SIGNIFIED A LINE NOT TO BE CROSSED.
MY BROTHER DAN WAS IN SHOCK. HE FELT THE SAME WAY I DID.
MA, *I CAN'T BEAT THAT BOY! IT'S NOT MY JACKET!* I CAN'T GET IT.
I CAN'T.
YOU GO OUT THERE AND GET YOUR BROTHER'S JACKET, OR WHEN YOU GET BACK, I'M GOING TO GIVE YOU A BEATING *TEN TIMES AS BAD* AS WHAT THAT LITTLE THIEF COULD DO!
AND JOHN, *YOU* GO WITH HIM!
BOTH OF YOU BETTER BRING THAT JACKET BACK HERE!
MY MOTHER ORDERED THEM OUT.
DAN HAD THIS LOOK ON HIS FACE THAT I HAD SEEN BEFORE. A STERN DETERMINATION SHOWED THROUGH THE TEARS.
FOR THE FIRST TIME I DIDN'T WANT TO GO WITH MY BROTHERS TO THE PARK.

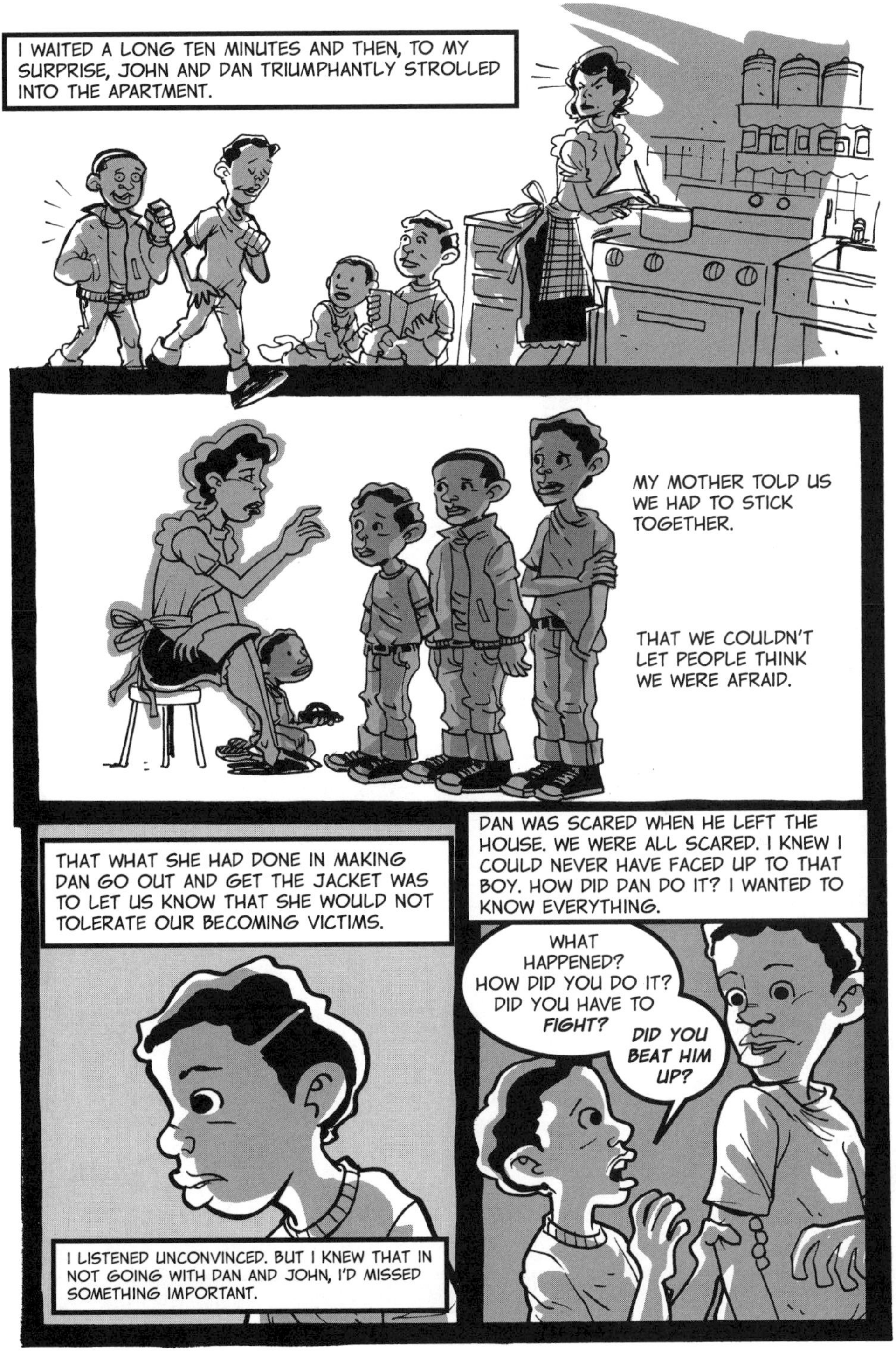
I WAITED A LONG TEN MINUTES AND THEN, TO MY SURPRISE, JOHN AND DAN TRIUMPHANTLY STROLLED INTO THE APARTMENT.
MY MOTHER TOLD US WE HAD TO STICK TOGETHER.
THAT WE COULDN'T LET PEOPLE THINK WE WERE AFRAID.
THAT WHAT SHE HAD DONE IN MAKING DAN GO OUT AND GET THE JACKET WAS TO LET US KNOW THAT SHE WOULD NOT TOLERATE OUR BECOMING VICTIMS.
I LISTENED UNCONVINCED. BUT I KNEW THAT IN NOT GOING WITH DAN AND JOHN, I'D MISSED SOMETHING IMPORTANT.
DAN WAS SCARED WHEN HE LEFT THE HOUSE. WE WERE ALL SCARED. I KNEW I COULD NEVER HAVE FACED UP TO THAT BOY. HOW DID DAN DO IT? I WANTED TO KNOW EVERYTHING.
WHAT HAPPENED? HOW DID YOU DO IT? DID YOU HAVE TO *FIGHT?*
DID YOU BEAT HIM UP?

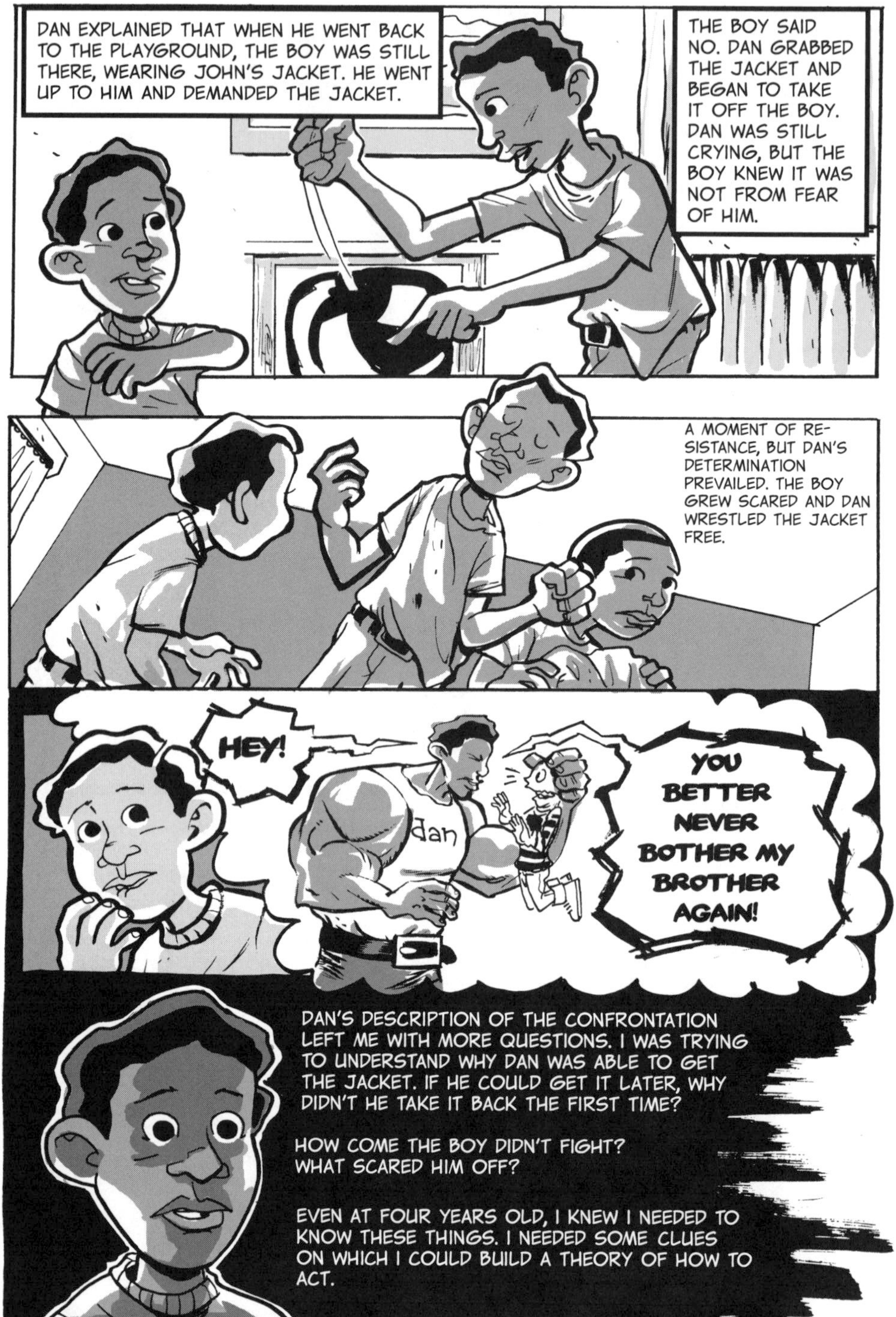
DAN EXPLAINED THAT WHEN HE WENT BACK TO THE PLAYGROUND, THE BOY WAS STILL THERE, WEARING JOHN'S JACKET. HE WENT UP TO HIM AND DEMANDED THE JACKET.
THE BOY SAID NO. DAN GRABBED THE JACKET AND BEGAN TO TAKE IT OFF THE BOY. DAN WAS STILL CRYING, BUT THE BOY KNEW IT WAS NOT FROM FEAR OF HIM.
A MOMENT OF RESISTANCE, BUT DAN'S DETERMINATION PREVAILED. THE BOY GREW SCARED AND DAN WRESTLED THE JACKET FREE.
HEY!
DAN
YOU BETTER NEVER BOTHER MY BROTHER AGAIN!
DAN'S DESCRIPTION OF THE CONFRONTATION LEFT ME WITH MORE QUESTIONS. I WAS TRYING TO UNDERSTAND WHY DAN WAS ABLE TO GET THE JACKET. IF HE COULD GET IT LATER, WHY DIDN'T HE TAKE IT BACK THE FIRST TIME?
HOW COME THE BOY DIDN'T FIGHT? WHAT SCARED HIM OFF?
EVEN AT FOUR YEARS OLD, I KNEW I NEEDED TO KNOW THESE THINGS. I NEEDED SOME CLUES ON WHICH I COULD BUILD A THEORY OF HOW TO ACT.

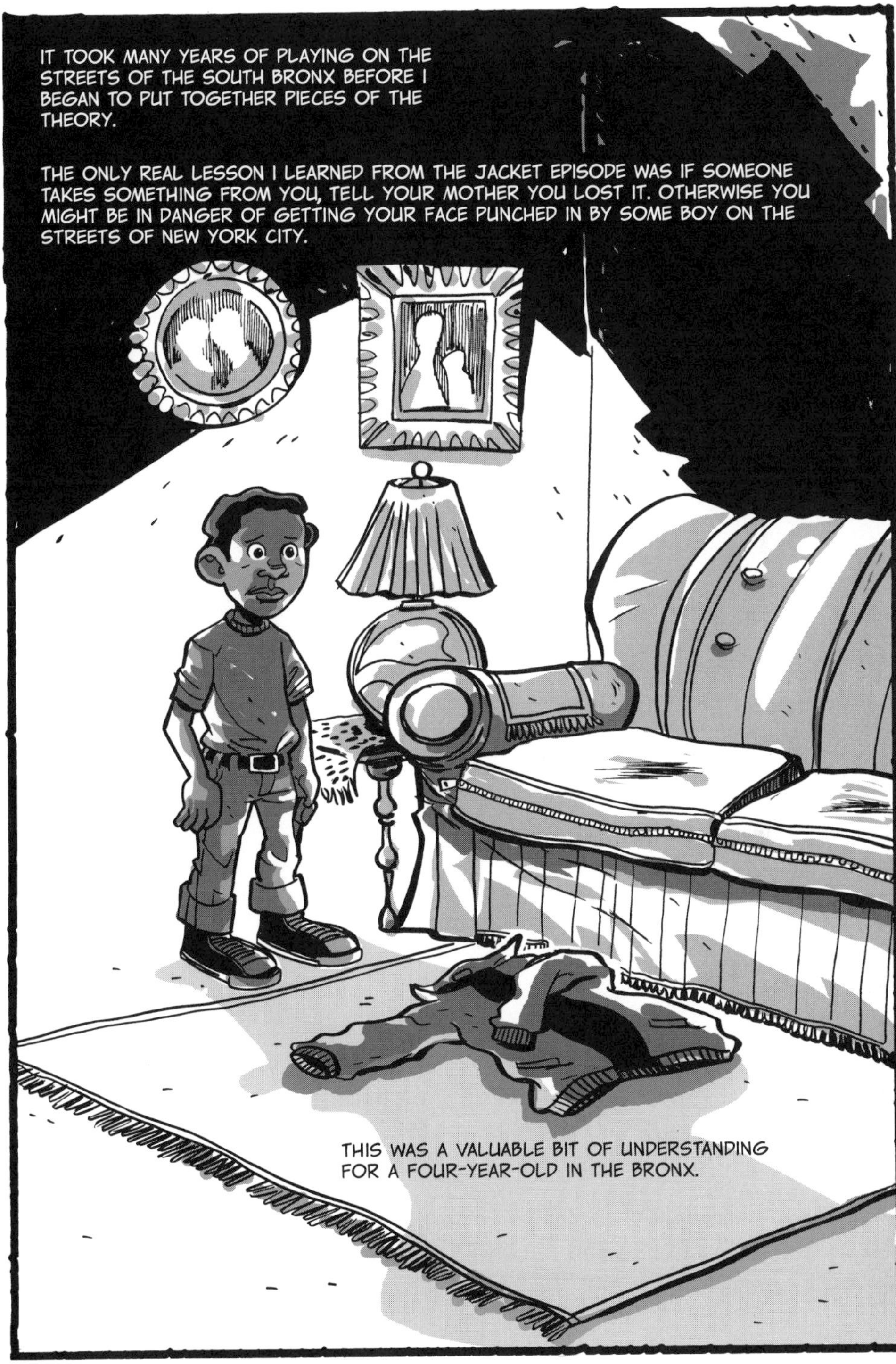
IT TOOK MANY YEARS OF PLAYING ON THE STREETS OF THE SOUTH BRONX BEFORE I BEGAN TO PUT TOGETHER PIECES OF THE THEORY.
THE ONLY REAL LESSON I LEARNED FROM THE JACKET EPISODE WAS IF SOMEONE TAKES SOMETHING FROM YOU, TELL YOUR MOTHER YOU LOST IT. OTHERWISE YOU MIGHT BE IN DANGER OF GETTING YOUR FACE PUNCHED IN BY SOME BOY ON THE STREETS OF NEW YORK CITY.
THIS WAS A VALUABLE BIT OF UNDERSTANDING FOR A FOUR-YEAR-OLD IN THE BRONX.

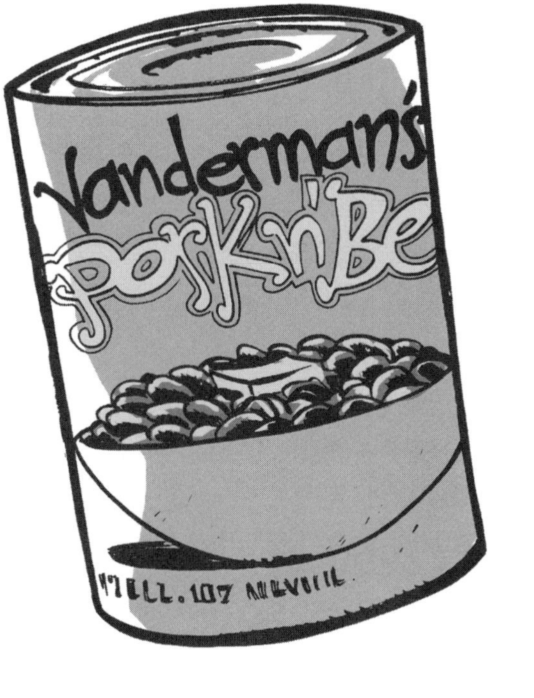
Vanderman's
Pork'n'Be

2

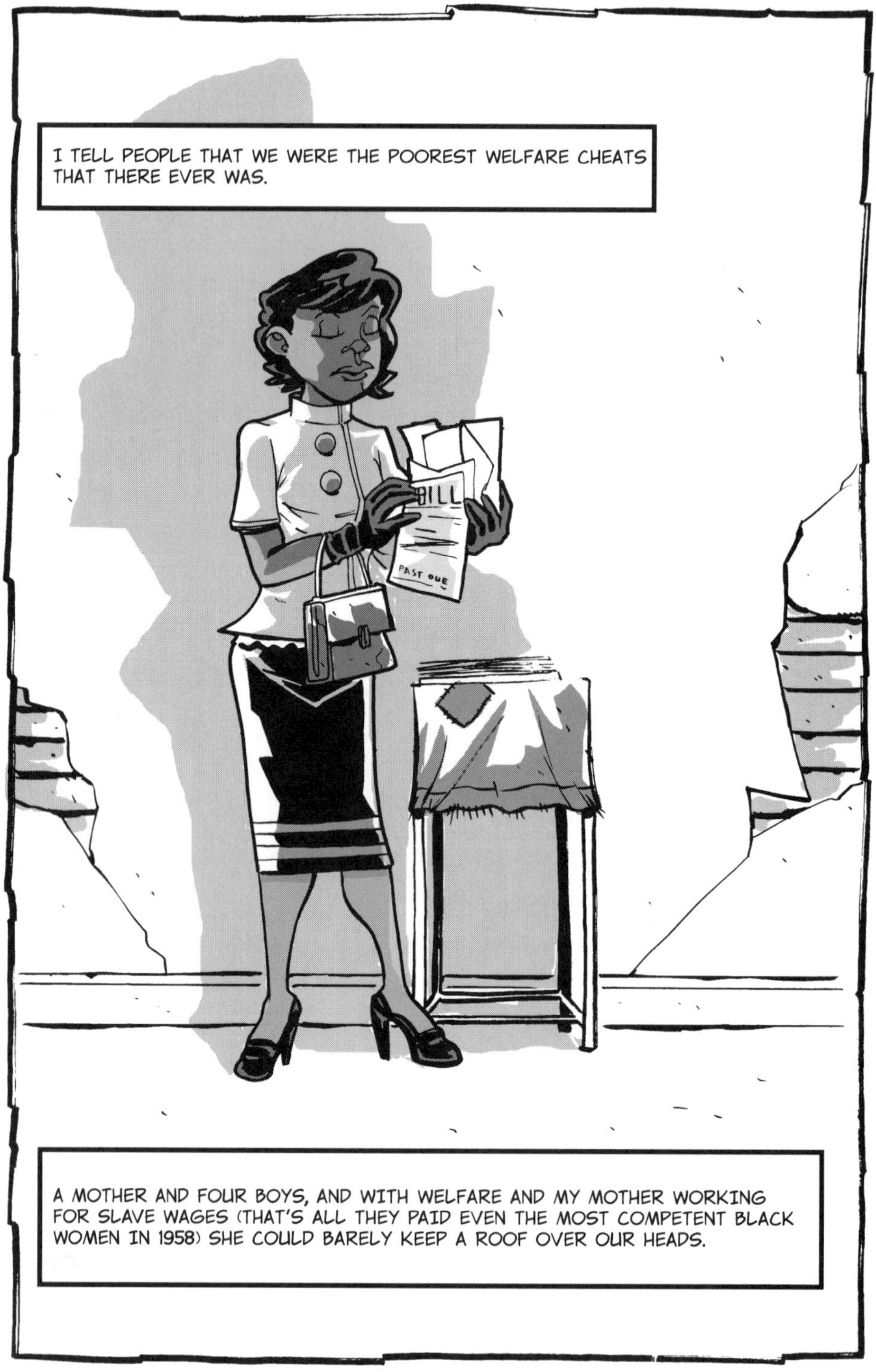
I TELL PEOPLE THAT WE WERE THE POOREST WELFARE CHEATS THAT THERE EVER WAS.
BILL
PAST DUE
A MOTHER AND FOUR BOYS, AND WITH WELFARE AND MY MOTHER WORKING FOR SLAVE WAGES (THAT'S ALL THEY PAID EVEN THE MOST COMPETENT BLACK WOMEN IN 1958) SHE COULD BARELY KEEP A ROOF OVER OUR HEADS.

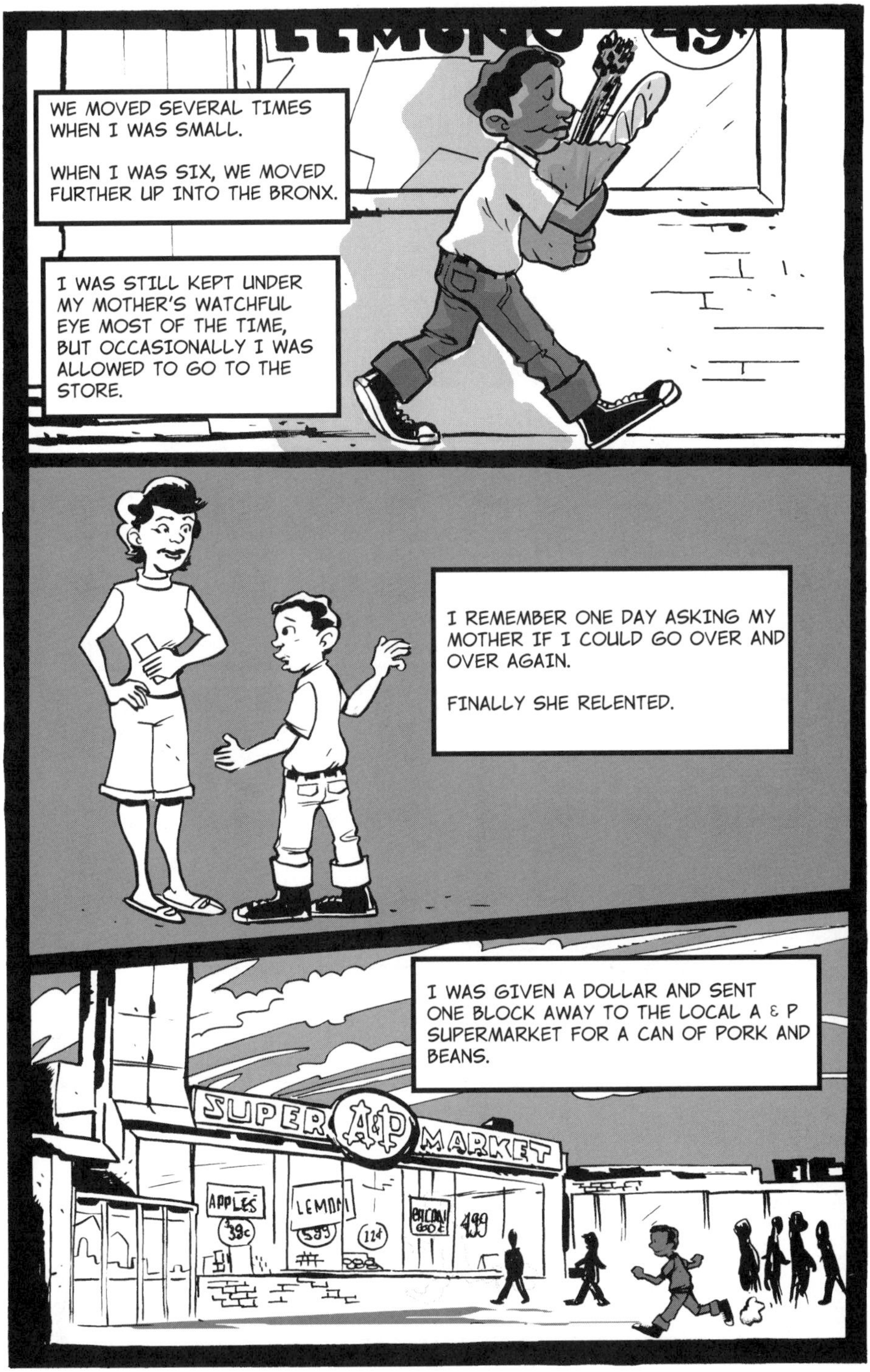
WE MOVED SEVERAL TIMES WHEN I WAS SMALL.
WHEN I WAS SIX, WE MOVED FURTHER UP INTO THE BRONX.
I WAS STILL KEPT UNDER MY MOTHER'S WATCHFUL EYE MOST OF THE TIME, BUT OCCASIONALLY I WAS ALLOWED TO GO TO THE STORE.
I REMEMBER ONE DAY ASKING MY MOTHER IF I COULD GO OVER AND OVER AGAIN.
FINALLY SHE RELENTED.
I WAS GIVEN A DOLLAR AND SENT ONE BLOCK AWAY TO THE LOCAL A & P SUPERMARKET FOR A CAN OF PORK AND BEANS.
SUPER A&P MARKET
APPLES
LEMON

HE WAS A RAGGEDY LITTLE BOY WITH A CIRCLE ON HIS HEAD WHERE NO HAIR GREW BECAUSE OF RINGWORM.

THE BOY WHO APPROACHED ME AS I PAID FOR MY PURCHASE WAS MAYBE EIGHT, AND SEEMED VERY INTERESTED IN BEING MY FRIEND.

HE ASKED IF WE COULD WALK BACK TO-GETHER. I WAS THRILLED. SINCE MOVING ONTO THIS BLOCK I HAD MET NO FRIENDS, AND NOW I COULDN'T BELIEVE MY GOOD FORTUNE.

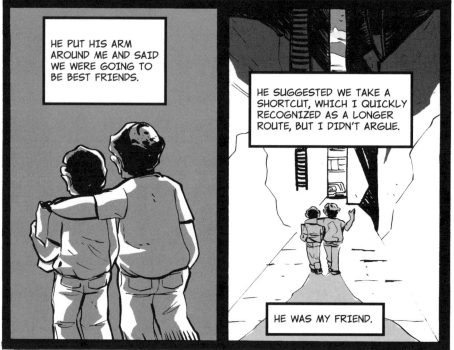

HE PUT HIS ARM AROUND ME AND SAID WE WERE GOING TO BE BEST FRIENDS.

HE SUGGESTED WE TAKE A SHORTCUT, WHICH I QUICKLY RECOGNIZED AS A LONGER ROUTE, BUT I DIDN'T ARGUE.

HE WAS MY FRIEND.

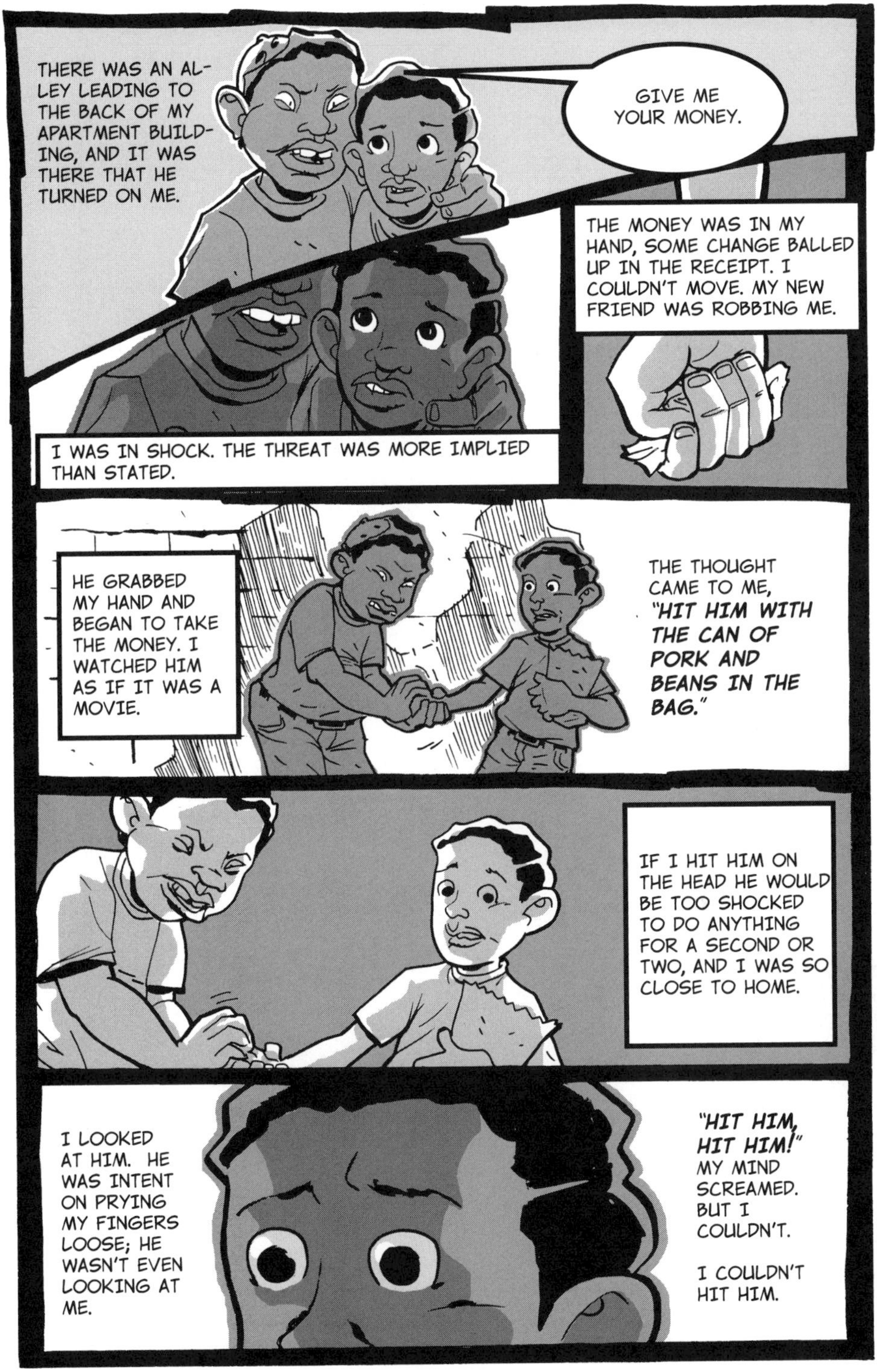
THERE WAS AN AL-LEY LEADING TO THE BACK OF MY APARTMENT BUILD-ING, AND IT WAS THERE THAT HE TURNED ON ME.
GIVE ME YOUR MONEY.
THE MONEY WAS IN MY HAND, SOME CHANGE BALLED UP IN THE RECEIPT. I COULDN'T MOVE. MY NEW FRIEND WAS ROBBING ME.
I WAS IN SHOCK. THE THREAT WAS MORE IMPLIED THAN STATED.
HE GRABBED MY HAND AND BEGAN TO TAKE THE MONEY. I WATCHED HIM AS IF IT WAS A MOVIE.
THE THOUGHT CAME TO ME, *"HIT HIM WITH THE CAN OF PORK AND BEANS IN THE BAG."*
IF I HIT HIM ON THE HEAD HE WOULD BE TOO SHOCKED TO DO ANYTHING FOR A SECOND OR TWO, AND I WAS SO CLOSE TO HOME.
I LOOKED AT HIM. HE WAS INTENT ON PRYING MY FINGERS LOOSE; HE WASN'T EVEN LOOKING AT ME.
"HIT HIM, HIT HIM!" MY MIND SCREAMED. BUT I COULDN'T.
I COULDN'T HIT HIM.

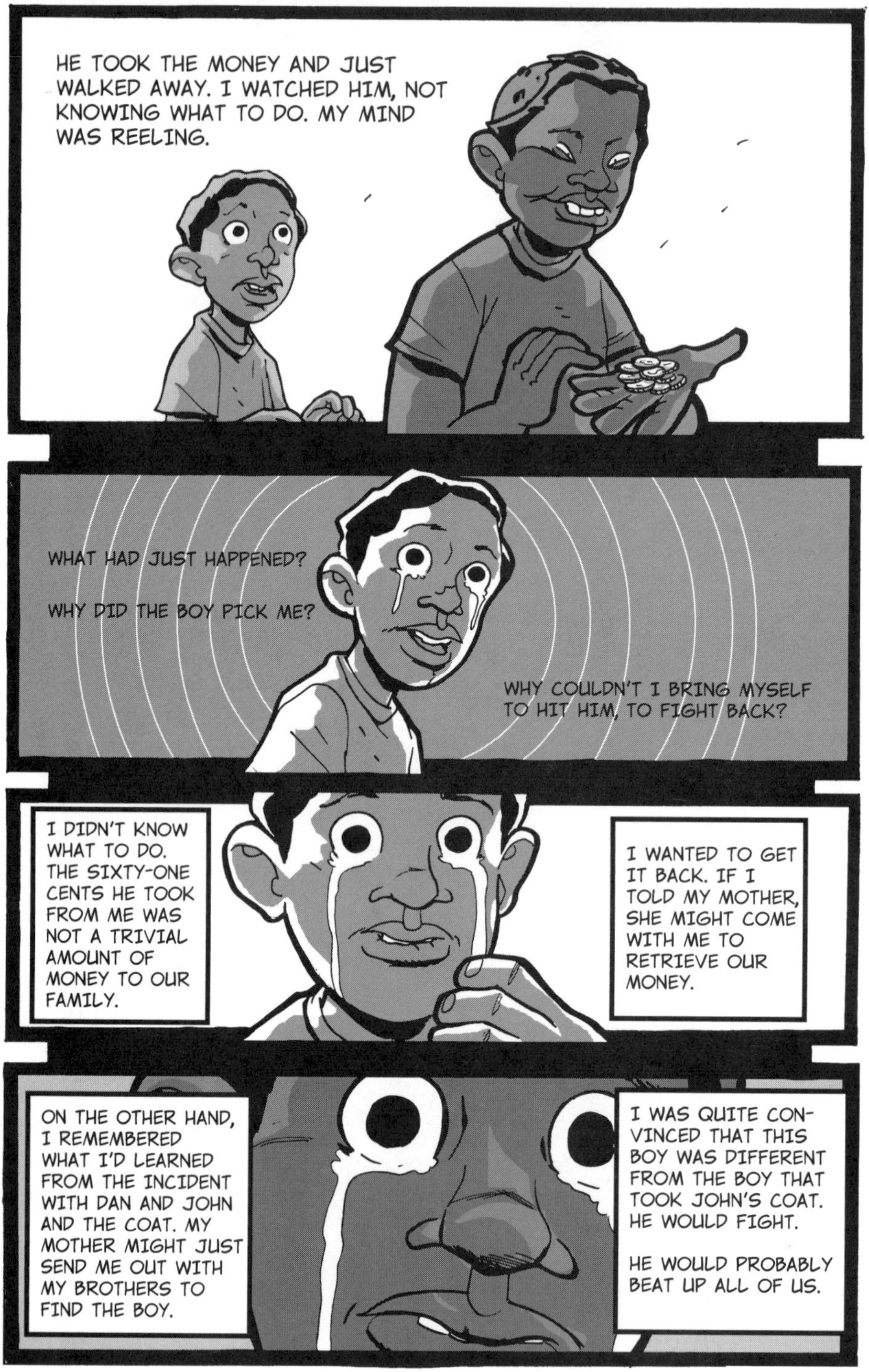
HE TOOK THE MONEY AND JUST WALKED AWAY. I WATCHED HIM, NOT KNOWING WHAT TO DO. MY MIND WAS REELING.
WHAT HAD JUST HAPPENED?
WHY DID THE BOY PICK ME?
WHY COULDN'T I BRING MYSELF TO HIT HIM, TO FIGHT BACK?
I DIDN'T KNOW WHAT TO DO. THE SIXTY-ONE CENTS HE TOOK FROM ME WAS NOT A TRIVIAL AMOUNT OF MONEY TO OUR FAMILY.
I WANTED TO GET IT BACK. IF I TOLD MY MOTHER, SHE MIGHT COME WITH ME TO RETRIEVE OUR MONEY.
ON THE OTHER HAND, I REMEMBERED WHAT I'D LEARNED FROM THE INCIDENT WITH DAN AND JOHN AND THE COAT. MY MOTHER MIGHT JUST SEND ME OUT WITH MY BROTHERS TO FIND THE BOY.
I WAS QUITE CONVINCED THAT THIS BOY WAS DIFFERENT FROM THE BOY THAT TOOK JOHN'S COAT. HE WOULD FIGHT.
HE WOULD PROBABLY BEAT UP ALL OF US.

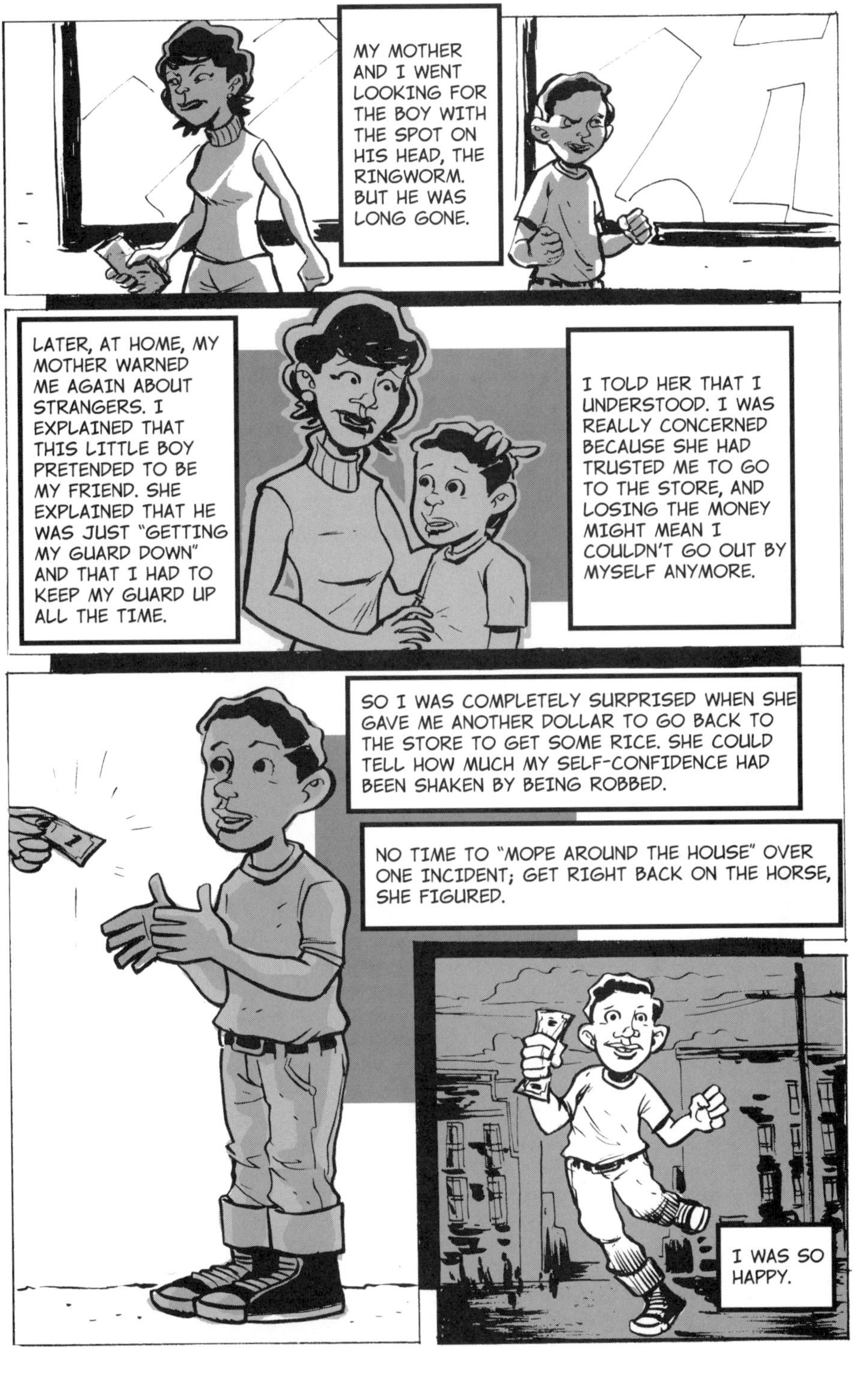
MY MOTHER AND I WENT LOOKING FOR THE BOY WITH THE SPOT ON HIS HEAD, THE RINGWORM. BUT HE WAS LONG GONE.
LATER, AT HOME, MY MOTHER WARNED ME AGAIN ABOUT STRANGERS. I EXPLAINED THAT THIS LITTLE BOY PRETENDED TO BE MY FRIEND. SHE EXPLAINED THAT HE WAS JUST "GETTING MY GUARD DOWN" AND THAT I HAD TO KEEP MY GUARD UP ALL THE TIME.
I TOLD HER THAT I UNDERSTOOD. I WAS REALLY CONCERNED BECAUSE SHE HAD TRUSTED ME TO GO TO THE STORE, AND LOSING THE MONEY MIGHT MEAN I COULDN'T GO OUT BY MYSELF ANYMORE.
SO I WAS COMPLETELY SURPRISED WHEN SHE GAVE ME ANOTHER DOLLAR TO GO BACK TO THE STORE TO GET SOME RICE. SHE COULD TELL HOW MUCH MY SELF-CONFIDENCE HAD BEEN SHAKEN BY BEING ROBBED.
NO TIME TO "MOPE AROUND THE HOUSE" OVER ONE INCIDENT; GET RIGHT BACK ON THE HORSE, SHE FIGURED.
I WAS SO HAPPY.

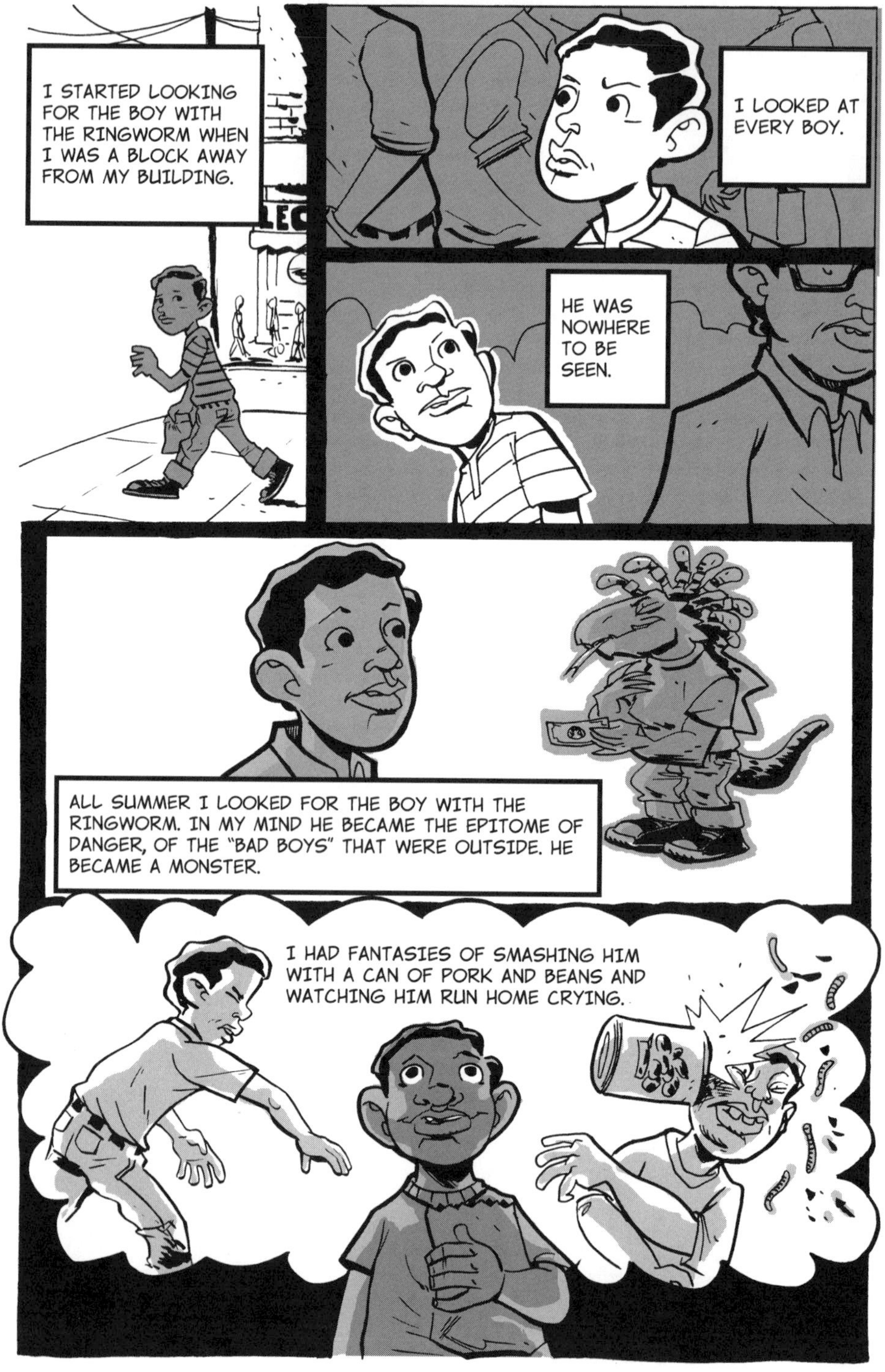

I STARTED LOOKING FOR THE BOY WITH THE RINGWORM WHEN I WAS A BLOCK AWAY FROM MY BUILDING.
I LOOKED AT EVERY BOY.
HE WAS NOWHERE TO BE SEEN.
ALL SUMMER I LOOKED FOR THE BOY WITH THE RINGWORM. IN MY MIND HE BECAME THE EPITOME OF DANGER, OF THE "BAD BOYS" THAT WERE OUTSIDE. HE BECAME A MONSTER.
I HAD FANTASIES OF SMASHING HIM WITH A CAN OF PORK AND BEANS AND WATCHING HIM RUN HOME CRYING.

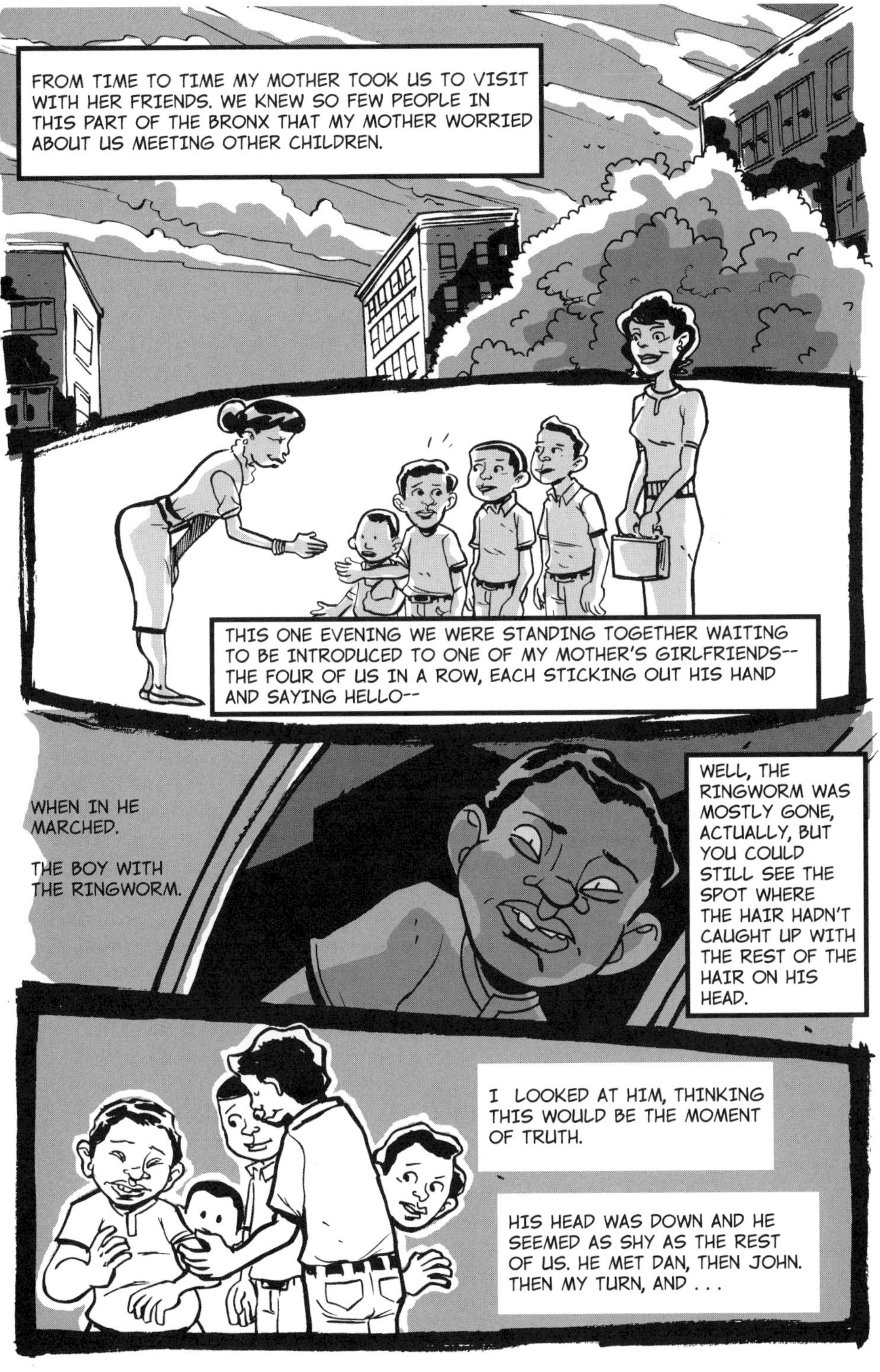
FROM TIME TO TIME MY MOTHER TOOK US TO VISIT WITH HER FRIENDS. WE KNEW SO FEW PEOPLE IN THIS PART OF THE BRONX THAT MY MOTHER WORRIED ABOUT US MEETING OTHER CHILDREN.
THIS ONE EVENING WE WERE STANDING TOGETHER WAITING TO BE INTRODUCED TO ONE OF MY MOTHER'S GIRLFRIENDS--THE FOUR OF US IN A ROW, EACH STICKING OUT HIS HAND AND SAYING HELLO--
WHEN IN HE MARCHED.
THE BOY WITH THE RINGWORM.
WELL, THE RINGWORM WAS MOSTLY GONE, ACTUALLY, BUT YOU COULD STILL SEE THE SPOT WHERE THE HAIR HADN'T CAUGHT UP WITH THE REST OF THE HAIR ON HIS HEAD.
I LOOKED AT HIM, THINKING THIS WOULD BE THE MOMENT OF TRUTH.
HIS HEAD WAS DOWN AND HE SEEMED AS SHY AS THE REST OF US. HE MET DAN, THEN JOHN. THEN MY TURN, AND . . .

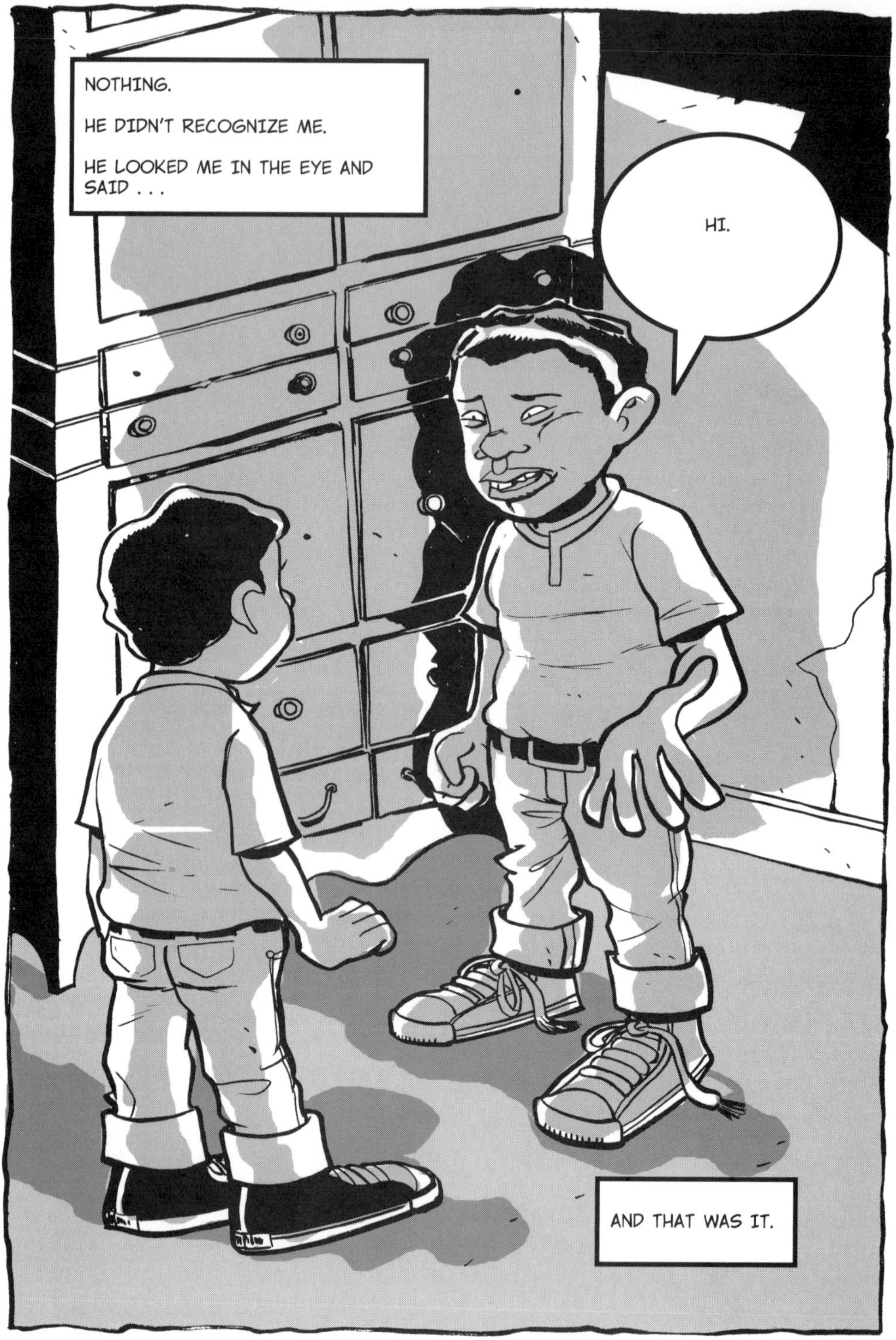
NOTHING.
HE DIDN'T RECOGNIZE ME.
HE LOOKED ME IN THE EYE AND SAID . . .
HI.
AND THAT WAS IT.

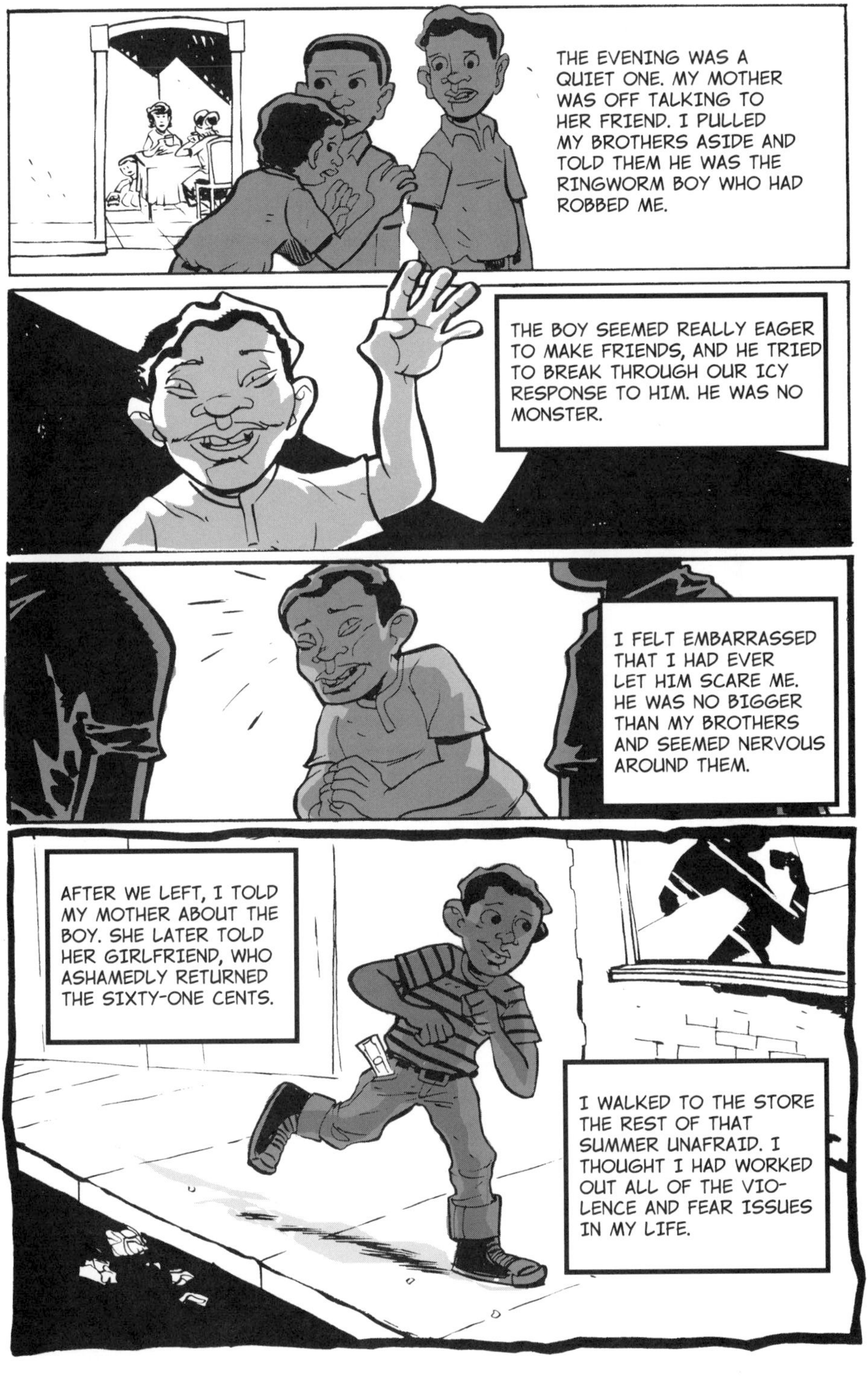
THE EVENING WAS A QUIET ONE. MY MOTHER WAS OFF TALKING TO HER FRIEND. I PULLED MY BROTHERS ASIDE AND TOLD THEM HE WAS THE RINGWORM BOY WHO HAD ROBBED ME.
THE BOY SEEMED REALLY EAGER TO MAKE FRIENDS, AND HE TRIED TO BREAK THROUGH OUR ICY RESPONSE TO HIM. HE WAS NO MONSTER.
I FELT EMBARRASSED THAT I HAD EVER LET HIM SCARE ME. HE WAS NO BIGGER THAN MY BROTHERS AND SEEMED NERVOUS AROUND THEM.
AFTER WE LEFT, I TOLD MY MOTHER ABOUT THE BOY. SHE LATER TOLD HER GIRLFRIEND, WHO ASHAMEDLY RETURNED THE SIXTY-ONE CENTS.
I WALKED TO THE STORE THE REST OF THAT SUMMER UNAFRAID. I THOUGHT I HAD WORKED OUT ALL OF THE VIOLENCE AND FEAR ISSUES IN MY LIFE.

3

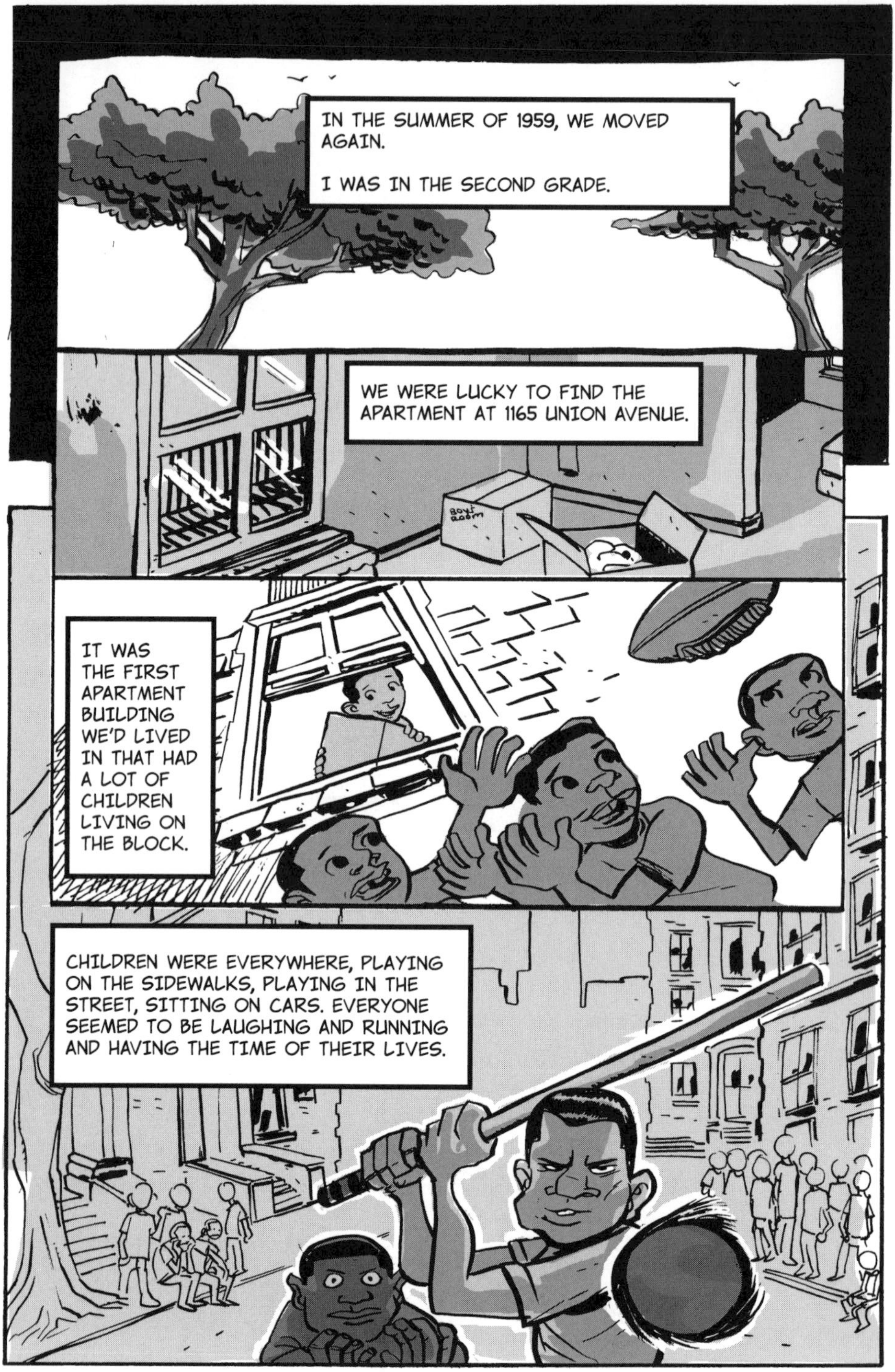
IN THE SUMMER OF 1959, WE MOVED AGAIN.
I WAS IN THE SECOND GRADE.
WE WERE LUCKY TO FIND THE APARTMENT AT 1165 UNION AVENUE.
IT WAS THE FIRST APARTMENT BUILDING WE'D LIVED IN THAT HAD A LOT OF CHILDREN LIVING ON THE BLOCK.
CHILDREN WERE EVERYWHERE, PLAYING ON THE SIDEWALKS, PLAYING IN THE STREET, SITTING ON CARS. EVERYONE SEEMED TO BE LAUGHING AND RUNNING AND HAVING THE TIME OF THEIR LIVES.

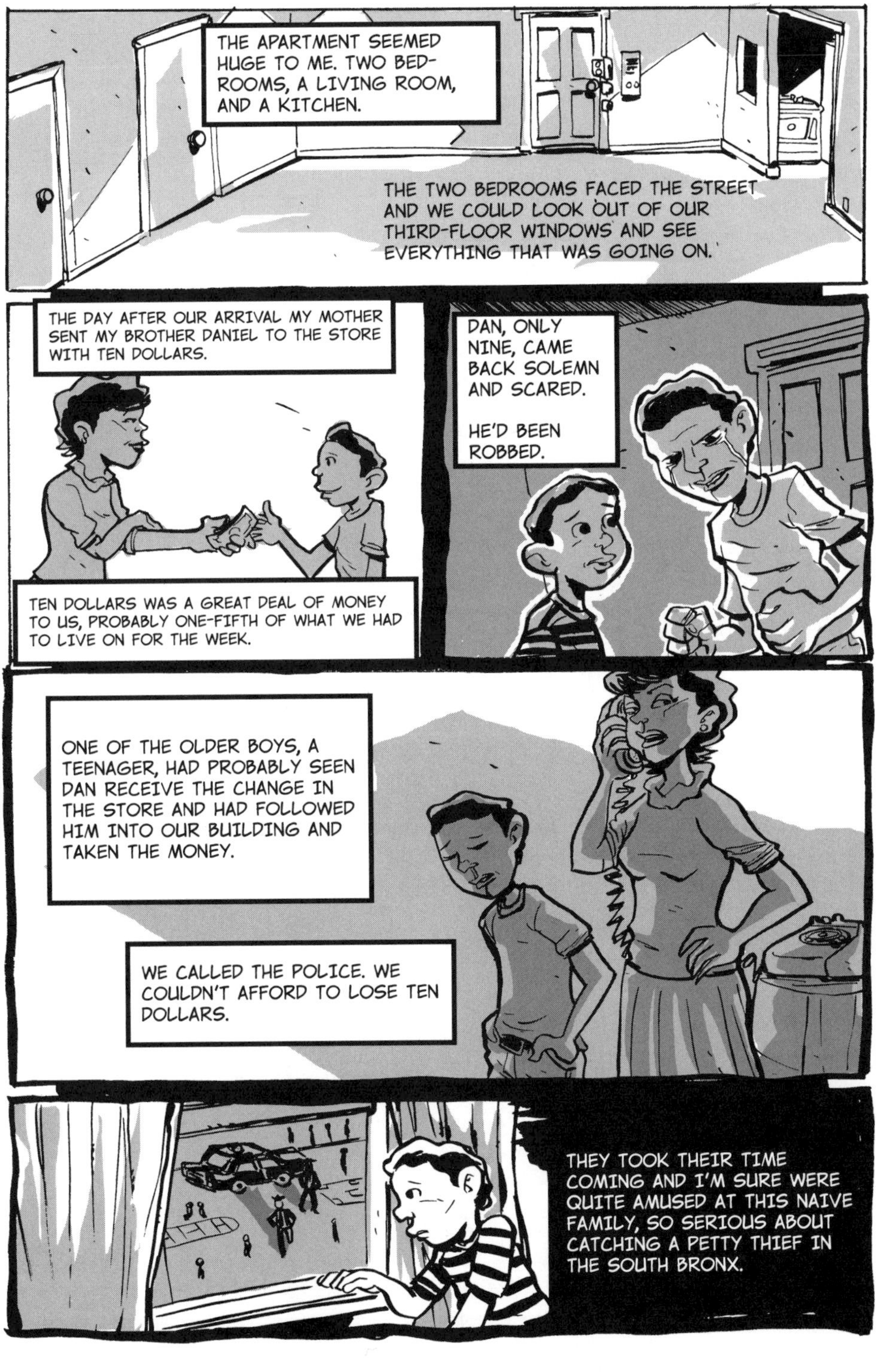
THE APARTMENT SEEMED HUGE TO ME. TWO BED-ROOMS, A LIVING ROOM, AND A KITCHEN.
THE TWO BEDROOMS FACED THE STREET AND WE COULD LOOK OUT OF OUR THIRD-FLOOR WINDOWS AND SEE EVERYTHING THAT WAS GOING ON.
THE DAY AFTER OUR ARRIVAL MY MOTHER SENT MY BROTHER DANIEL TO THE STORE WITH TEN DOLLARS.
TEN DOLLARS WAS A GREAT DEAL OF MONEY TO US, PROBABLY ONE-FIFTH OF WHAT WE HAD TO LIVE ON FOR THE WEEK.
DAN, ONLY NINE, CAME BACK SOLEMN AND SCARED.
HE'D BEEN ROBBED.
ONE OF THE OLDER BOYS, A TEENAGER, HAD PROBABLY SEEN DAN RECEIVE THE CHANGE IN THE STORE AND HAD FOLLOWED HIM INTO OUR BUILDING AND TAKEN THE MONEY.
WE CALLED THE POLICE. WE COULDN'T AFFORD TO LOSE TEN DOLLARS.
THEY TOOK THEIR TIME COMING AND I'M SURE WERE QUITE AMUSED AT THIS NAIVE FAMILY, SO SERIOUS ABOUT CATCHING A PETTY THIEF IN THE SOUTH BRONX.

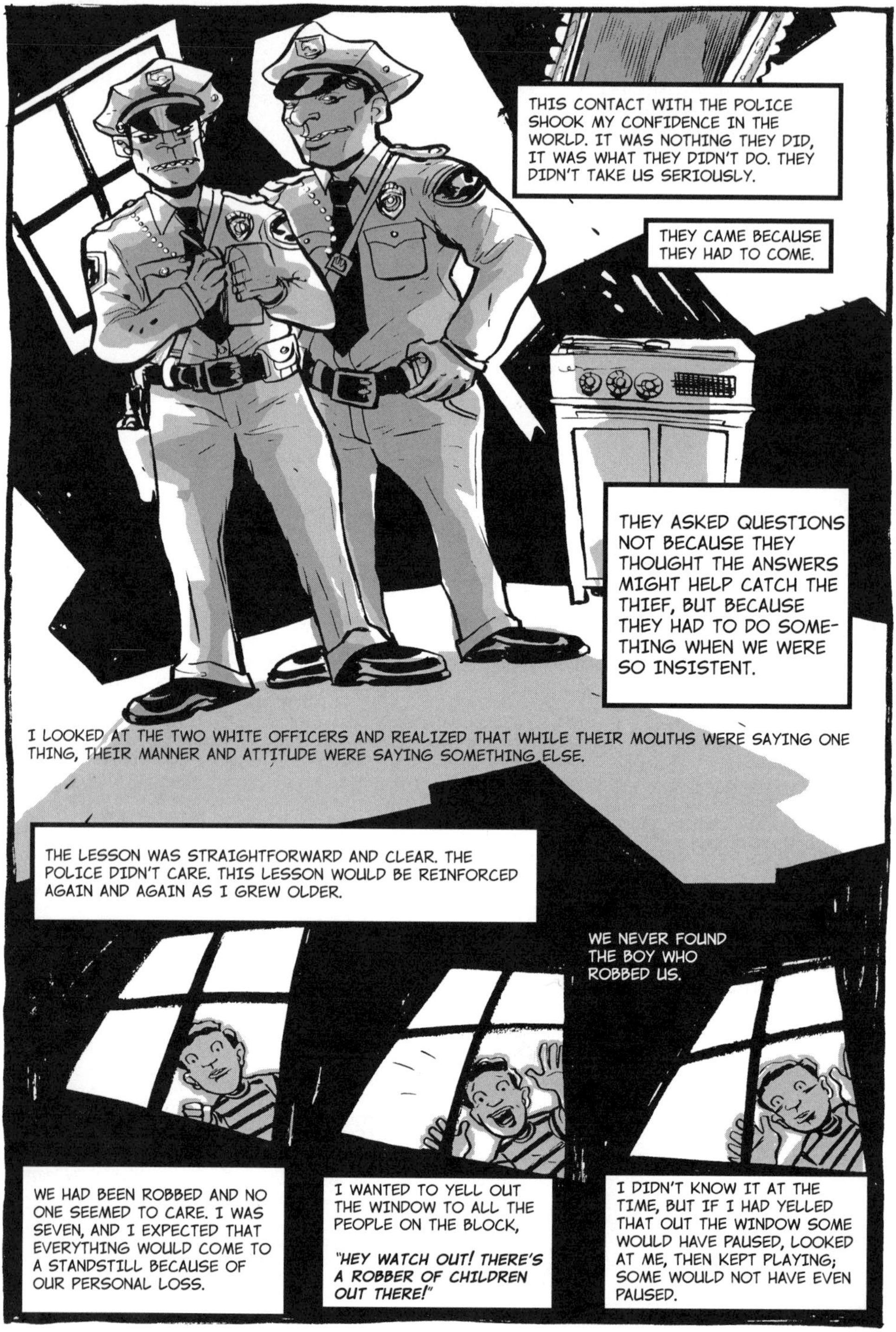
THIS CONTACT WITH THE POLICE SHOOK MY CONFIDENCE IN THE WORLD. IT WAS NOTHING THEY DID, IT WAS WHAT THEY DIDN'T DO. THEY DIDN'T TAKE US SERIOUSLY.
THEY CAME BECAUSE THEY HAD TO COME.
THEY ASKED QUESTIONS NOT BECAUSE THEY THOUGHT THE ANSWERS MIGHT HELP CATCH THE THIEF, BUT BECAUSE THEY HAD TO DO SOMETHING WHEN WE WERE SO INSISTENT.
I LOOKED AT THE TWO WHITE OFFICERS AND REALIZED THAT WHILE THEIR MOUTHS WERE SAYING ONE THING, THEIR MANNER AND ATTITUDE WERE SAYING SOMETHING ELSE.
THE LESSON WAS STRAIGHTFORWARD AND CLEAR. THE POLICE DIDN'T CARE. THIS LESSON WOULD BE REINFORCED AGAIN AND AGAIN AS I GREW OLDER.
WE HAD BEEN ROBBED AND NO ONE SEEMED TO CARE. I WAS SEVEN, AND I EXPECTED THAT EVERYTHING WOULD COME TO A STANDSTILL BECAUSE OF OUR PERSONAL LOSS.
I WANTED TO YELL OUT THE WINDOW TO ALL THE PEOPLE ON THE BLOCK,
"HEY WATCH OUT! THERE'S A ROBBER OF CHILDREN OUT THERE!"
WE NEVER FOUND THE BOY WHO ROBBED US.
I DIDN'T KNOW IT AT THE TIME, BUT IF I HAD YELLED THAT OUT THE WINDOW SOME WOULD HAVE PAUSED, LOOKED AT ME, THEN KEPT PLAYING; SOME WOULD NOT HAVE EVEN PAUSED.

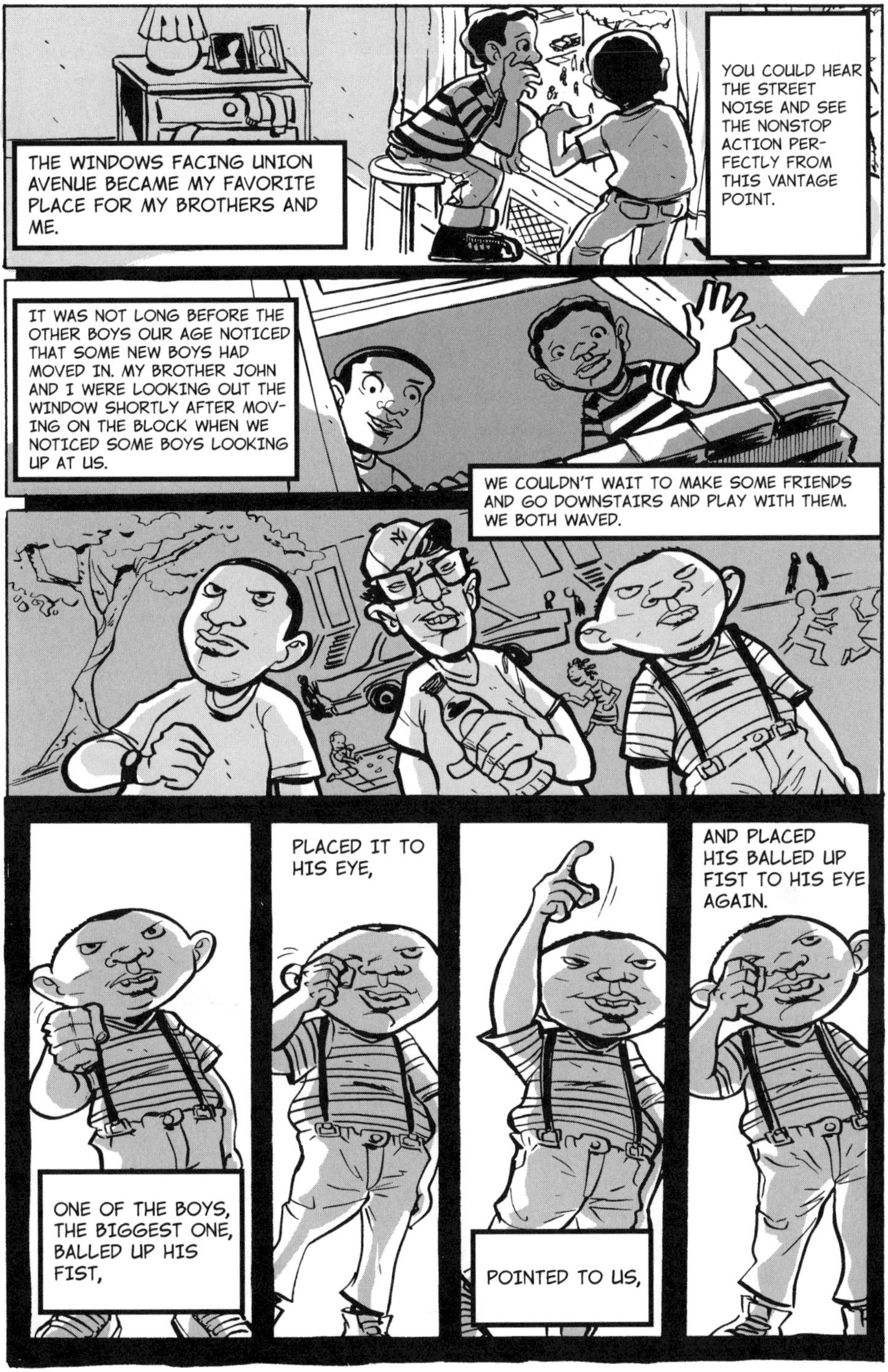
THE WINDOWS FACING UNION AVENUE BECAME MY FAVORITE PLACE FOR MY BROTHERS AND ME.
YOU COULD HEAR THE STREET NOISE AND SEE THE NONSTOP ACTION PERFECTLY FROM THIS VANTAGE POINT.
IT WAS NOT LONG BEFORE THE OTHER BOYS OUR AGE NOTICED THAT SOME NEW BOYS HAD MOVED IN. MY BROTHER JOHN AND I WERE LOOKING OUT THE WINDOW SHORTLY AFTER MOVING ON THE BLOCK WHEN WE NOTICED SOME BOYS LOOKING UP AT US.
WE COULDN'T WAIT TO MAKE SOME FRIENDS AND GO DOWNSTAIRS AND PLAY WITH THEM. WE BOTH WAVED.
ONE OF THE BOYS, THE BIGGEST ONE, BALLED UP HIS FIST,
PLACED IT TO HIS EYE,
POINTED TO US,
AND PLACED HIS BALLED UP FIST TO HIS EYE AGAIN.

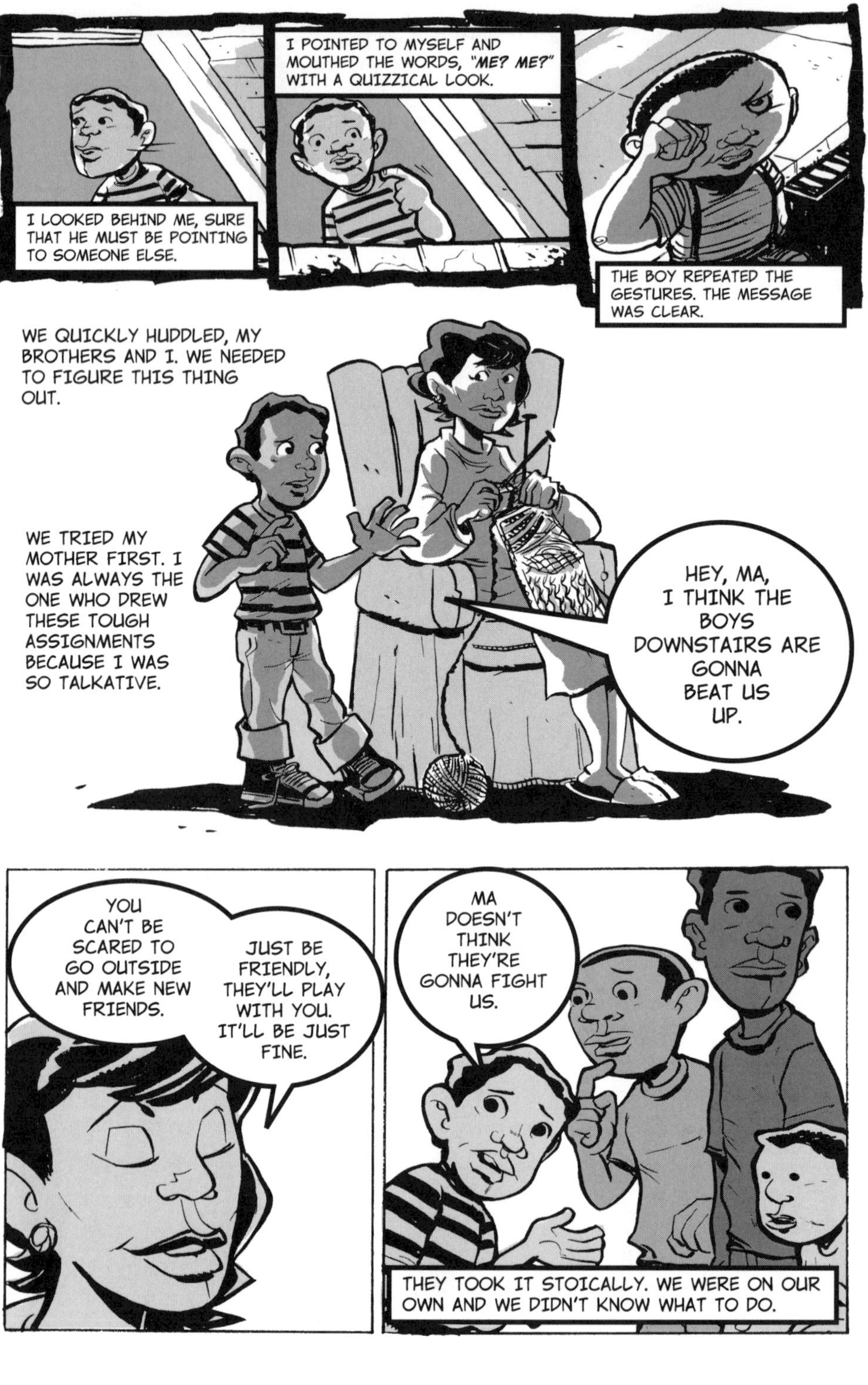
I LOOKED BEHIND ME, SURE THAT HE MUST BE POINTING TO SOMEONE ELSE.
I POINTED TO MYSELF AND MOUTHED THE WORDS, *"ME? ME?"* WITH A QUIZZICAL LOOK.
THE BOY REPEATED THE GESTURES. THE MESSAGE WAS CLEAR.
WE QUICKLY HUDDLED, MY BROTHERS AND I. WE NEEDED TO FIGURE THIS THING OUT.
WE TRIED MY MOTHER FIRST. I WAS ALWAYS THE ONE WHO DREW THESE TOUGH ASSIGNMENTS BECAUSE I WAS SO TALKATIVE.
HEY, MA, I THINK THE BOYS DOWNSTAIRS ARE GONNA BEAT US UP.
YOU CAN'T BE SCARED TO GO OUTSIDE AND MAKE NEW FRIENDS.
JUST BE FRIENDLY, THEY'LL PLAY WITH YOU. IT'LL BE JUST FINE.
MA DOESN'T THINK THEY'RE GONNA FIGHT US.
THEY TOOK IT STOICALLY. WE WERE ON OUR OWN AND WE DIDN'T KNOW WHAT TO DO.

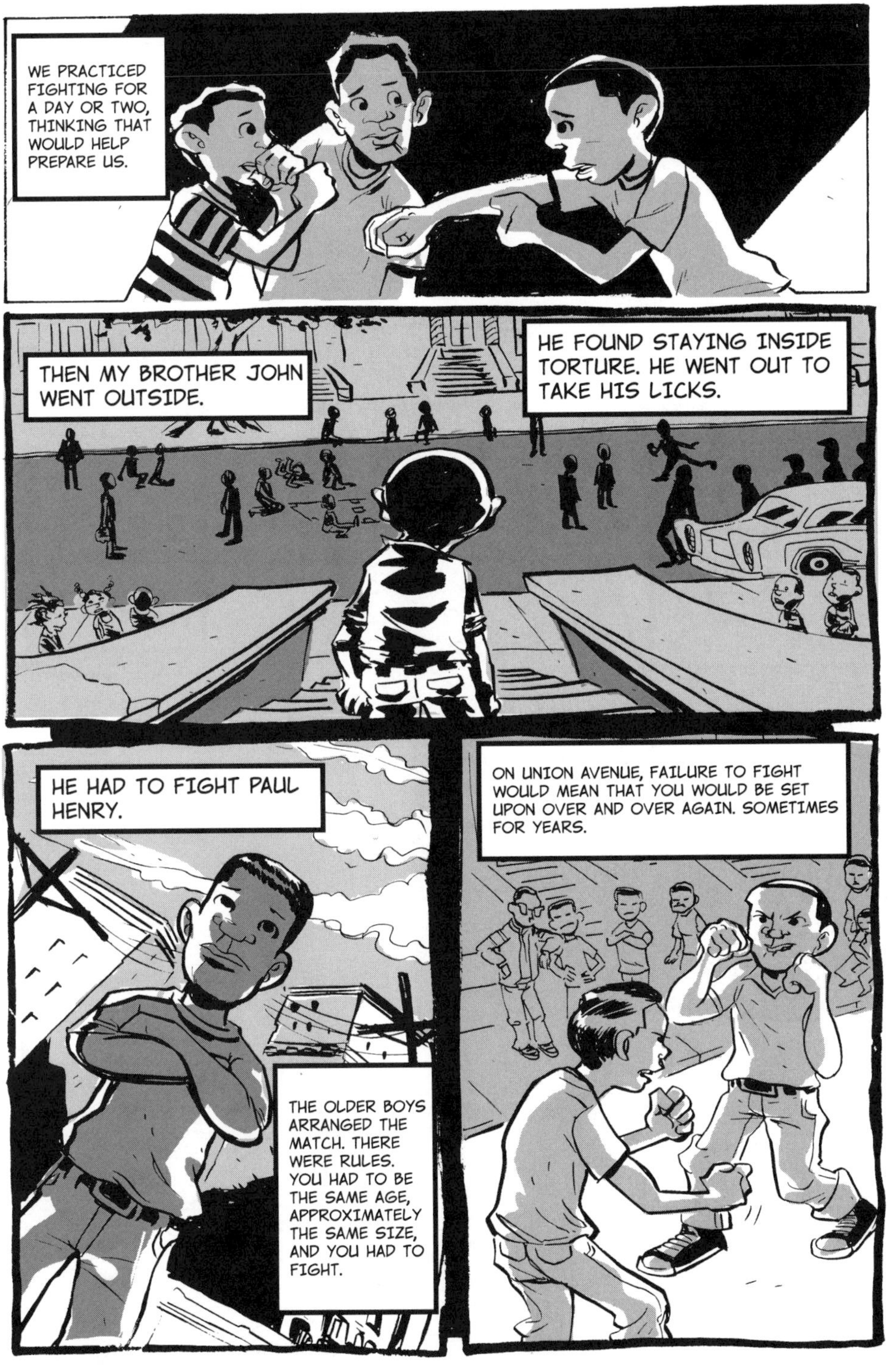
WE PRACTICED FIGHTING FOR A DAY OR TWO, THINKING THAT WOULD HELP PREPARE US.
THEN MY BROTHER JOHN WENT OUTSIDE.
HE FOUND STAYING INSIDE TORTURE. HE WENT OUT TO TAKE HIS LICKS.
HE HAD TO FIGHT PAUL HENRY.
THE OLDER BOYS ARRANGED THE MATCH. THERE WERE RULES. YOU HAD TO BE THE SAME AGE, APPROXIMATELY THE SAME SIZE, AND YOU HAD TO FIGHT.
ON UNION AVENUE, FAILURE TO FIGHT WOULD MEAN THAT YOU WOULD BE SET UPON OVER AND OVER AGAIN. SOMETIMES FOR YEARS.

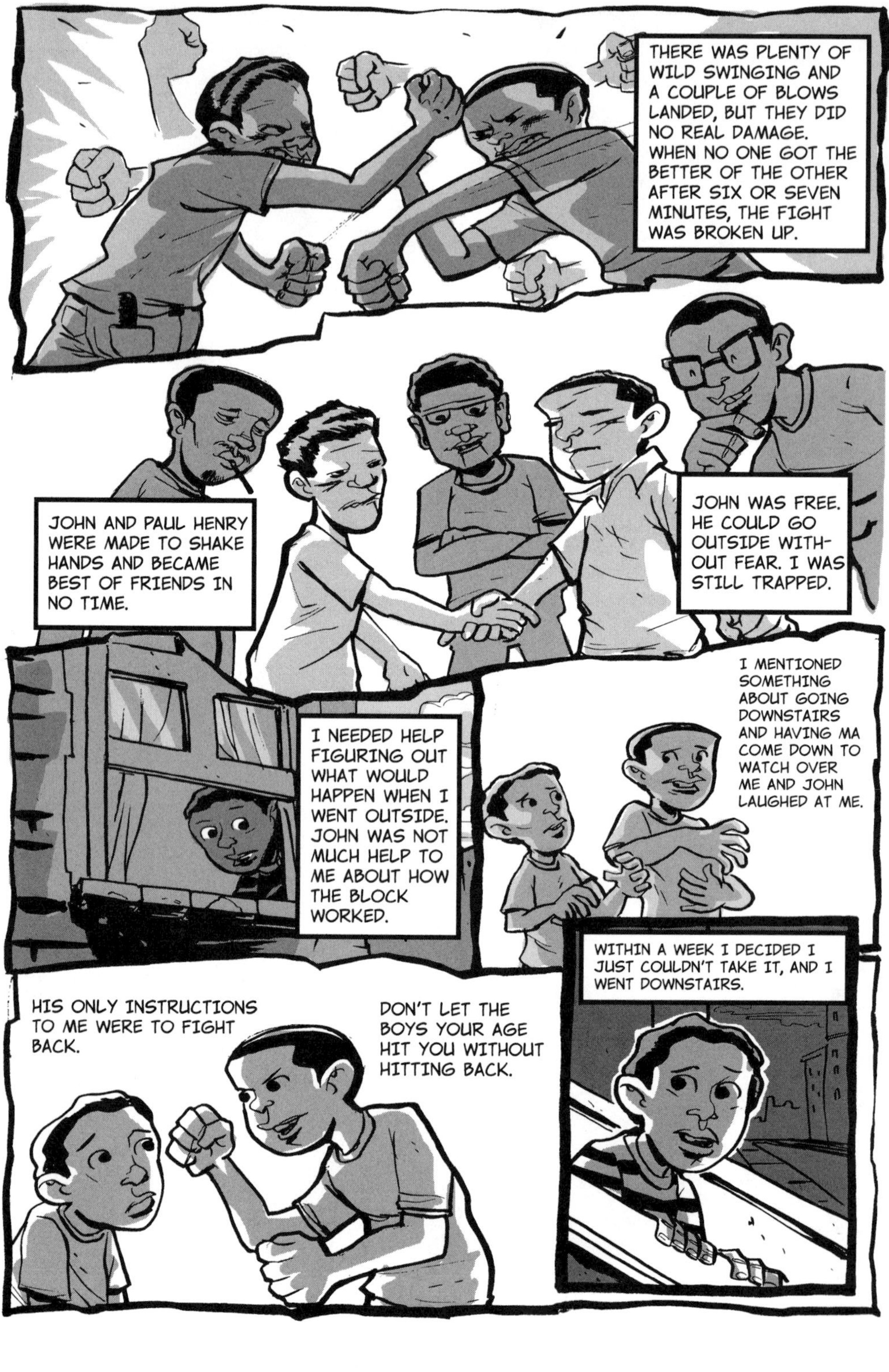
THERE WAS PLENTY OF WILD SWINGING AND A COUPLE OF BLOWS LANDED, BUT THEY DID NO REAL DAMAGE. WHEN NO ONE GOT THE BETTER OF THE OTHER AFTER SIX OR SEVEN MINUTES, THE FIGHT WAS BROKEN UP.
JOHN AND PAUL HENRY WERE MADE TO SHAKE HANDS AND BECAME BEST OF FRIENDS IN NO TIME.
JOHN WAS FREE. HE COULD GO OUTSIDE WITHOUT FEAR. I WAS STILL TRAPPED.
I NEEDED HELP FIGURING OUT WHAT WOULD HAPPEN WHEN I WENT OUTSIDE. JOHN WAS NOT MUCH HELP TO ME ABOUT HOW THE BLOCK WORKED.
I MENTIONED SOMETHING ABOUT GOING DOWNSTAIRS AND HAVING MA COME DOWN TO WATCH OVER ME AND JOHN LAUGHED AT ME.
HIS ONLY INSTRUCTIONS TO ME WERE TO FIGHT BACK.
DON'T LET THE BOYS YOUR AGE HIT YOU WITHOUT HITTING BACK.
WITHIN A WEEK I DECIDED I JUST COULDN'T TAKE IT, AND I WENT DOWNSTAIRS.

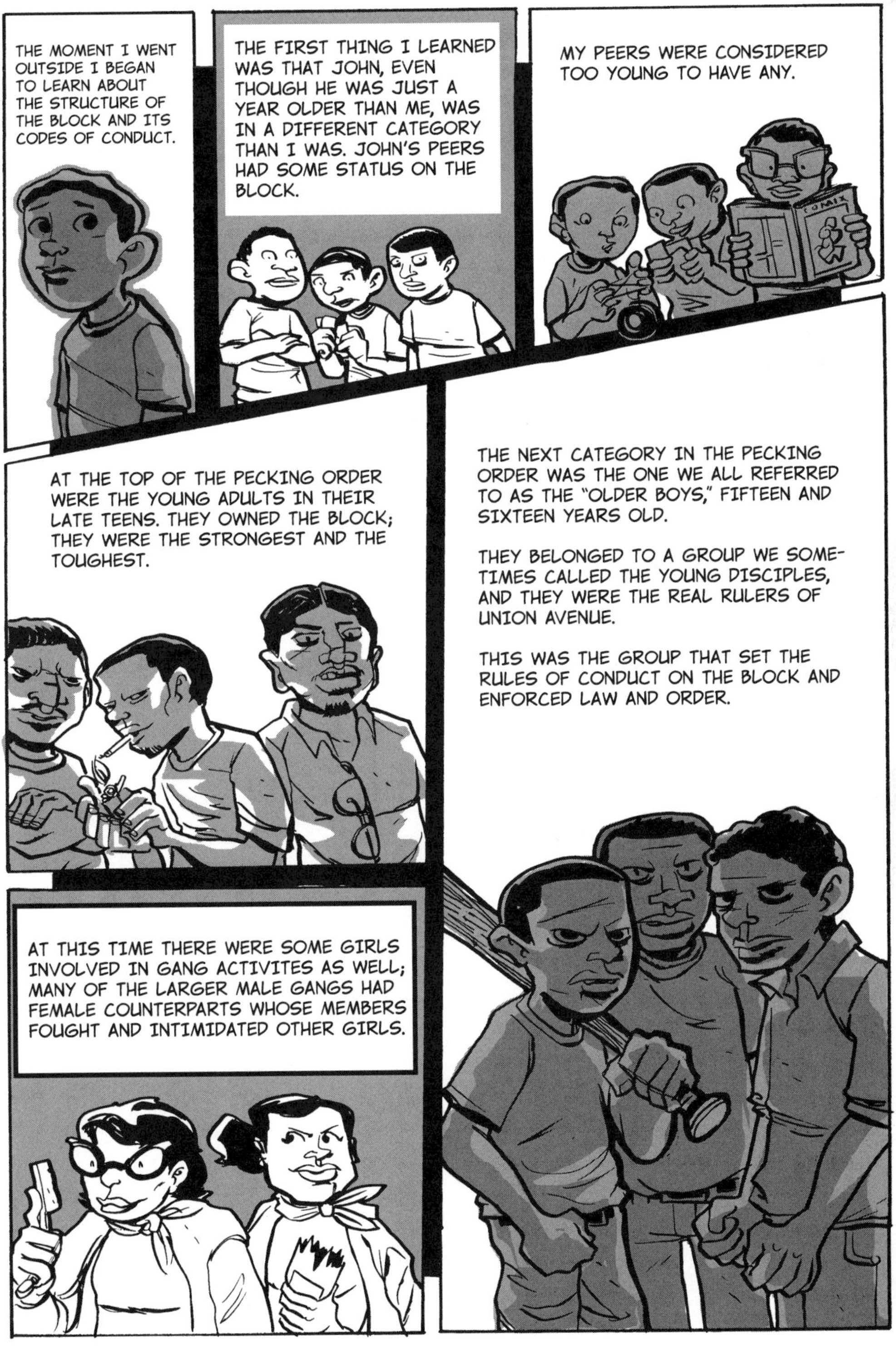
THE MOMENT I WENT OUTSIDE I BEGAN TO LEARN ABOUT THE STRUCTURE OF THE BLOCK AND ITS CODES OF CONDUCT.
THE FIRST THING I LEARNED WAS THAT JOHN, EVEN THOUGH HE WAS JUST A YEAR OLDER THAN ME, WAS IN A DIFFERENT CATEGORY THAN I WAS. JOHN'S PEERS HAD SOME STATUS ON THE BLOCK.
MY PEERS WERE CONSIDERED TOO YOUNG TO HAVE ANY.
COMIX
AT THE TOP OF THE PECKING ORDER WERE THE YOUNG ADULTS IN THEIR LATE TEENS. THEY OWNED THE BLOCK; THEY WERE THE STRONGEST AND THE TOUGHEST.
THE NEXT CATEGORY IN THE PECKING ORDER WAS THE ONE WE ALL REFERRED TO AS THE "OLDER BOYS," FIFTEEN AND SIXTEEN YEARS OLD.
THEY BELONGED TO A GROUP WE SOMETIMES CALLED THE YOUNG DISCIPLES, AND THEY WERE THE REAL RULERS OF UNION AVENUE.
THIS WAS THE GROUP THAT SET THE RULES OF CONDUCT ON THE BLOCK AND ENFORCED LAW AND ORDER.
AT THIS TIME THERE WERE SOME GIRLS INVOLVED IN GANG ACTIVITES AS WELL; MANY OF THE LARGER MALE GANGS HAD FEMALE COUNTERPARTS WHOSE MEMBERS FOUGHT AND INTIMIDATED OTHER GIRLS.

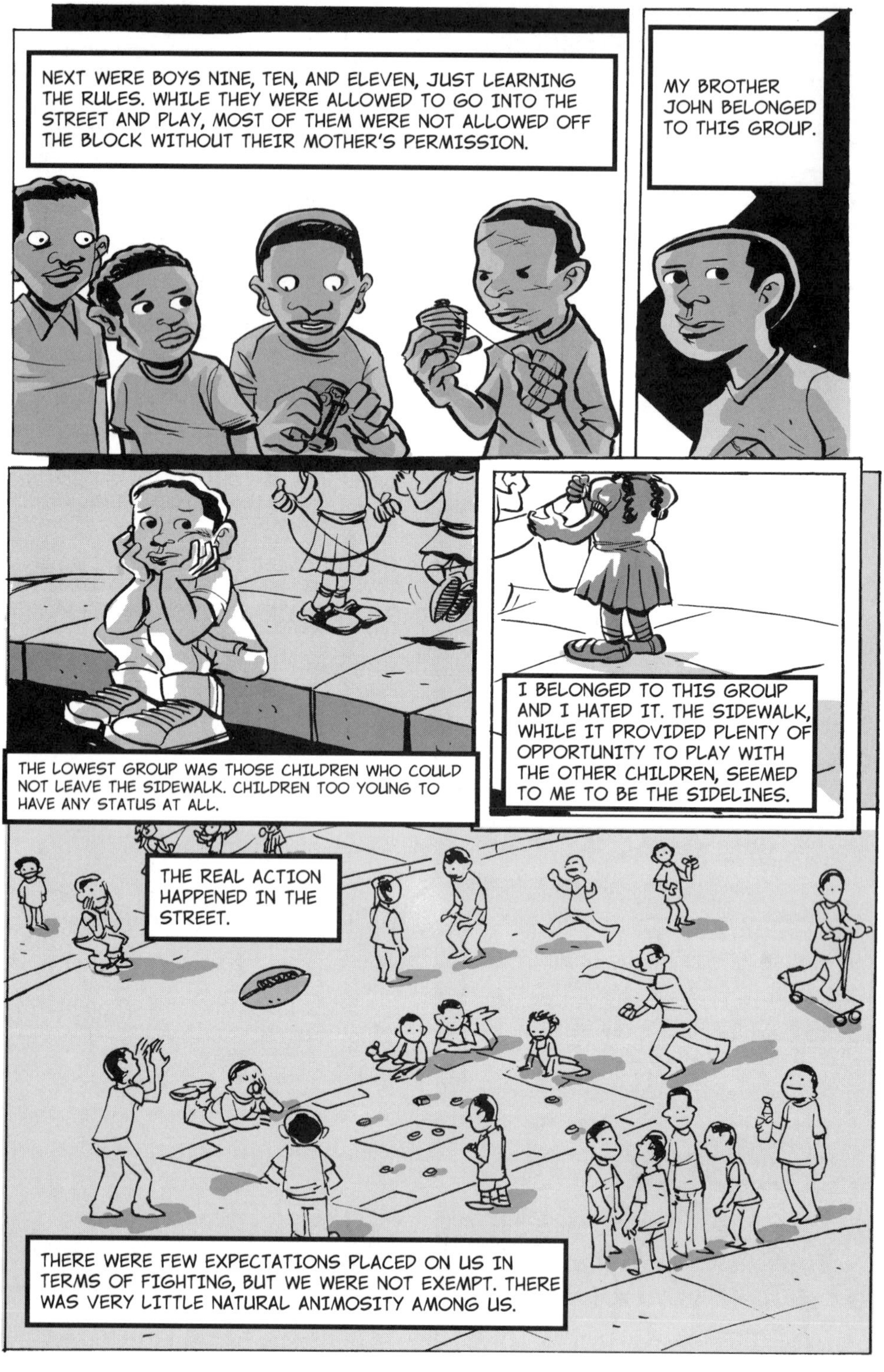
NEXT WERE BOYS NINE, TEN, AND ELEVEN, JUST LEARNING THE RULES. WHILE THEY WERE ALLOWED TO GO INTO THE STREET AND PLAY, MOST OF THEM WERE NOT ALLOWED OFF THE BLOCK WITHOUT THEIR MOTHER'S PERMISSION.
MY BROTHER JOHN BELONGED TO THIS GROUP.
THE LOWEST GROUP WAS THOSE CHILDREN WHO COULD NOT LEAVE THE SIDEWALK. CHILDREN TOO YOUNG TO HAVE ANY STATUS AT ALL.
I BELONGED TO THIS GROUP AND I HATED IT. THE SIDEWALK, WHILE IT PROVIDED PLENTY OF OPPORTUNITY TO PLAY WITH THE OTHER CHILDREN, SEEMED TO ME TO BE THE SIDELINES.
THE REAL ACTION HAPPENED IN THE STREET.
THERE WERE FEW EXPECTATIONS PLACED ON US IN TERMS OF FIGHTING, BUT WE WERE NOT EXEMPT. THERE WAS VERY LITTLE NATURAL ANIMOSITY AMONG US.

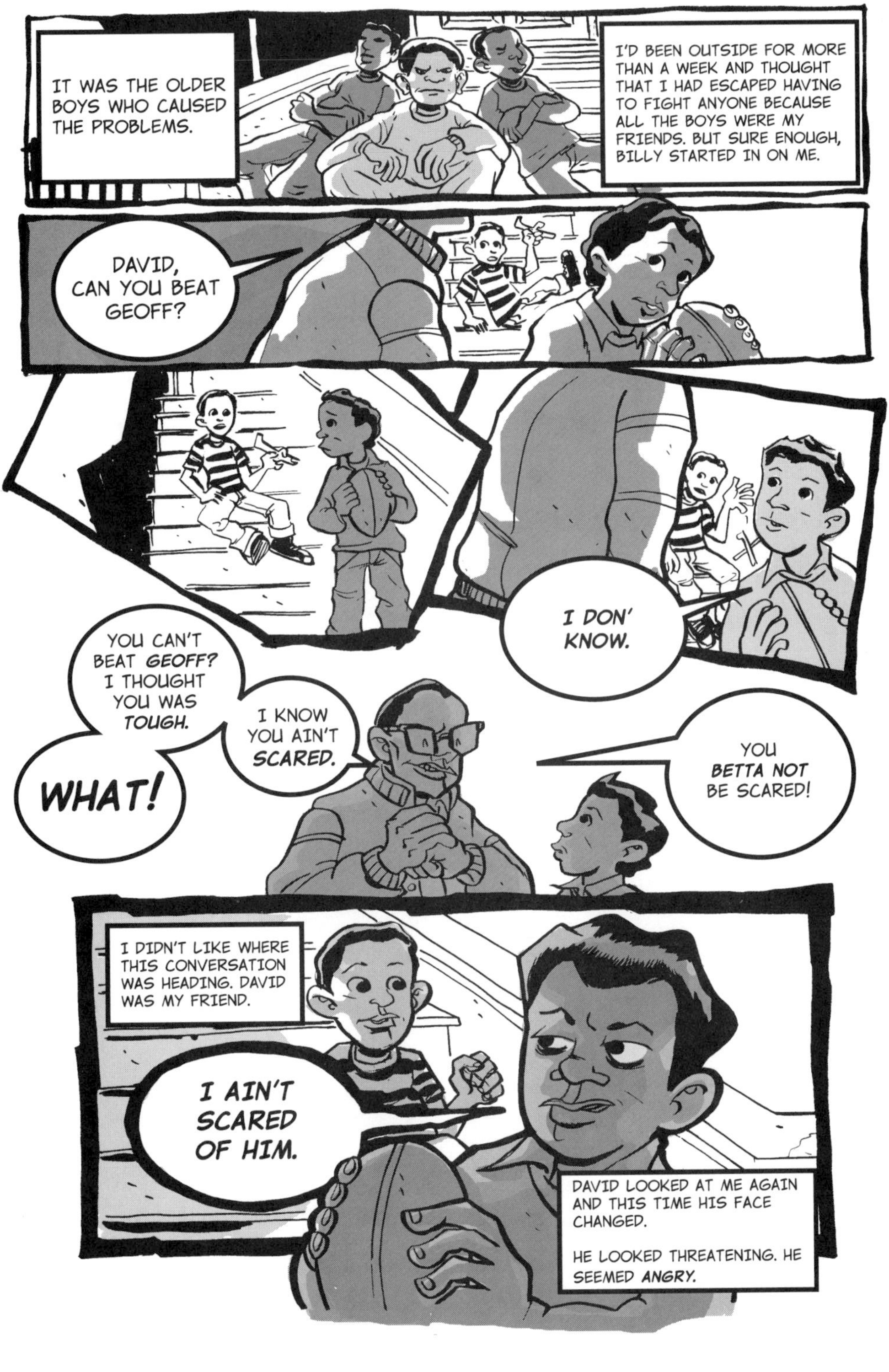
IT WAS THE OLDER BOYS WHO CAUSED THE PROBLEMS.
I'D BEEN OUTSIDE FOR MORE THAN A WEEK AND THOUGHT THAT I HAD ESCAPED HAVING TO FIGHT ANYONE BECAUSE ALL THE BOYS WERE MY FRIENDS. BUT SURE ENOUGH, BILLY STARTED IN ON ME.
DAVID, CAN YOU BEAT GEOFF?
I DON' KNOW.
YOU CAN'T BEAT GEOFF? I THOUGHT YOU WAS TOUGH.
WHAT!
I KNOW YOU AIN'T SCARED.
YOU BETTA NOT BE SCARED!
I DIDN'T LIKE WHERE THIS CONVERSATION WAS HEADING. DAVID WAS MY FRIEND.
I AIN'T SCARED OF HIM.
DAVID LOOKED AT ME AGAIN AND THIS TIME HIS FACE CHANGED.
HE LOOKED THREATENING. HE SEEMED ANGRY.

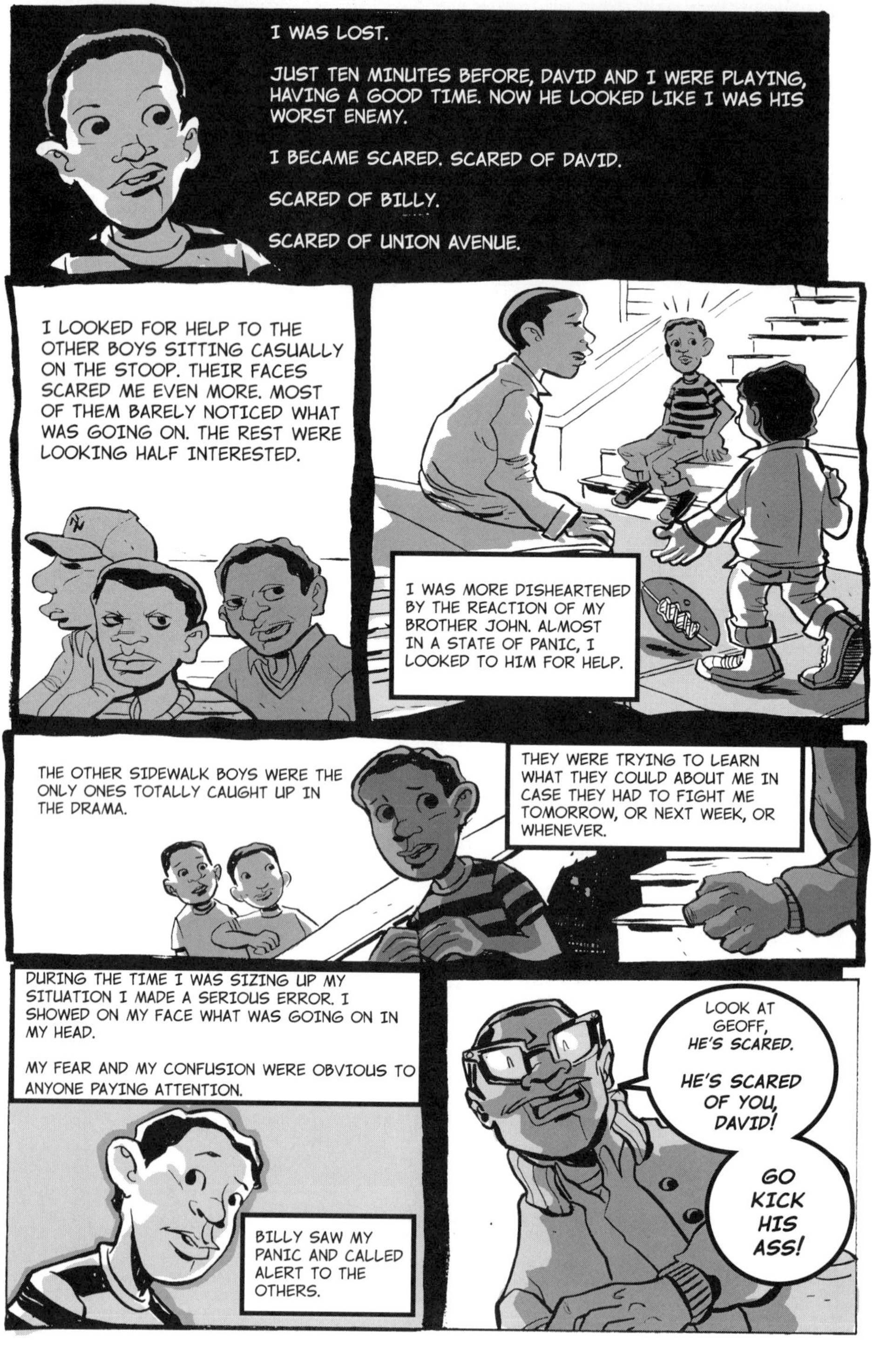
I WAS LOST.
JUST TEN MINUTES BEFORE, DAVID AND I WERE PLAYING, HAVING A GOOD TIME. NOW HE LOOKED LIKE I WAS HIS WORST ENEMY.
I BECAME SCARED. SCARED OF DAVID.
SCARED OF BILLY.
SCARED OF UNION AVENUE.
I LOOKED FOR HELP TO THE OTHER BOYS SITTING CASUALLY ON THE STOOP. THEIR FACES SCARED ME EVEN MORE. MOST OF THEM BARELY NOTICED WHAT WAS GOING ON. THE REST WERE LOOKING HALF INTERESTED.
I WAS MORE DISHEARTENED BY THE REACTION OF MY BROTHER JOHN. ALMOST IN A STATE OF PANIC, I LOOKED TO HIM FOR HELP.
THE OTHER SIDEWALK BOYS WERE THE ONLY ONES TOTALLY CAUGHT UP IN THE DRAMA.
THEY WERE TRYING TO LEARN WHAT THEY COULD ABOUT ME IN CASE THEY HAD TO FIGHT ME TOMORROW, OR NEXT WEEK, OR WHENEVER.
DURING THE TIME I WAS SIZING UP MY SITUATION I MADE A SERIOUS ERROR. I SHOWED ON MY FACE WHAT WAS GOING ON IN MY HEAD.
MY FEAR AND MY CONFUSION WERE OBVIOUS TO ANYONE PAYING ATTENTION.
BILLY SAW MY PANIC AND CALLED ALERT TO THE OTHERS.
LOOK AT GEOFF, HE'S SCARED.
HE'S SCARED OF YOU, DAVID!
GO KICK HIS ASS!

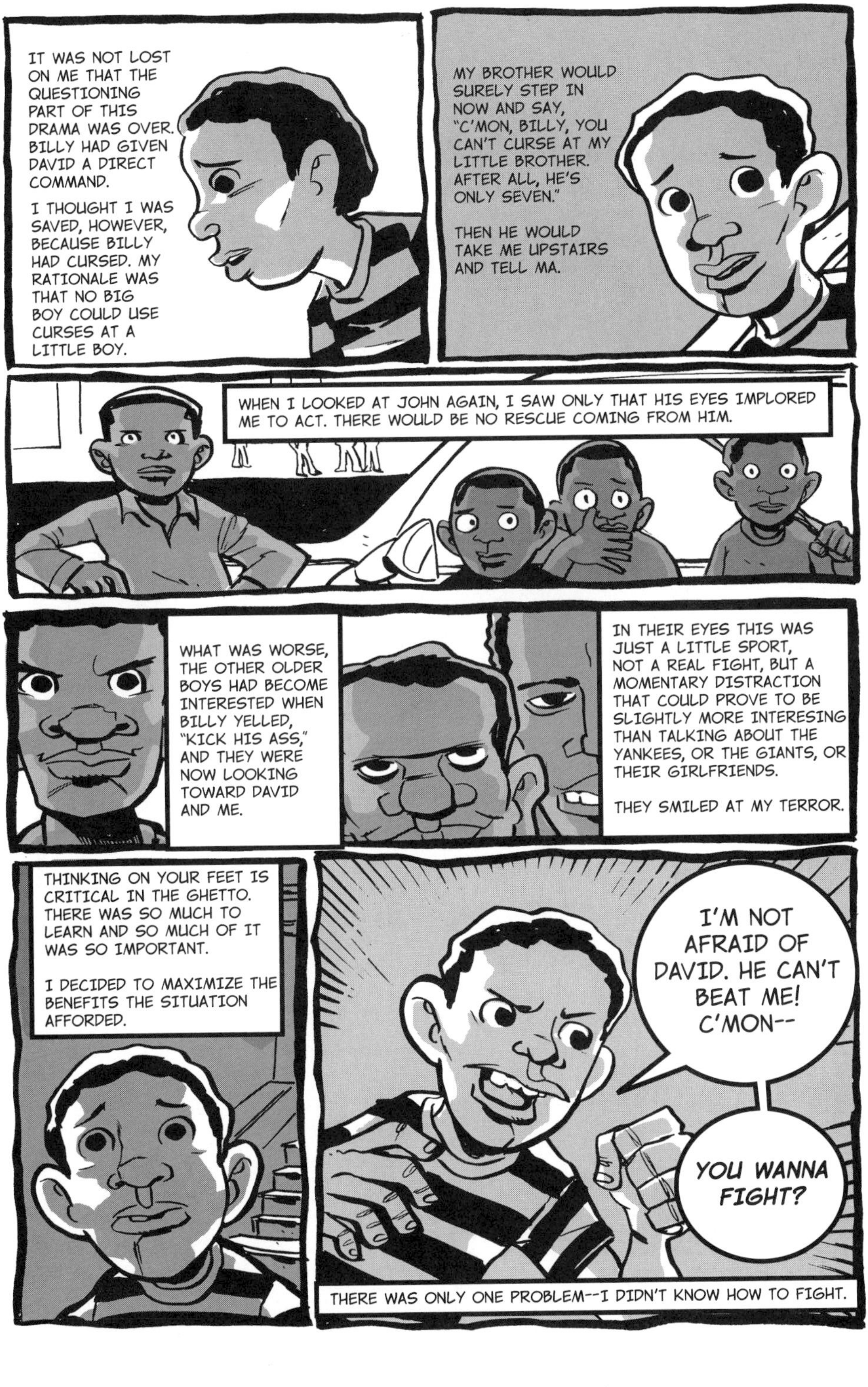

IT WAS NOT LOST ON ME THAT THE QUESTIONING PART OF THIS DRAMA WAS OVER. BILLY HAD GIVEN DAVID A DIRECT COMMAND.
I THOUGHT I WAS SAVED, HOWEVER, BECAUSE BILLY HAD CURSED. MY RATIONALE WAS THAT NO BIG BOY COULD USE CURSES AT A LITTLE BOY.
MY BROTHER WOULD SURELY STEP IN NOW AND SAY, "C'MON, BILLY, YOU CAN'T CURSE AT MY LITTLE BROTHER. AFTER ALL, HE'S ONLY SEVEN."
THEN HE WOULD TAKE ME UPSTAIRS AND TELL MA.
WHEN I LOOKED AT JOHN AGAIN, I SAW ONLY THAT HIS EYES IMPLORED ME TO ACT. THERE WOULD BE NO RESCUE COMING FROM HIM.
WHAT WAS WORSE, THE OTHER OLDER BOYS HAD BECOME INTERESTED WHEN BILLY YELLED, "KICK HIS ASS," AND THEY WERE NOW LOOKING TOWARD DAVID AND ME.
IN THEIR EYES THIS WAS JUST A LITTLE SPORT, NOT A REAL FIGHT, BUT A MOMENTARY DISTRACTION THAT COULD PROVE TO BE SLIGHTLY MORE INTERESING THAN TALKING ABOUT THE YANKEES, OR THE GIANTS, OR THEIR GIRLFRIENDS.
THEY SMILED AT MY TERROR.
THINKING ON YOUR FEET IS CRITICAL IN THE GHETTO. THERE WAS SO MUCH TO LEARN AND SO MUCH OF IT WAS SO IMPORTANT.
I DECIDED TO MAXIMIZE THE BENEFITS THE SITUATION AFFORDED.
I'M NOT AFRAID OF DAVID. HE CAN'T BEAT ME! C'MON--
YOU WANNA FIGHT?
THERE WAS ONLY ONE PROBLEM--I DIDN'T KNOW HOW TO FIGHT.

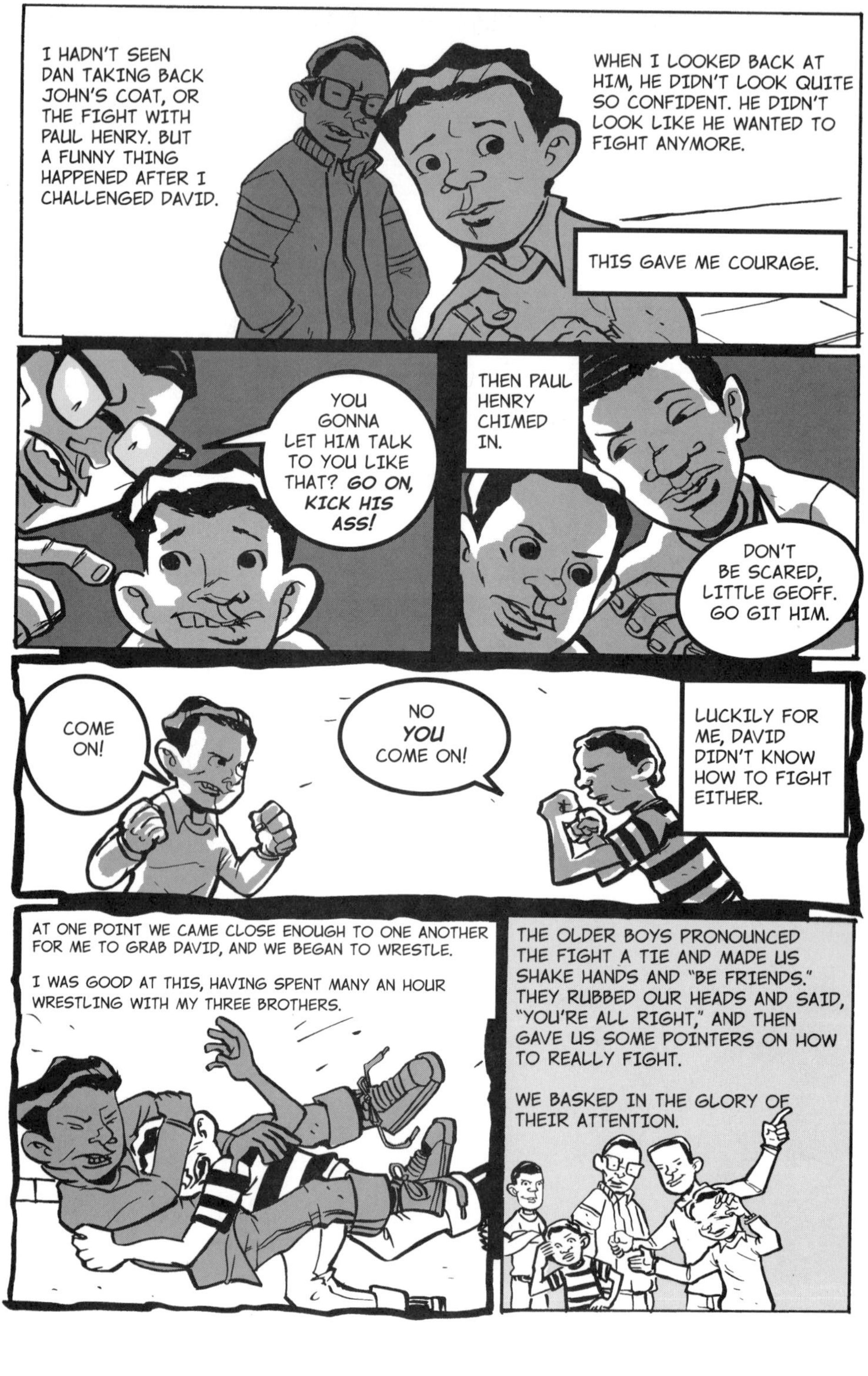
I HADN'T SEEN DAN TAKING BACK JOHN'S COAT, OR THE FIGHT WITH PAUL HENRY. BUT A FUNNY THING HAPPENED AFTER I CHALLENGED DAVID.
WHEN I LOOKED BACK AT HIM, HE DIDN'T LOOK QUITE SO CONFIDENT. HE DIDN'T LOOK LIKE HE WANTED TO FIGHT ANYMORE.
THIS GAVE ME COURAGE.
YOU GONNA LET HIM TALK TO YOU LIKE THAT? GO ON, KICK HIS ASS!
THEN PAUL HENRY CHIMED IN.
DON'T BE SCARED, LITTLE GEOFF. GO GIT HIM.
COME ON!
NO YOU COME ON!
LUCKILY FOR ME, DAVID DIDN'T KNOW HOW TO FIGHT EITHER.
AT ONE POINT WE CAME CLOSE ENOUGH TO ONE ANOTHER FOR ME TO GRAB DAVID, AND WE BEGAN TO WRESTLE.
I WAS GOOD AT THIS, HAVING SPENT MANY AN HOUR WRESTLING WITH MY THREE BROTHERS.
THE OLDER BOYS PRONOUNCED THE FIGHT A TIE AND MADE US SHAKE HANDS AND "BE FRIENDS." THEY RUBBED OUR HEADS AND SAID, "YOU'RE ALL RIGHT," AND THEN GAVE US SOME POINTERS ON HOW TO REALLY FIGHT.
WE BASKED IN THE GLORY OF THEIR ATTENTION.

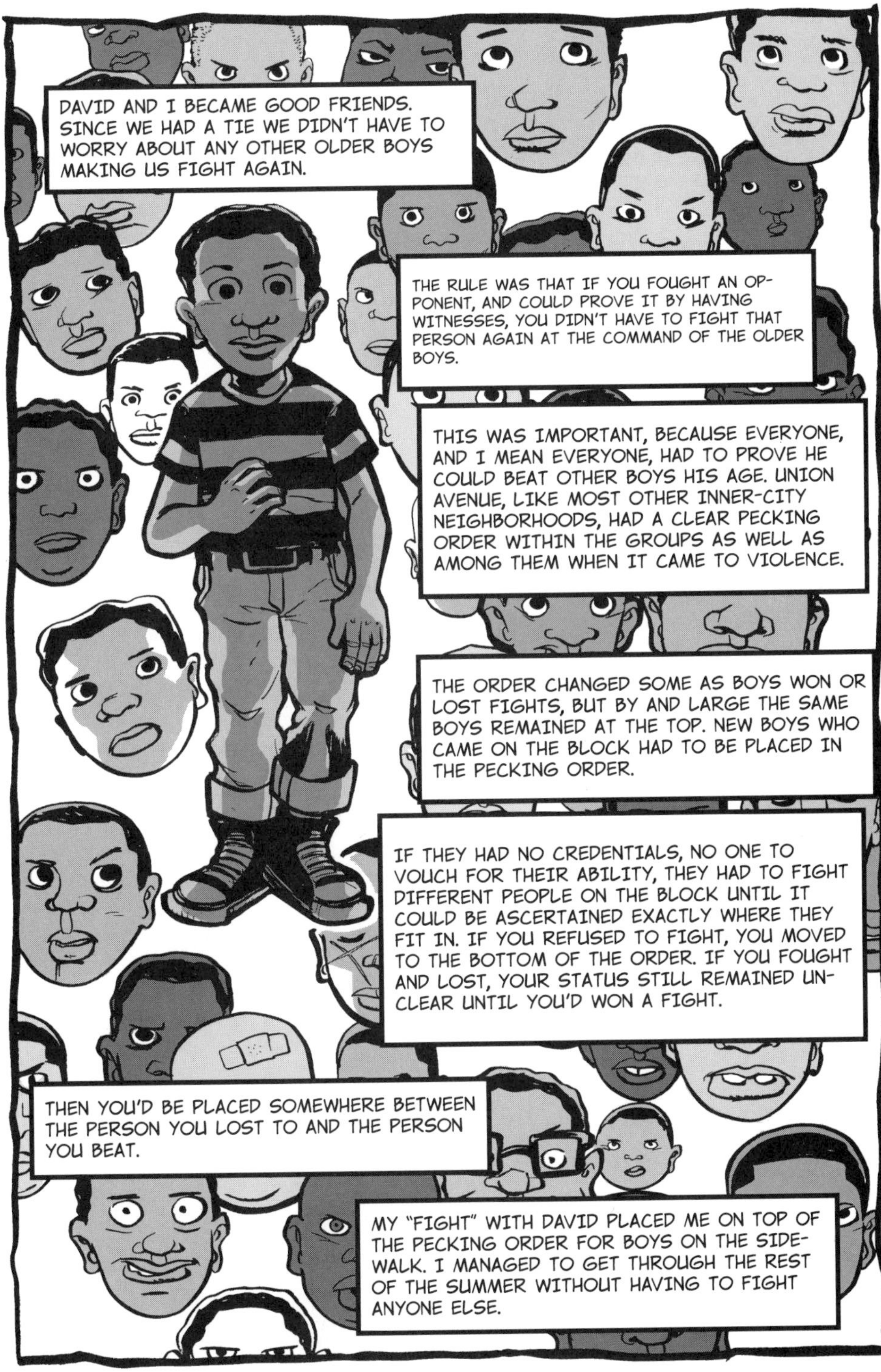
DAVID AND I BECAME GOOD FRIENDS. SINCE WE HAD A TIE WE DIDN'T HAVE TO WORRY ABOUT ANY OTHER OLDER BOYS MAKING US FIGHT AGAIN.
THE RULE WAS THAT IF YOU FOUGHT AN OPPONENT, AND COULD PROVE IT BY HAVING WITNESSES, YOU DIDN'T HAVE TO FIGHT THAT PERSON AGAIN AT THE COMMAND OF THE OLDER BOYS.
THIS WAS IMPORTANT, BECAUSE EVERYONE, AND I MEAN EVERYONE, HAD TO PROVE HE COULD BEAT OTHER BOYS HIS AGE. UNION AVENUE, LIKE MOST OTHER INNER-CITY NEIGHBORHOODS, HAD A CLEAR PECKING ORDER WITHIN THE GROUPS AS WELL AS AMONG THEM WHEN IT CAME TO VIOLENCE.
THE ORDER CHANGED SOME AS BOYS WON OR LOST FIGHTS, BUT BY AND LARGE THE SAME BOYS REMAINED AT THE TOP. NEW BOYS WHO CAME ON THE BLOCK HAD TO BE PLACED IN THE PECKING ORDER.
IF THEY HAD NO CREDENTIALS, NO ONE TO VOUCH FOR THEIR ABILITY, THEY HAD TO FIGHT DIFFERENT PEOPLE ON THE BLOCK UNTIL IT COULD BE ASCERTAINED EXACTLY WHERE THEY FIT IN. IF YOU REFUSED TO FIGHT, YOU MOVED TO THE BOTTOM OF THE ORDER. IF YOU FOUGHT AND LOST, YOUR STATUS STILL REMAINED UNCLEAR UNTIL YOU'D WON A FIGHT.
THEN YOU'D BE PLACED SOMEWHERE BETWEEN THE PERSON YOU LOST TO AND THE PERSON YOU BEAT.
MY "FIGHT" WITH DAVID PLACED ME ON TOP OF THE PECKING ORDER FOR BOYS ON THE SIDEWALK. I MANAGED TO GET THROUGH THE REST OF THE SUMMER WITHOUT HAVING TO FIGHT ANYONE ELSE.

4

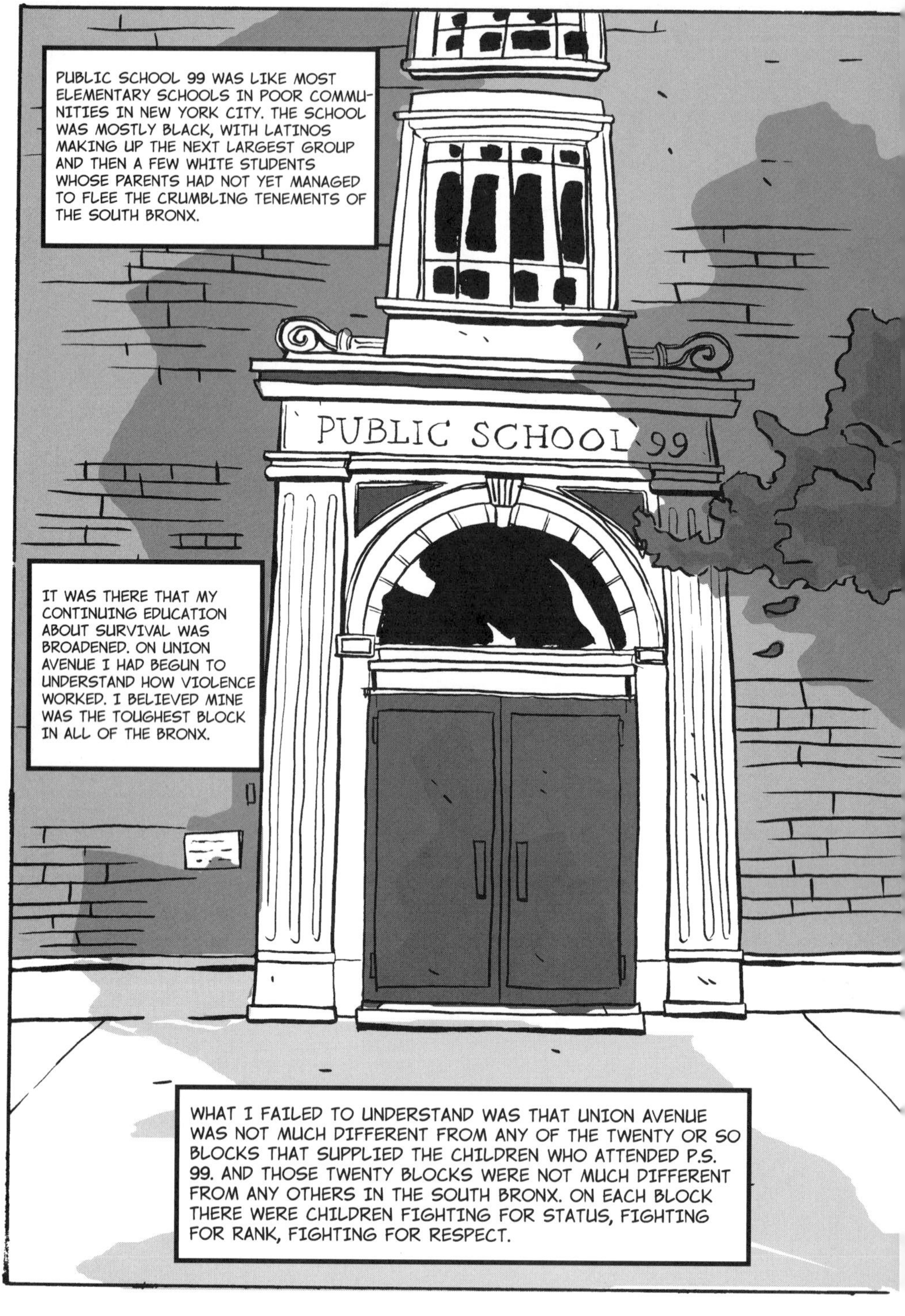
PUBLIC SCHOOL 99 WAS LIKE MOST ELEMENTARY SCHOOLS IN POOR COMMUNITIES IN NEW YORK CITY. THE SCHOOL WAS MOSTLY BLACK, WITH LATINOS MAKING UP THE NEXT LARGEST GROUP AND THEN A FEW WHITE STUDENTS WHOSE PARENTS HAD NOT YET MANAGED TO FLEE THE CRUMBLING TENEMENTS OF THE SOUTH BRONX.
PUBLIC SCHOOL 99
IT WAS THERE THAT MY CONTINUING EDUCATION ABOUT SURVIVAL WAS BROADENED. ON UNION AVENUE I HAD BEGUN TO UNDERSTAND HOW VIOLENCE WORKED. I BELIEVED MINE WAS THE TOUGHEST BLOCK IN ALL OF THE BRONX.
WHAT I FAILED TO UNDERSTAND WAS THAT UNION AVENUE WAS NOT MUCH DIFFERENT FROM ANY OF THE TWENTY OR SO BLOCKS THAT SUPPLIED THE CHILDREN WHO ATTENDED P.S. 99. AND THOSE TWENTY BLOCKS WERE NOT MUCH DIFFERENT FROM ANY OTHERS IN THE SOUTH BRONX. ON EACH BLOCK THERE WERE CHILDREN FIGHTING FOR STATUS, FIGHTING FOR RANK, FIGHTING FOR RESPECT.

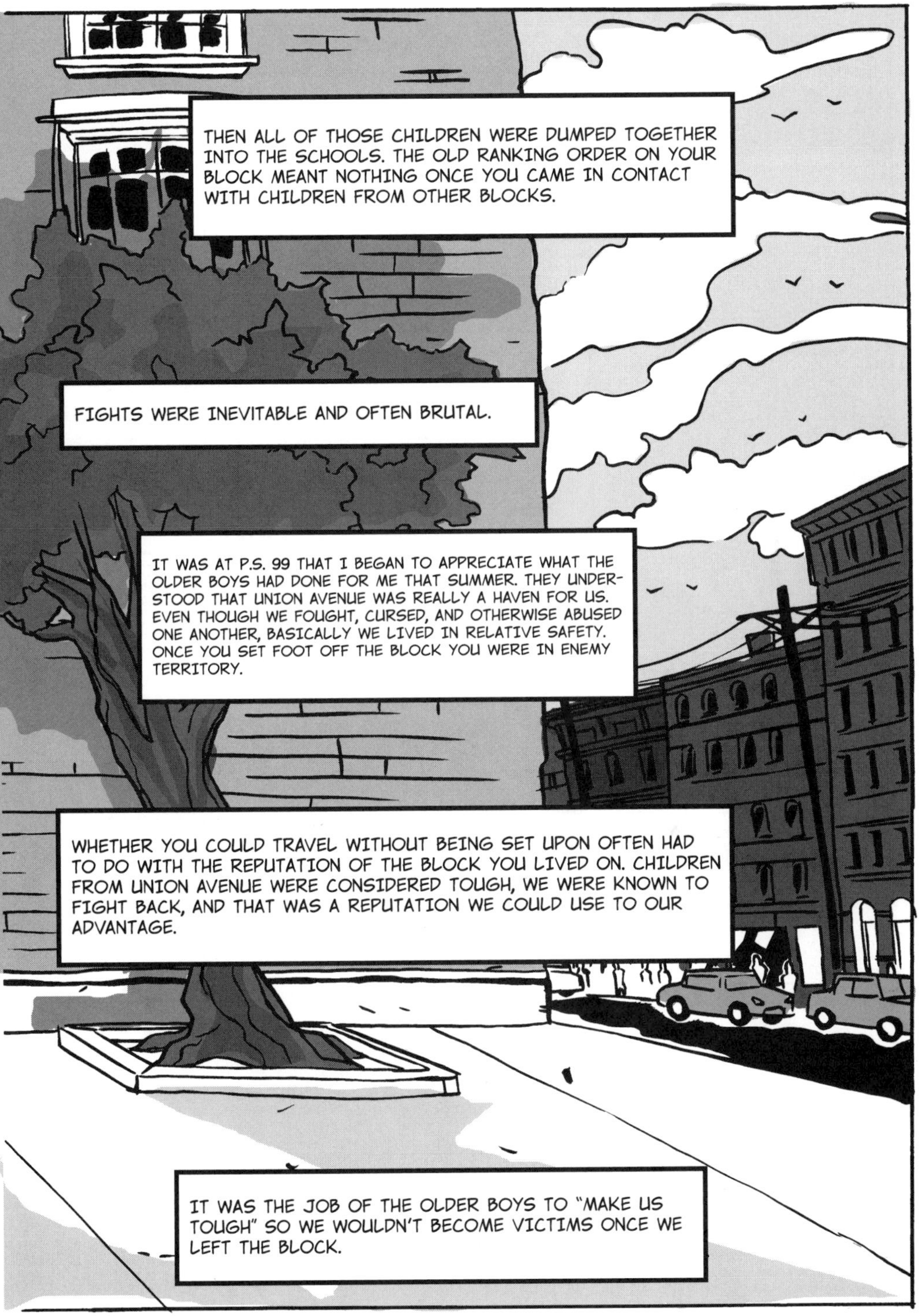
THEN ALL OF THOSE CHILDREN WERE DUMPED TOGETHER INTO THE SCHOOLS. THE OLD RANKING ORDER ON YOUR BLOCK MEANT NOTHING ONCE YOU CAME IN CONTACT WITH CHILDREN FROM OTHER BLOCKS.
FIGHTS WERE INEVITABLE AND OFTEN BRUTAL.
IT WAS AT P.S. 99 THAT I BEGAN TO APPRECIATE WHAT THE OLDER BOYS HAD DONE FOR ME THAT SUMMER. THEY UNDERSTOOD THAT UNION AVENUE WAS REALLY A HAVEN FOR US. EVEN THOUGH WE FOUGHT, CURSED, AND OTHERWISE ABUSED ONE ANOTHER, BASICALLY WE LIVED IN RELATIVE SAFETY. ONCE YOU SET FOOT OFF THE BLOCK YOU WERE IN ENEMY TERRITORY.
WHETHER YOU COULD TRAVEL WITHOUT BEING SET UPON OFTEN HAD TO DO WITH THE REPUTATION OF THE BLOCK YOU LIVED ON. CHILDREN FROM UNION AVENUE WERE CONSIDERED TOUGH, WE WERE KNOWN TO FIGHT BACK, AND THAT WAS A REPUTATION WE COULD USE TO OUR ADVANTAGE.
IT WAS THE JOB OF THE OLDER BOYS TO "MAKE US TOUGH" SO WE WOULDN'T BECOME VICTIMS ONCE WE LEFT THE BLOCK.

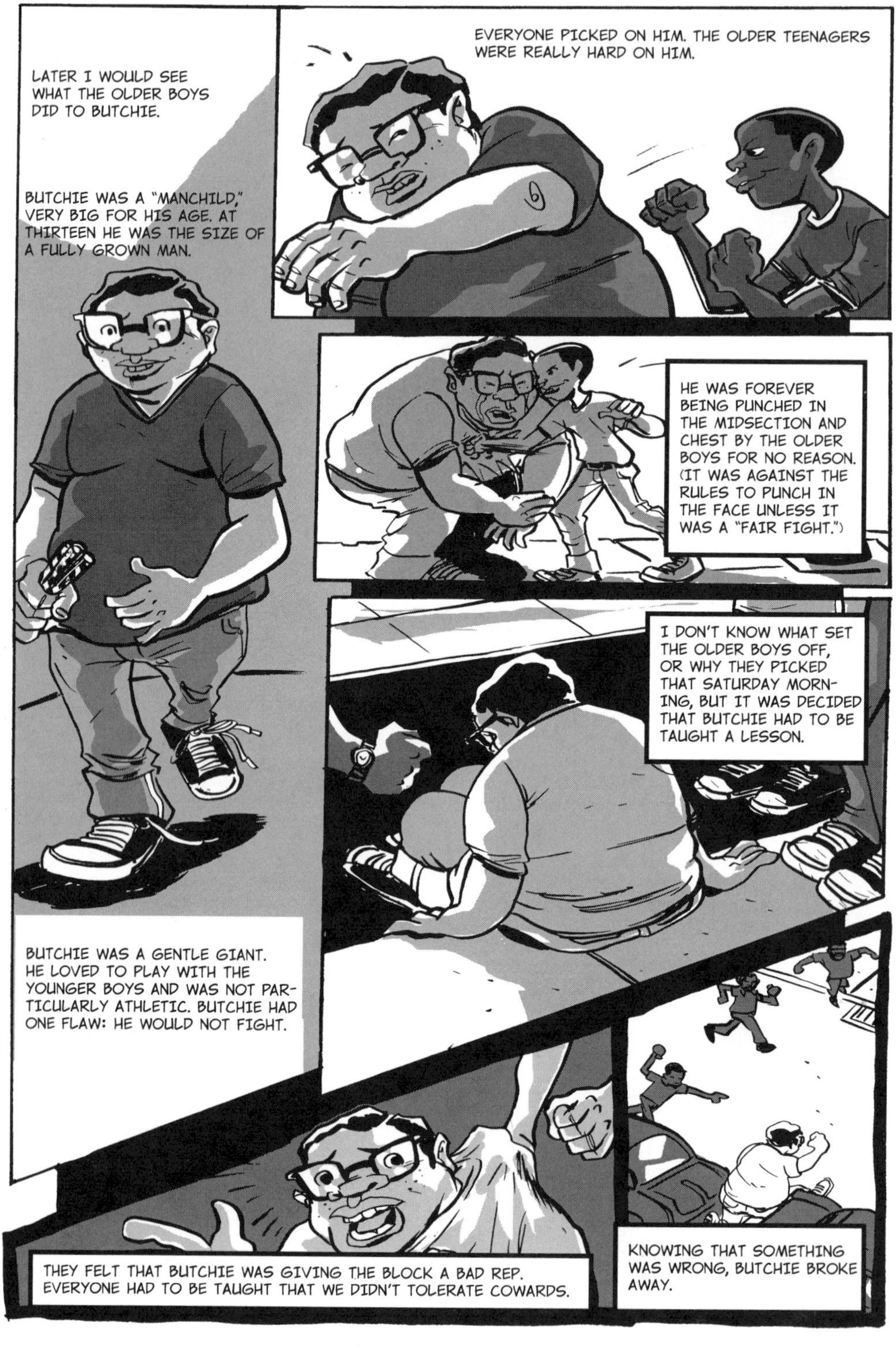
LATER I WOULD SEE WHAT THE OLDER BOYS DID TO BUTCHIE.
BUTCHIE WAS A "MANCHILD," VERY BIG FOR HIS AGE. AT THIRTEEN HE WAS THE SIZE OF A FULLY GROWN MAN.
EVERYONE PICKED ON HIM. THE OLDER TEENAGERS WERE REALLY HARD ON HIM.
HE WAS FOREVER BEING PUNCHED IN THE MIDSECTION AND CHEST BY THE OLDER BOYS FOR NO REASON. (IT WAS AGAINST THE RULES TO PUNCH IN THE FACE UNLESS IT WAS A "FAIR FIGHT.")
I DON'T KNOW WHAT SET THE OLDER BOYS OFF, OR WHY THEY PICKED THAT SATURDAY MORNING, BUT IT WAS DECIDED THAT BUTCHIE HAD TO BE TAUGHT A LESSON.
BUTCHIE WAS A GENTLE GIANT. HE LOVED TO PLAY WITH THE YOUNGER BOYS AND WAS NOT PARTICULARLY ATHLETIC. BUTCHIE HAD ONE FLAW: HE WOULD NOT FIGHT.
THEY FELT THAT BUTCHIE WAS GIVING THE BLOCK A BAD REP. EVERYONE HAD TO BE TAUGHT THAT WE DIDN'T TOLERATE COWARDS.
KNOWING THAT SOMETHING WAS WRONG, BUTCHIE BROKE AWAY.

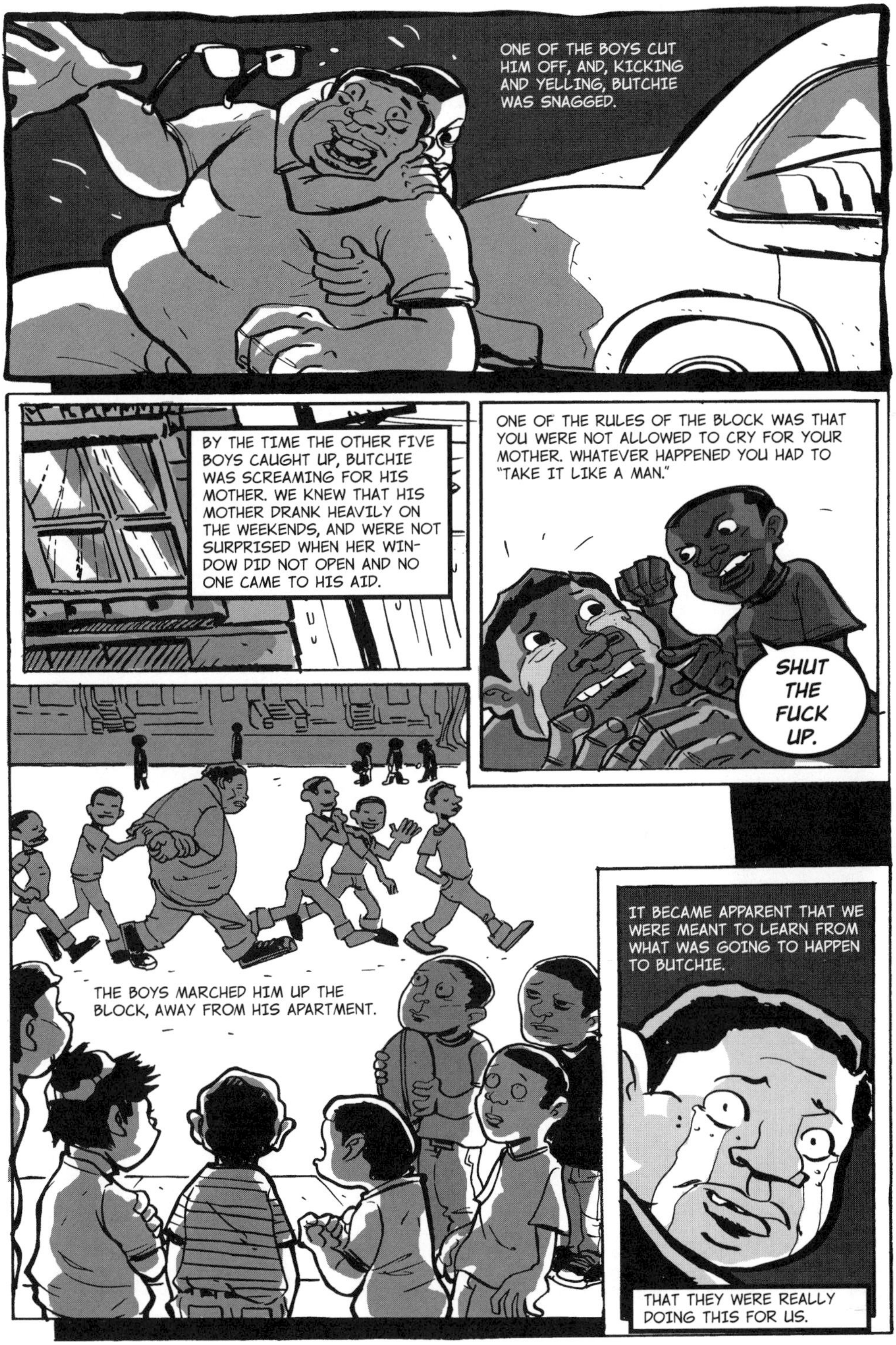
ONE OF THE BOYS CUT HIM OFF, AND, KICKING AND YELLING, BUTCHIE WAS SNAGGED.
BY THE TIME THE OTHER FIVE BOYS CAUGHT UP, BUTCHIE WAS SCREAMING FOR HIS MOTHER. WE KNEW THAT HIS MOTHER DRANK HEAVILY ON THE WEEKENDS, AND WERE NOT SURPRISED WHEN HER WIN-DOW DID NOT OPEN AND NO ONE CAME TO HIS AID.
ONE OF THE RULES OF THE BLOCK WAS THAT YOU WERE NOT ALLOWED TO CRY FOR YOUR MOTHER. WHATEVER HAPPENED YOU HAD TO "TAKE IT LIKE A MAN."
SHUT THE FUCK UP.
THE BOYS MARCHED HIM UP THE BLOCK, AWAY FROM HIS APARTMENT.
IT BECAME APPARENT THAT WE WERE MEANT TO LEARN FROM WHAT WAS GOING TO HAPPEN TO BUTCHIE.
THAT THEY WERE REALLY DOING THIS FOR US.

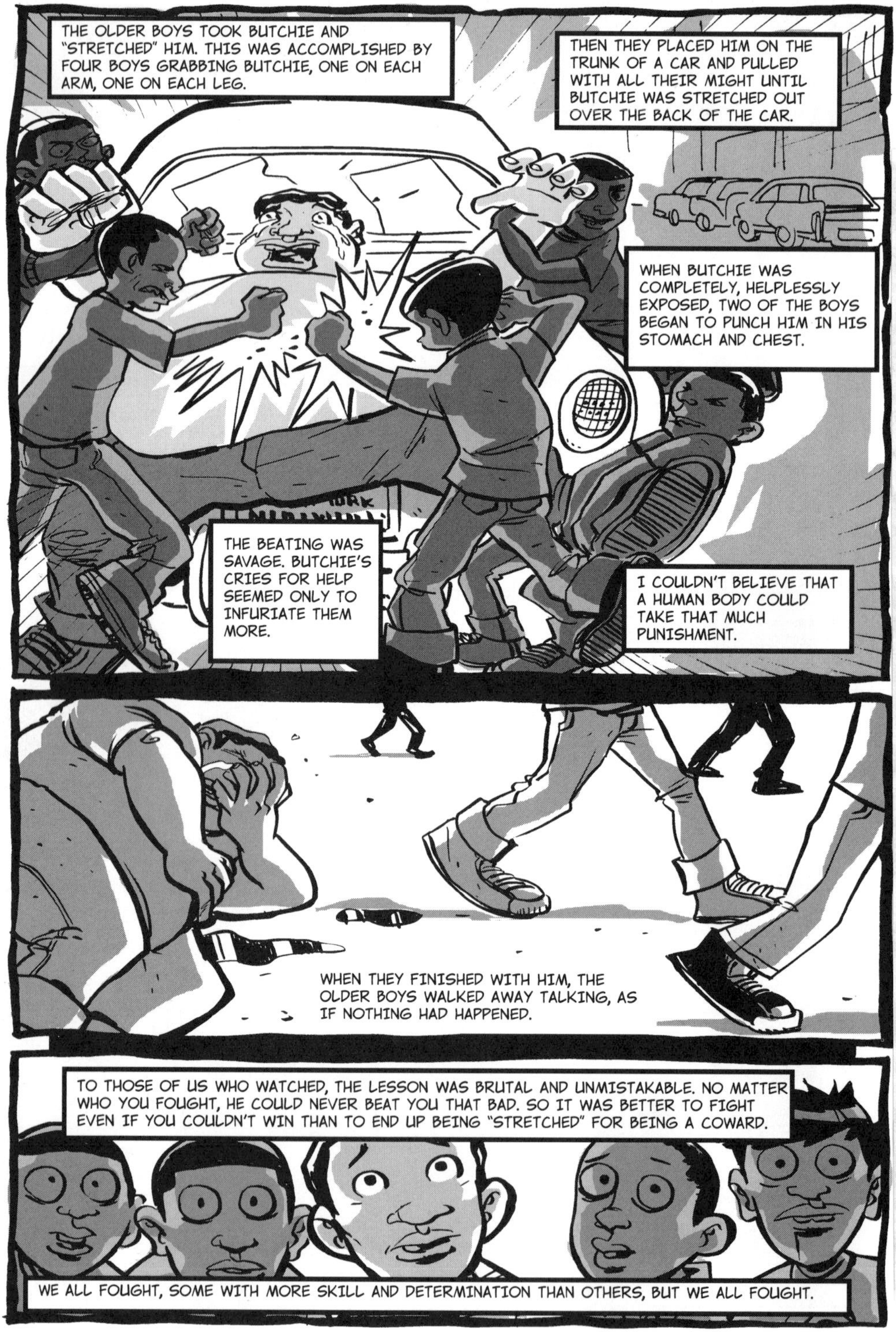
THE OLDER BOYS TOOK BUTCHIE AND "STRETCHED" HIM. THIS WAS ACCOMPLISHED BY FOUR BOYS GRABBING BUTCHIE, ONE ON EACH ARM, ONE ON EACH LEG.
THEN THEY PLACED HIM ON THE TRUNK OF A CAR AND PULLED WITH ALL THEIR MIGHT UNTIL BUTCHIE WAS STRETCHED OUT OVER THE BACK OF THE CAR.
WHEN BUTCHIE WAS COMPLETELY, HELPLESSLY EXPOSED, TWO OF THE BOYS BEGAN TO PUNCH HIM IN HIS STOMACH AND CHEST.
THE BEATING WAS SAVAGE. BUTCHIE'S CRIES FOR HELP SEEMED ONLY TO INFURIATE THEM MORE.
I COULDN'T BELIEVE THAT A HUMAN BODY COULD TAKE THAT MUCH PUNISHMENT.
WHEN THEY FINISHED WITH HIM, THE OLDER BOYS WALKED AWAY TALKING, AS IF NOTHING HAD HAPPENED.
TO THOSE OF US WHO WATCHED, THE LESSON WAS BRUTAL AND UNMISTAKABLE. NO MATTER WHO YOU FOUGHT, HE COULD NEVER BEAT YOU THAT BAD. SO IT WAS BETTER TO FIGHT EVEN IF YOU COULDN'T WIN THAN TO END UP BEING "STRETCHED" FOR BEING A COWARD.
WE ALL FOUGHT, SOME WITH MORE SKILL AND DETERMINATION THAN OTHERS, BUT WE ALL FOUGHT.

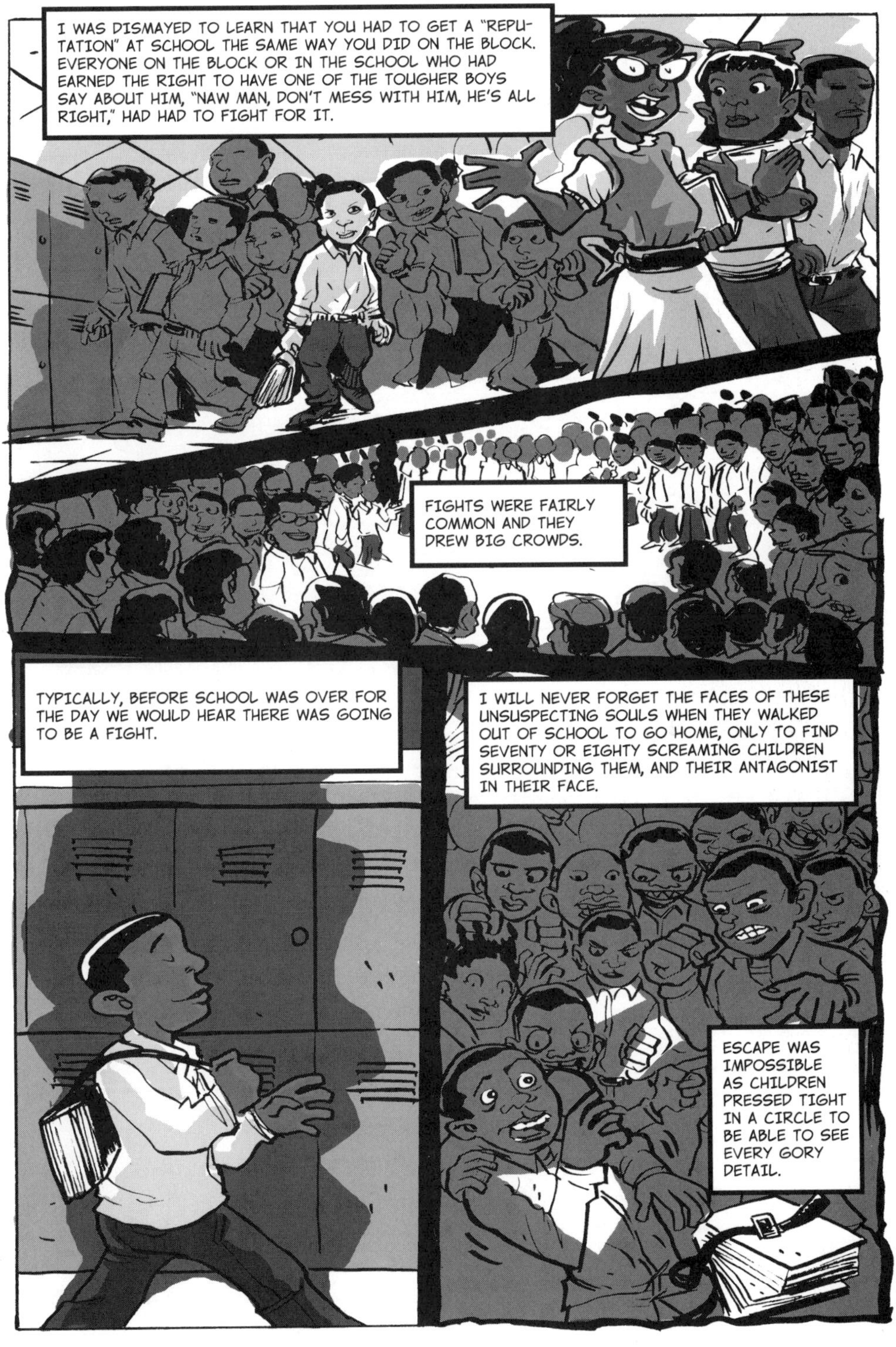
I WAS DISMAYED TO LEARN THAT YOU HAD TO GET A "REPUTATION" AT SCHOOL THE SAME WAY YOU DID ON THE BLOCK. EVERYONE ON THE BLOCK OR IN THE SCHOOL WHO HAD EARNED THE RIGHT TO HAVE ONE OF THE TOUGHER BOYS SAY ABOUT HIM, "NAW MAN, DON'T MESS WITH HIM, HE'S ALL RIGHT," HAD HAD TO FIGHT FOR IT.
FIGHTS WERE FAIRLY COMMON AND THEY DREW BIG CROWDS.
TYPICALLY, BEFORE SCHOOL WAS OVER FOR THE DAY WE WOULD HEAR THERE WAS GOING TO BE A FIGHT.
I WILL NEVER FORGET THE FACES OF THESE UNSUSPECTING SOULS WHEN THEY WALKED OUT OF SCHOOL TO GO HOME, ONLY TO FIND SEVENTY OR EIGHTY SCREAMING CHILDREN SURROUNDING THEM, AND THEIR ANTAGONIST IN THEIR FACE.
ESCAPE WAS IMPOSSIBLE AS CHILDREN PRESSED TIGHT IN A CIRCLE TO BE ABLE TO SEE EVERY GORY DETAIL.

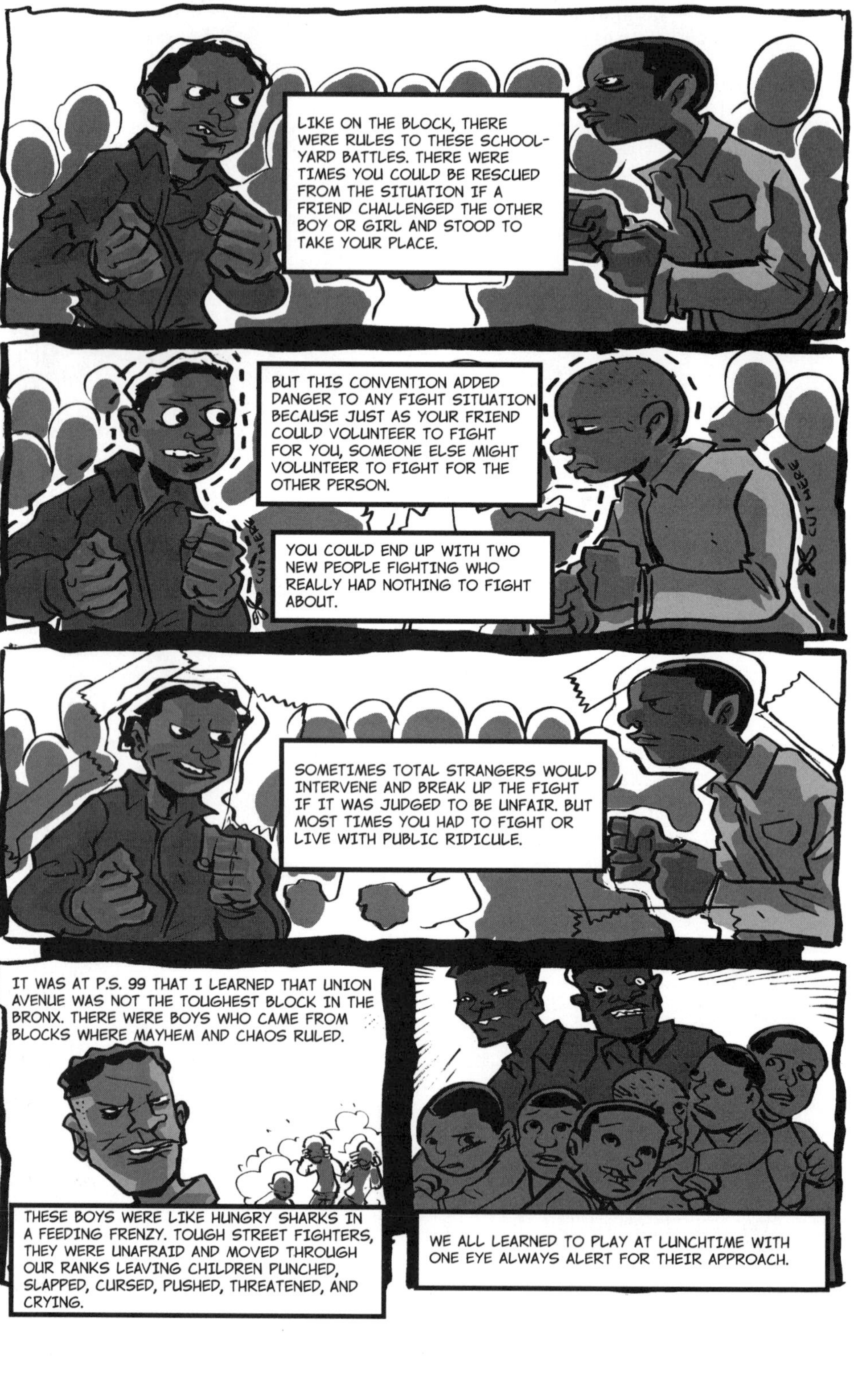
LIKE ON THE BLOCK, THERE WERE RULES TO THESE SCHOOL-YARD BATTLES. THERE WERE TIMES YOU COULD BE RESCUED FROM THE SITUATION IF A FRIEND CHALLENGED THE OTHER BOY OR GIRL AND STOOD TO TAKE YOUR PLACE.
BUT THIS CONVENTION ADDED DANGER TO ANY FIGHT SITUATION BECAUSE JUST AS YOUR FRIEND COULD VOLUNTEER TO FIGHT FOR YOU, SOMEONE ELSE MIGHT VOLUNTEER TO FIGHT FOR THE OTHER PERSON.
YOU COULD END UP WITH TWO NEW PEOPLE FIGHTING WHO REALLY HAD NOTHING TO FIGHT ABOUT.
SOMETIMES TOTAL STRANGERS WOULD INTERVENE AND BREAK UP THE FIGHT IF IT WAS JUDGED TO BE UNFAIR. BUT MOST TIMES YOU HAD TO FIGHT OR LIVE WITH PUBLIC RIDICULE.
IT WAS AT P.S. 99 THAT I LEARNED THAT UNION AVENUE WAS NOT THE TOUGHEST BLOCK IN THE BRONX. THERE WERE BOYS WHO CAME FROM BLOCKS WHERE MAYHEM AND CHAOS RULED.
THESE BOYS WERE LIKE HUNGRY SHARKS IN A FEEDING FRENZY. TOUGH STREET FIGHTERS, THEY WERE UNAFRAID AND MOVED THROUGH OUR RANKS LEAVING CHILDREN PUNCHED, SLAPPED, CURSED, PUSHED, THREATENED, AND CRYING.
WE ALL LEARNED TO PLAY AT LUNCHTIME WITH ONE EYE ALWAYS ALERT FOR THEIR APPROACH.

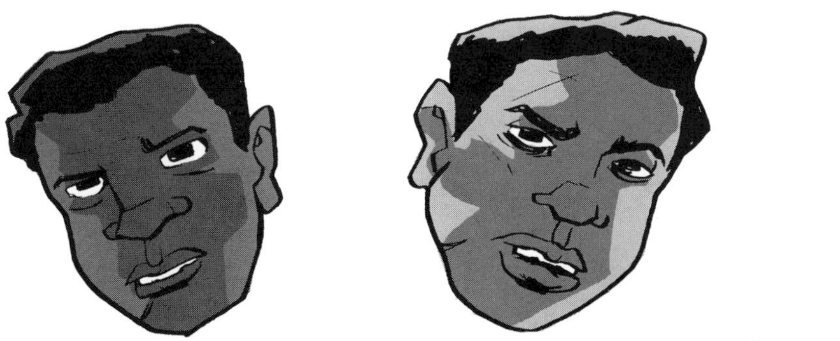

THE SCHOOL WAS RULED FROM THE TOP BY TWO BOYS NAMED TYRONNE AND ANTHONY, WHO WERE SAID TO BE TWINS, ALTHOUGH NO ONE SEEMED TO KNOW FOR SURE. THEY WERE FAIRLY BENEVOLENT RULERS, AS THEY TENDED TO LEAVE MOST OF THE YOUNGER BOYS ALONE.

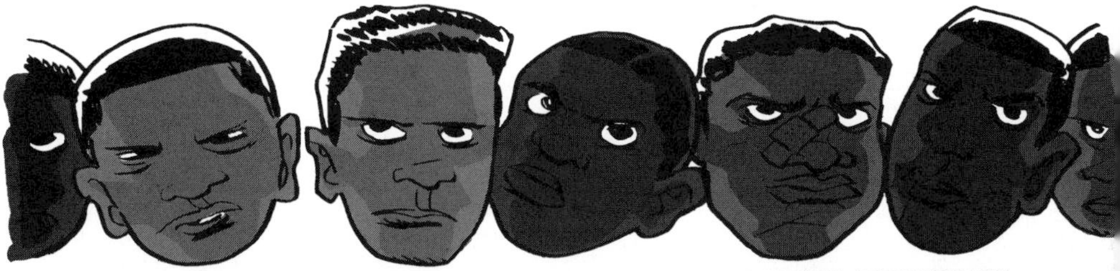

DIRECTLY UNDER THE TWINS WAS A GROUP OF MEAN, HARDENED LITTLE BOYS. THEY WOULD USE THEIR ASSOCIATION WITH TYRONNE AND ANTHONY TO BULLY ANYONE WHO MAY STAND UP TO THEM OTHERWISE.

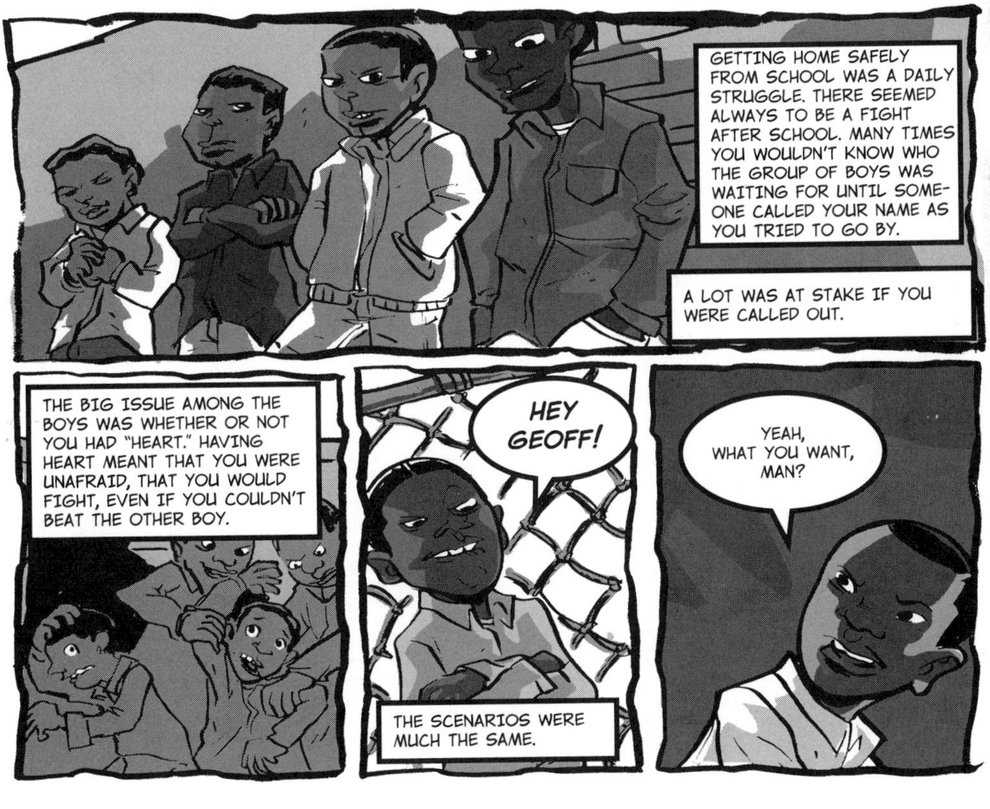
GETTING HOME SAFELY FROM SCHOOL WAS A DAILY STRUGGLE. THERE SEEMED ALWAYS TO BE A FIGHT AFTER SCHOOL. MANY TIMES YOU WOULDN'T KNOW WHO THE GROUP OF BOYS WAS WAITING FOR UNTIL SOME-ONE CALLED YOUR NAME AS YOU TRIED TO GO BY.
A LOT WAS AT STAKE IF YOU WERE CALLED OUT.
THE BIG ISSUE AMONG THE BOYS WAS WHETHER OR NOT YOU HAD "HEART." HAVING HEART MEANT THAT YOU WERE UNAFRAID, THAT YOU WOULD FIGHT, EVEN IF YOU COULDN'T BEAT THE OTHER BOY.
HEY GEOFF!
THE SCENARIOS WERE MUCH THE SAME.
YEAH, WHAT YOU WANT, MAN?

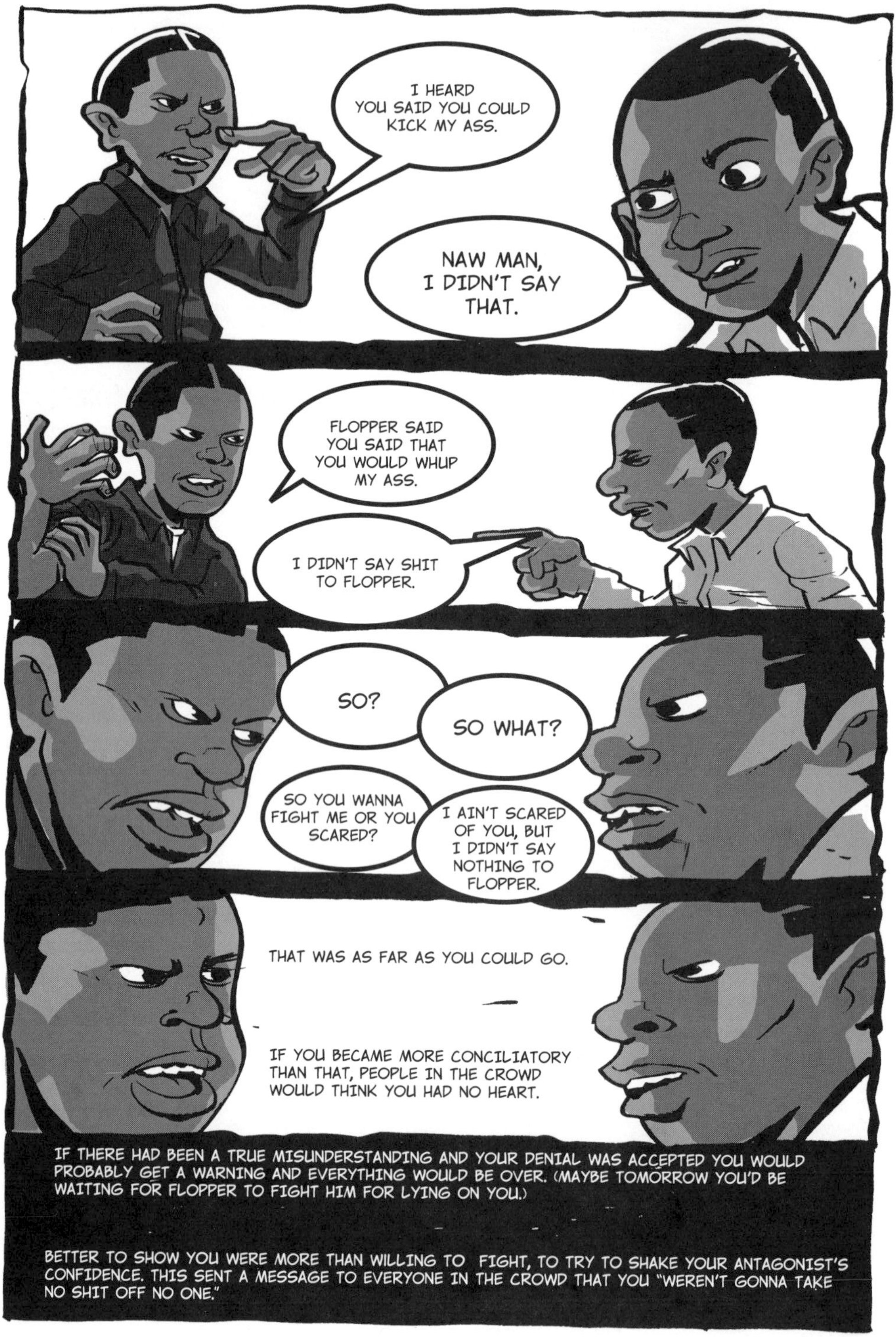
I HEARD YOU SAID YOU COULD KICK MY ASS.
NAW MAN, I DIDN'T SAY THAT.
FLOPPER SAID YOU SAID THAT YOU WOULD WHUP MY ASS.
I DIDN'T SAY SHIT TO FLOPPER.
SO?
SO WHAT?
SO YOU WANNA FIGHT ME OR YOU SCARED?
I AIN'T SCARED OF YOU, BUT I DIDN'T SAY NOTHING TO FLOPPER.
THAT WAS AS FAR AS YOU COULD GO.
IF YOU BECAME MORE CONCILIATORY THAN THAT, PEOPLE IN THE CROWD WOULD THINK YOU HAD NO HEART.
IF THERE HAD BEEN A TRUE MISUNDERSTANDING AND YOUR DENIAL WAS ACCEPTED YOU WOULD PROBABLY GET A WARNING AND EVERYTHING WOULD BE OVER. (MAYBE TOMORROW YOU'D BE WAITING FOR FLOPPER TO FIGHT HIM FOR LYING ON YOU.)
BETTER TO SHOW YOU WERE MORE THAN WILLING TO FIGHT, TO TRY TO SHAKE YOUR ANTAGONIST'S CONFIDENCE. THIS SENT A MESSAGE TO EVERYONE IN THE CROWD THAT YOU "WEREN'T GONNA TAKE NO SHIT OFF NO ONE."

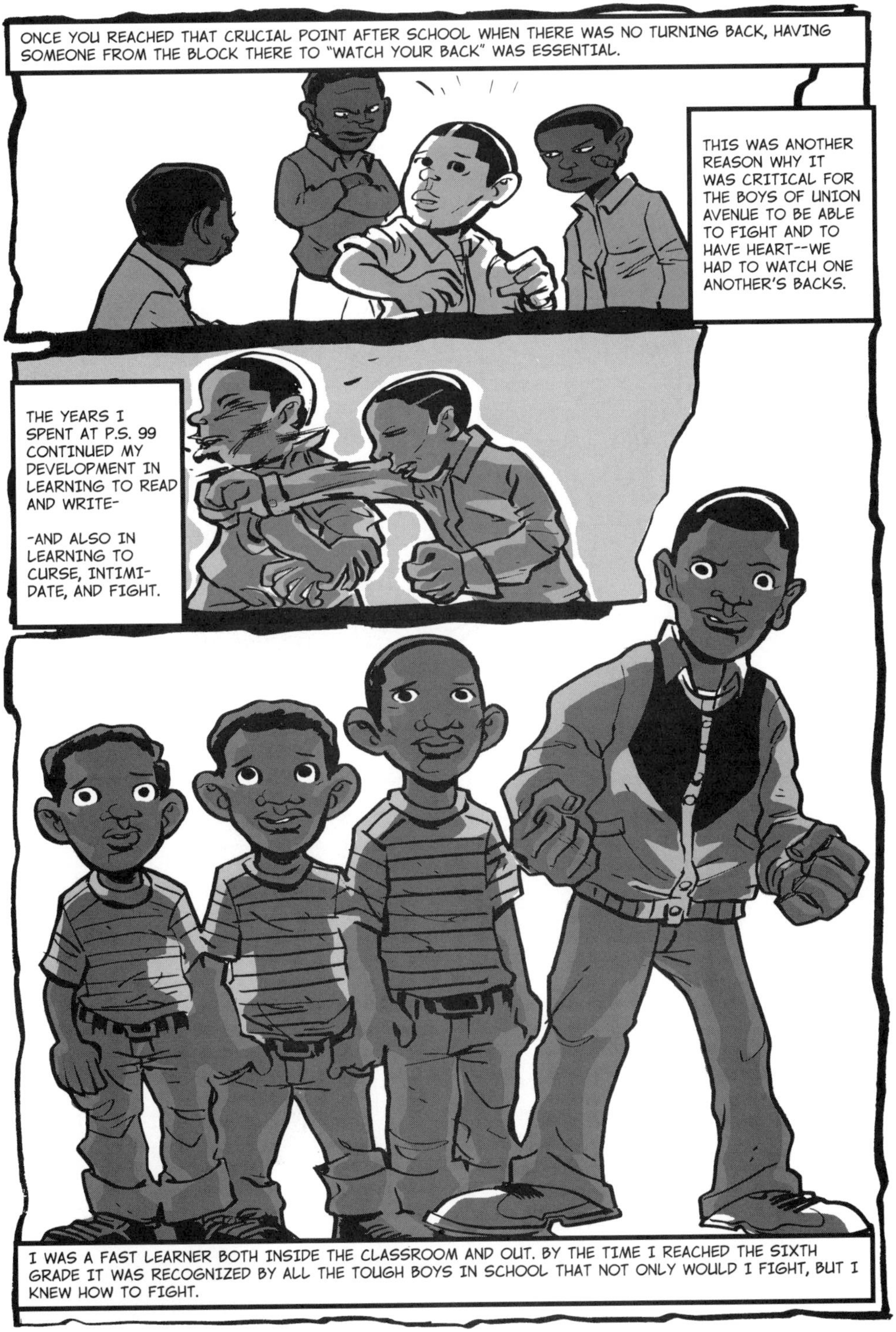
ONCE YOU REACHED THAT CRUCIAL POINT AFTER SCHOOL WHEN THERE WAS NO TURNING BACK, HAVING SOMEONE FROM THE BLOCK THERE TO "WATCH YOUR BACK" WAS ESSENTIAL.
THIS WAS ANOTHER REASON WHY IT WAS CRITICAL FOR THE BOYS OF UNION AVENUE TO BE ABLE TO FIGHT AND TO HAVE HEART--WE HAD TO WATCH ONE ANOTHER'S BACKS.
THE YEARS I SPENT AT P.S. 99 CONTINUED MY DEVELOPMENT IN LEARNING TO READ AND WRITE-
-AND ALSO IN LEARNING TO CURSE, INTIMIDATE, AND FIGHT.
I WAS A FAST LEARNER BOTH INSIDE THE CLASSROOM AND OUT. BY THE TIME I REACHED THE SIXTH GRADE IT WAS RECOGNIZED BY ALL THE TOUGH BOYS IN SCHOOL THAT NOT ONLY WOULD I FIGHT, BUT I KNEW HOW TO FIGHT.

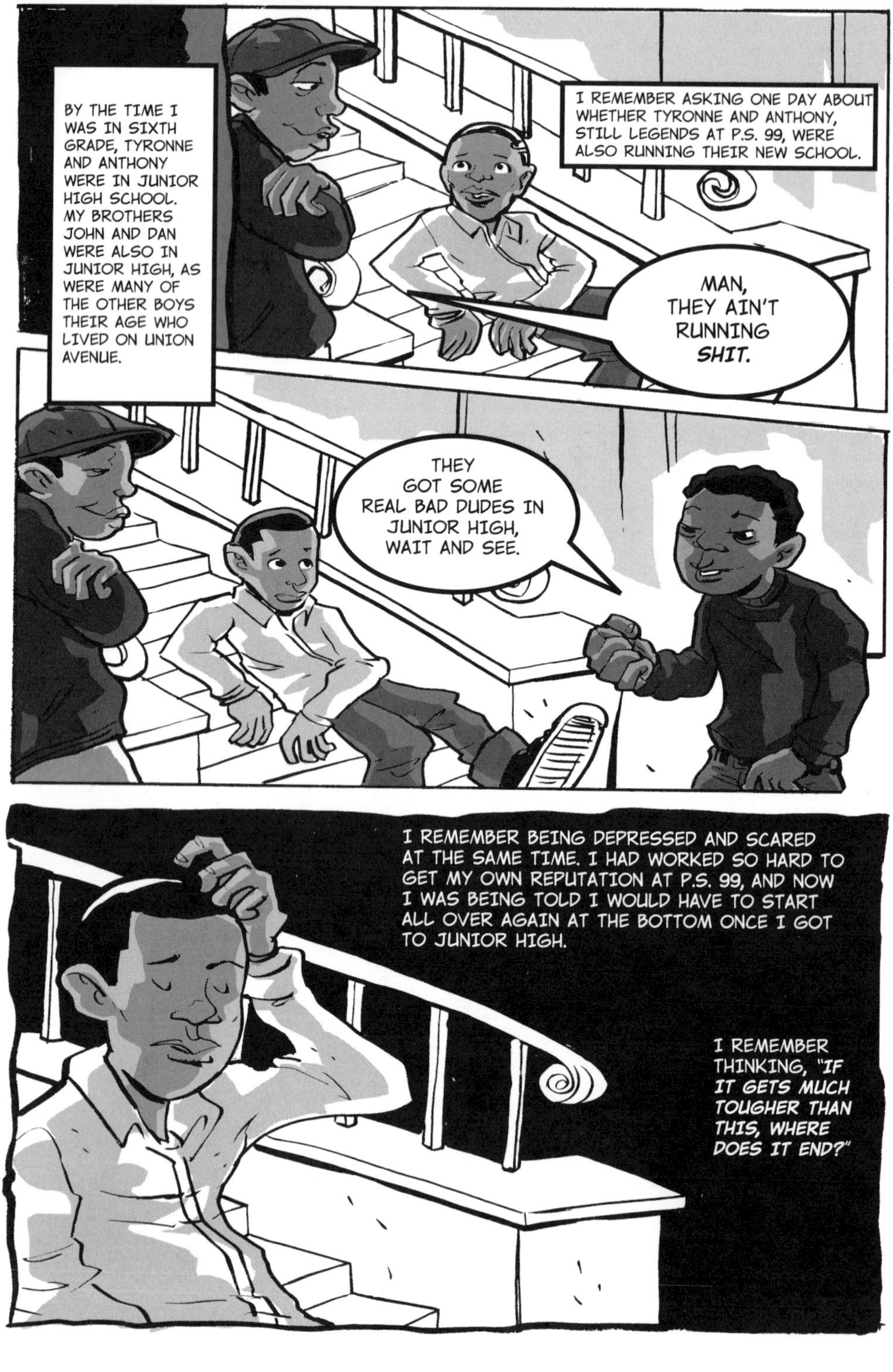
BY THE TIME I WAS IN SIXTH GRADE, TYRONNE AND ANTHONY WERE IN JUNIOR HIGH SCHOOL. MY BROTHERS JOHN AND DAN WERE ALSO IN JUNIOR HIGH, AS WERE MANY OF THE OTHER BOYS THEIR AGE WHO LIVED ON UNION AVENUE.
I REMEMBER ASKING ONE DAY ABOUT WHETHER TYRONNE AND ANTHONY, STILL LEGENDS AT P.S. 99, WERE ALSO RUNNING THEIR NEW SCHOOL.
MAN, THEY AIN'T RUNNING *SHIT.*
THEY GOT SOME REAL BAD DUDES IN JUNIOR HIGH, WAIT AND SEE.
I REMEMBER BEING DEPRESSED AND SCARED AT THE SAME TIME. I HAD WORKED SO HARD TO GET MY OWN REPUTATION AT P.S. 99, AND NOW I WAS BEING TOLD I WOULD HAVE TO START ALL OVER AGAIN AT THE BOTTOM ONCE I GOT TO JUNIOR HIGH.
I REMEMBER THINKING, *"IF IT GETS MUCH TOUGHER THAN THIS, WHERE DOES IT END?"*

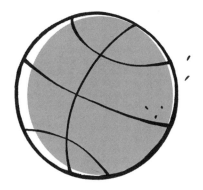

5

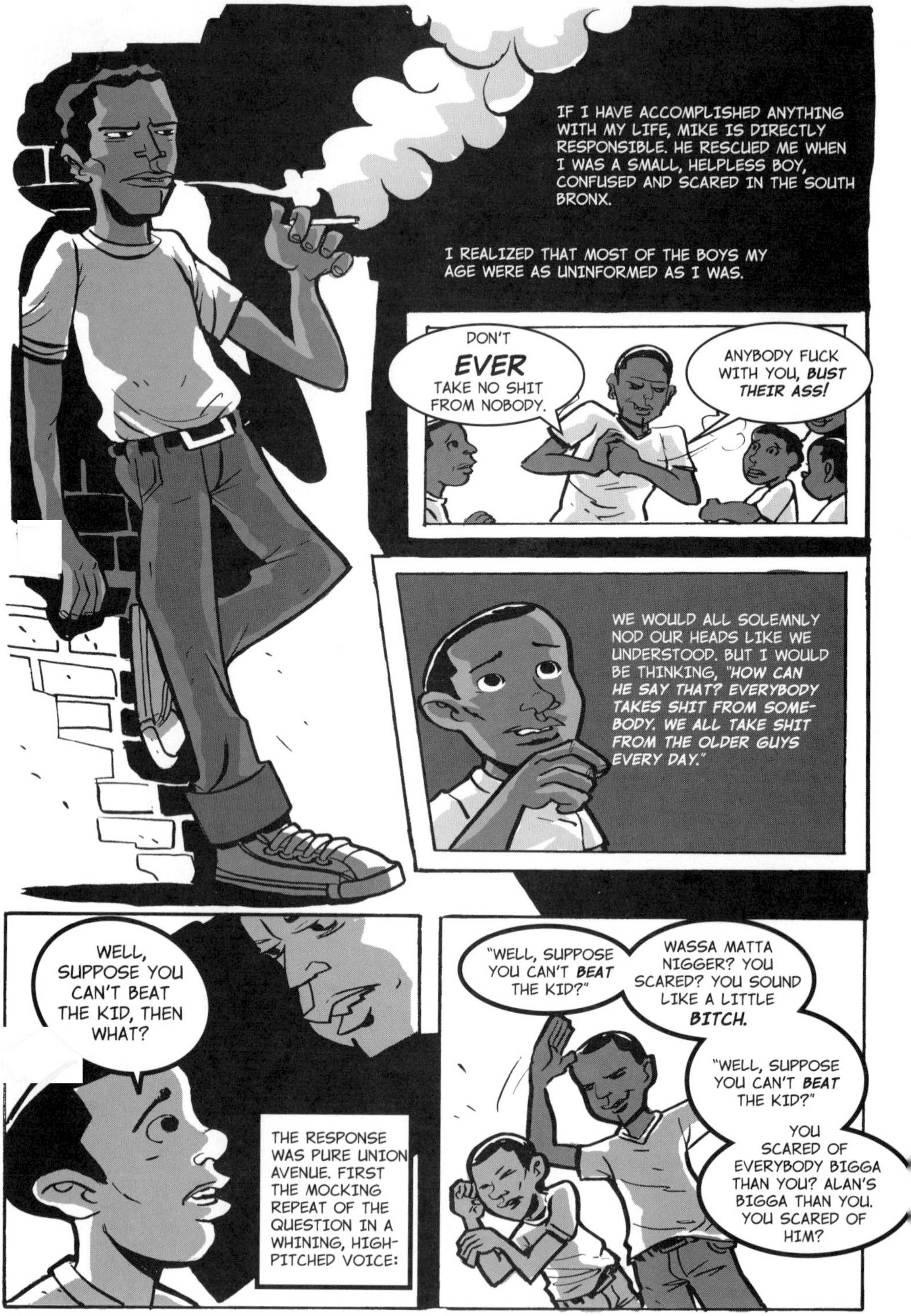
IF I HAVE ACCOMPLISHED ANYTHING WITH MY LIFE, MIKE IS DIRECTLY RESPONSIBLE. HE RESCUED ME WHEN I WAS A SMALL, HELPLESS BOY, CONFUSED AND SCARED IN THE SOUTH BRONX.
I REALIZED THAT MOST OF THE BOYS MY AGE WERE AS UNINFORMED AS I WAS.
DON'T EVER TAKE NO SHIT FROM NOBODY.
ANYBODY FUCK WITH YOU, BUST THEIR ASS!
WE WOULD ALL SOLEMNLY NOD OUR HEADS LIKE WE UNDERSTOOD. BUT I WOULD BE THINKING, "HOW CAN HE SAY THAT? EVERYBODY TAKES SHIT FROM SOMEBODY. WE ALL TAKE SHIT FROM THE OLDER GUYS EVERY DAY."
WELL, SUPPOSE YOU CAN'T BEAT THE KID, THEN WHAT?
THE RESPONSE WAS PURE UNION AVENUE. FIRST THE MOCKING REPEAT OF THE QUESTION IN A WHINING, HIGH-PITCHED VOICE:
"WELL, SUPPOSE YOU CAN'T BEAT THE KID?"
WASSA MATTA NIGGER? YOU SCARED? YOU SOUND LIKE A LITTLE BITCH.
"WELL, SUPPOSE YOU CAN'T BEAT THE KID?"
YOU SCARED OF EVERYBODY BIGGA THAN YOU? ALAN'S BIGGA THAN YOU. YOU SCARED OF HIM?

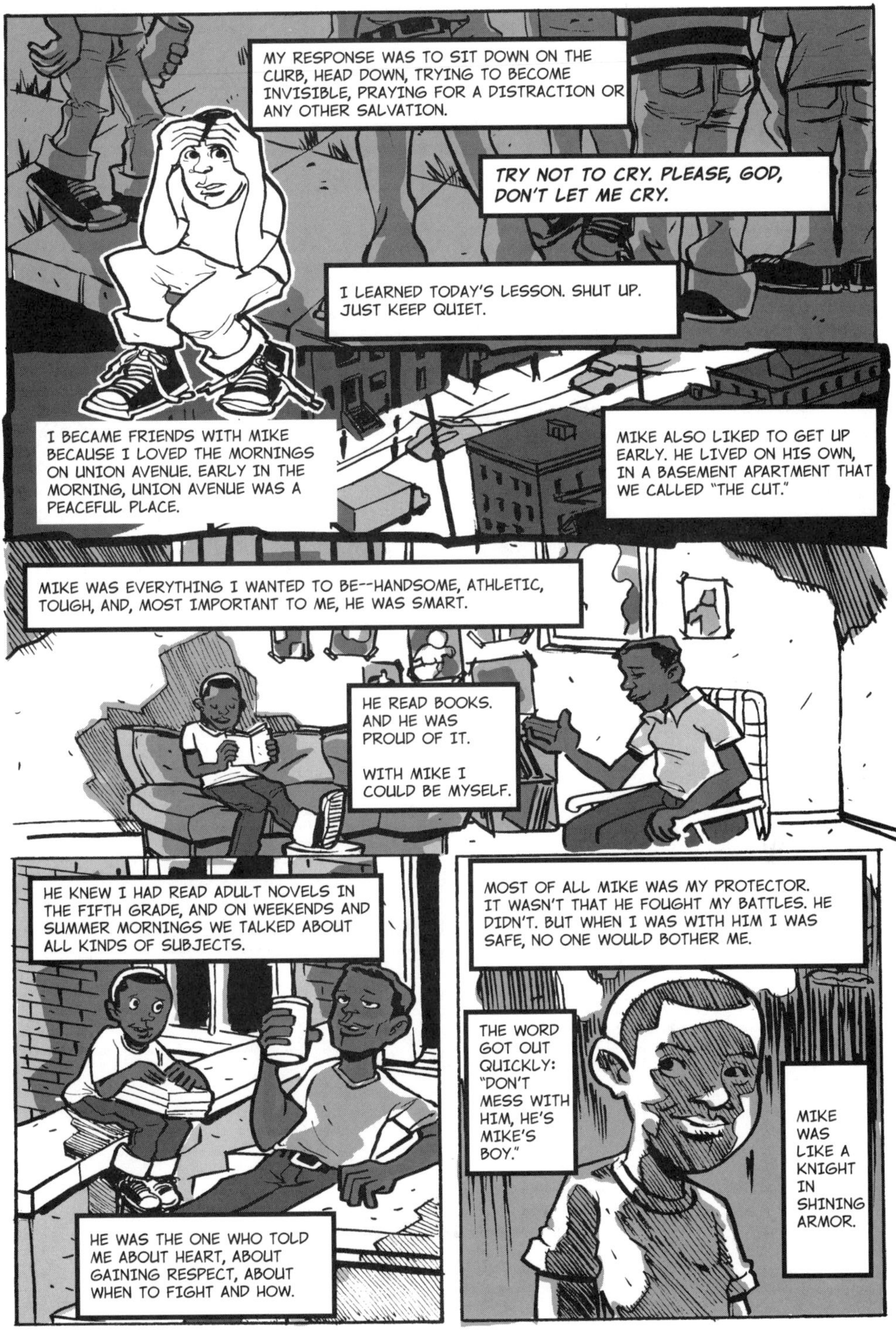
MY RESPONSE WAS TO SIT DOWN ON THE CURB, HEAD DOWN, TRYING TO BECOME INVISIBLE, PRAYING FOR A DISTRACTION OR ANY OTHER SALVATION.
TRY NOT TO CRY. PLEASE, GOD, DON'T LET ME CRY.
I LEARNED TODAY'S LESSON. SHUT UP. JUST KEEP QUIET.
I BECAME FRIENDS WITH MIKE BECAUSE I LOVED THE MORNINGS ON UNION AVENUE. EARLY IN THE MORNING, UNION AVENUE WAS A PEACEFUL PLACE.
MIKE ALSO LIKED TO GET UP EARLY. HE LIVED ON HIS OWN, IN A BASEMENT APARTMENT THAT WE CALLED "THE CUT."
MIKE WAS EVERYTHING I WANTED TO BE--HANDSOME, ATHLETIC, TOUGH, AND, MOST IMPORTANT TO ME, HE WAS SMART.
HE READ BOOKS. AND HE WAS PROUD OF IT.
WITH MIKE I COULD BE MYSELF.
HE KNEW I HAD READ ADULT NOVELS IN THE FIFTH GRADE, AND ON WEEKENDS AND SUMMER MORNINGS WE TALKED ABOUT ALL KINDS OF SUBJECTS.
HE WAS THE ONE WHO TOLD ME ABOUT HEART, ABOUT GAINING RESPECT, ABOUT WHEN TO FIGHT AND HOW.
MOST OF ALL MIKE WAS MY PROTECTOR. IT WASN'T THAT HE FOUGHT MY BATTLES. HE DIDN'T. BUT WHEN I WAS WITH HIM I WAS SAFE, NO ONE WOULD BOTHER ME.
THE WORD GOT OUT QUICKLY: "DON'T MESS WITH HIM, HE'S MIKE'S BOY."
MIKE WAS LIKE A KNIGHT IN SHINING ARMOR.

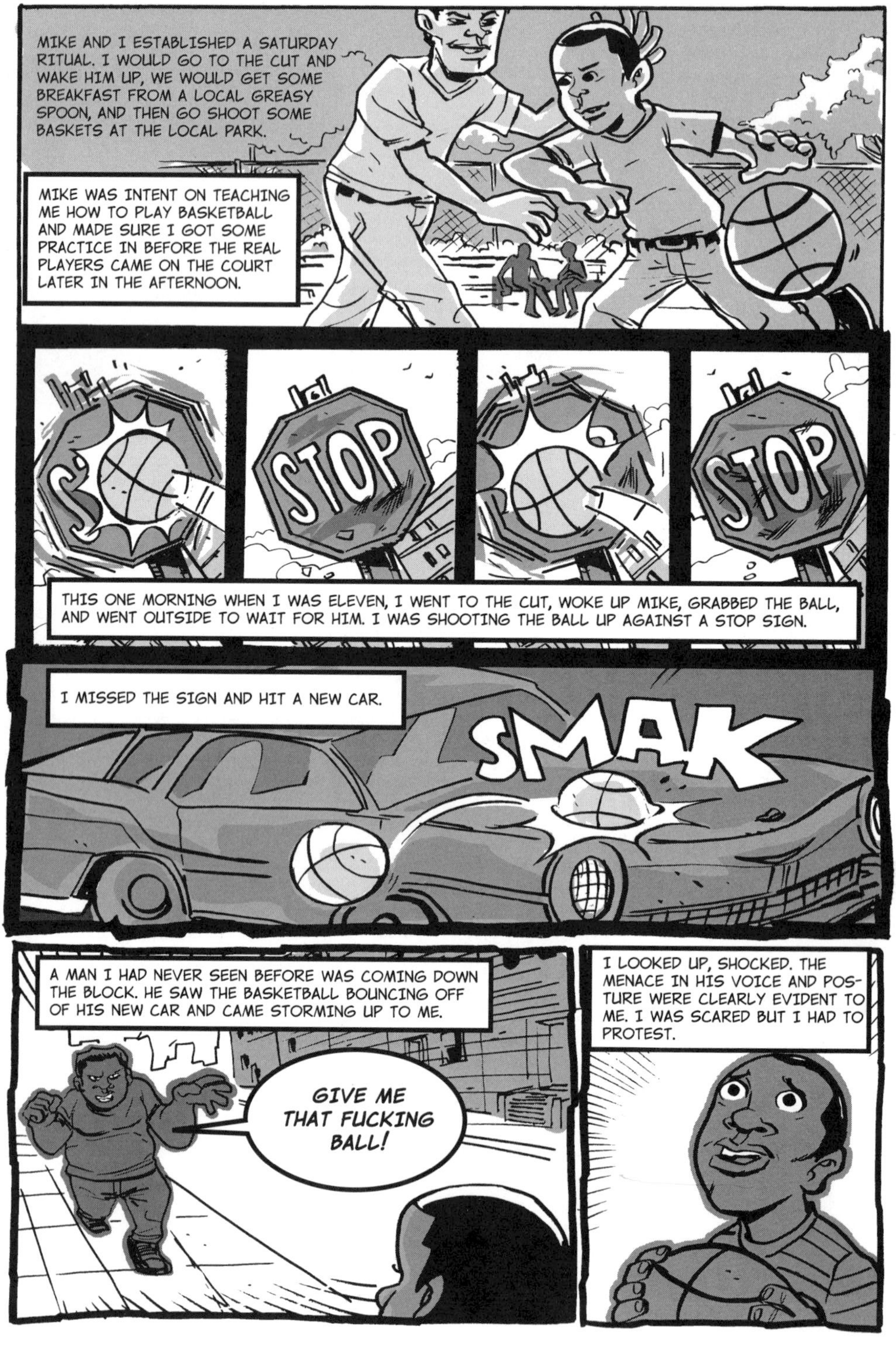
MIKE AND I ESTABLISHED A SATURDAY RITUAL. I WOULD GO TO THE CUT AND WAKE HIM UP, WE WOULD GET SOME BREAKFAST FROM A LOCAL GREASY SPOON, AND THEN GO SHOOT SOME BASKETS AT THE LOCAL PARK.
MIKE WAS INTENT ON TEACHING ME HOW TO PLAY BASKETBALL AND MADE SURE I GOT SOME PRACTICE IN BEFORE THE REAL PLAYERS CAME ON THE COURT LATER IN THE AFTERNOON.
STOP
STOP
THIS ONE MORNING WHEN I WAS ELEVEN, I WENT TO THE CUT, WOKE UP MIKE, GRABBED THE BALL, AND WENT OUTSIDE TO WAIT FOR HIM. I WAS SHOOTING THE BALL UP AGAINST A STOP SIGN.
I MISSED THE SIGN AND HIT A NEW CAR.
SMAK
A MAN I HAD NEVER SEEN BEFORE WAS COMING DOWN THE BLOCK. HE SAW THE BASKETBALL BOUNCING OFF OF HIS NEW CAR AND CAME STORMING UP TO ME.
GIVE ME THAT FUCKING BALL!
I LOOKED UP, SHOCKED. THE MENACE IN HIS VOICE AND POSTURE WERE CLEARLY EVIDENT TO ME. I WAS SCARED BUT I HAD TO PROTEST.

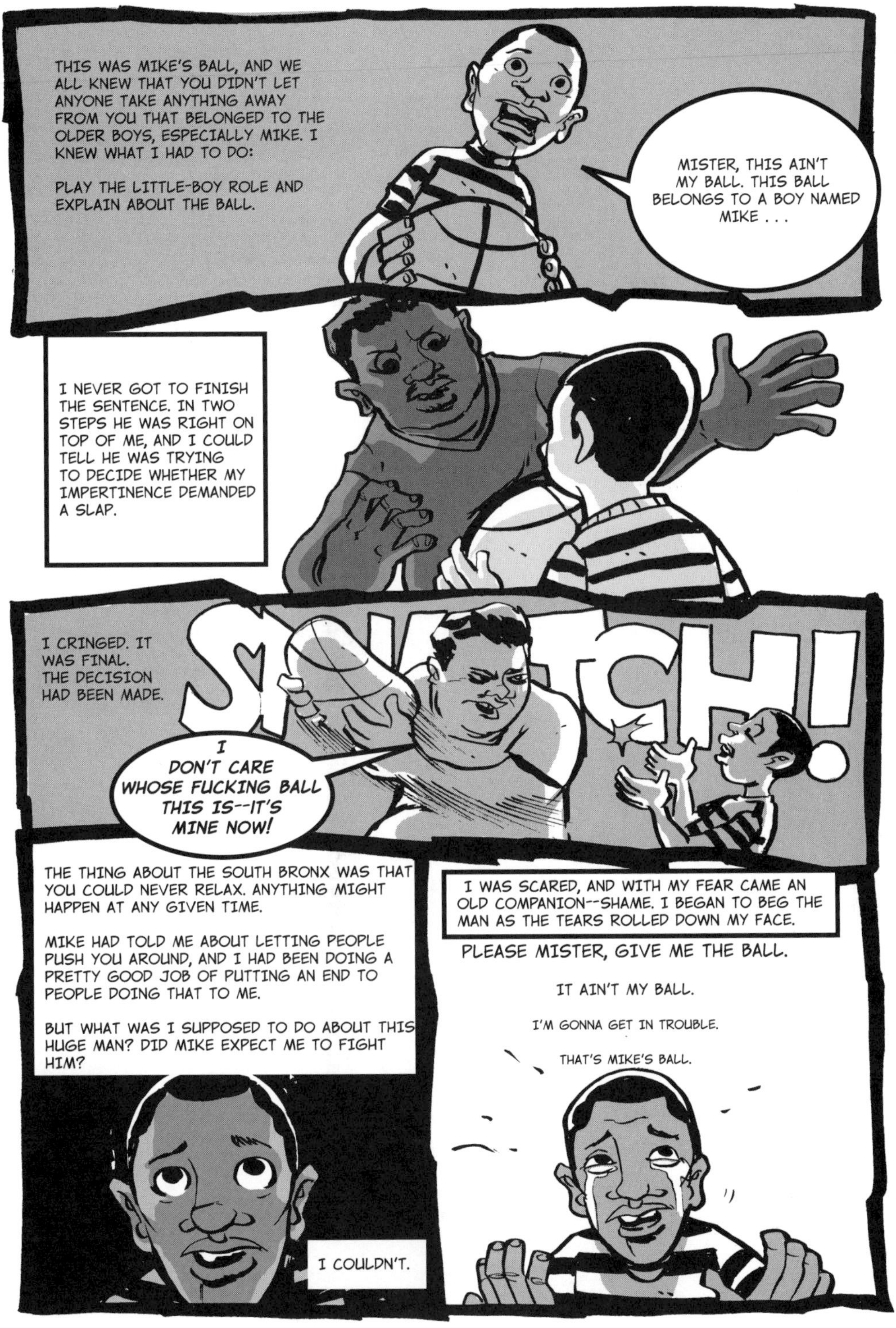
THIS WAS MIKE'S BALL, AND WE ALL KNEW THAT YOU DIDN'T LET ANYONE TAKE ANYTHING AWAY FROM YOU THAT BELONGED TO THE OLDER BOYS, ESPECIALLY MIKE. I KNEW WHAT I HAD TO DO:
PLAY THE LITTLE-BOY ROLE AND EXPLAIN ABOUT THE BALL.
MISTER, THIS AIN'T MY BALL. THIS BALL BELONGS TO A BOY NAMED MIKE . . .
I NEVER GOT TO FINISH THE SENTENCE. IN TWO STEPS HE WAS RIGHT ON TOP OF ME, AND I COULD TELL HE WAS TRYING TO DECIDE WHETHER MY IMPERTINENCE DEMANDED A SLAP.
I CRINGED. IT WAS FINAL. THE DECISION HAD BEEN MADE.
SNATCH!
I DON'T CARE WHOSE FUCKING BALL THIS IS--IT'S MINE NOW!
THE THING ABOUT THE SOUTH BRONX WAS THAT YOU COULD NEVER RELAX. ANYTHING MIGHT HAPPEN AT ANY GIVEN TIME.
MIKE HAD TOLD ME ABOUT LETTING PEOPLE PUSH YOU AROUND, AND I HAD BEEN DOING A PRETTY GOOD JOB OF PUTTING AN END TO PEOPLE DOING THAT TO ME.
BUT WHAT WAS I SUPPOSED TO DO ABOUT THIS HUGE MAN? DID MIKE EXPECT ME TO FIGHT HIM?
I COULDN'T.
I WAS SCARED, AND WITH MY FEAR CAME AN OLD COMPANION--SHAME. I BEGAN TO BEG THE MAN AS THE TEARS ROLLED DOWN MY FACE.
PLEASE MISTER, GIVE ME THE BALL.
IT AIN'T MY BALL.
I'M GONNA GET IN TROUBLE.
THAT'S MIKE'S BALL.

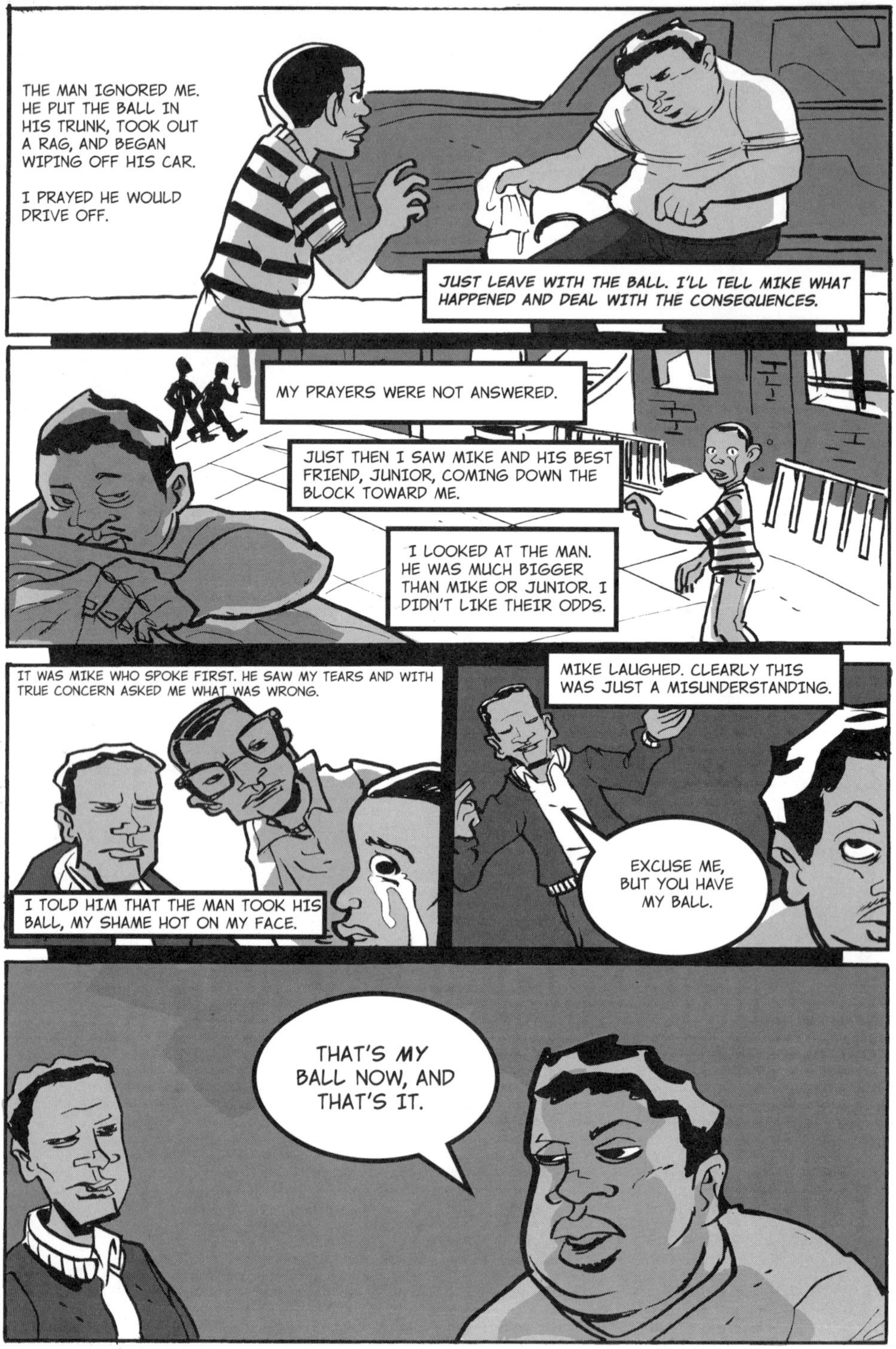
THE MAN IGNORED ME. HE PUT THE BALL IN HIS TRUNK, TOOK OUT A RAG, AND BEGAN WIPING OFF HIS CAR.
I PRAYED HE WOULD DRIVE OFF.
JUST LEAVE WITH THE BALL. I'LL TELL MIKE WHAT HAPPENED AND DEAL WITH THE CONSEQUENCES.
MY PRAYERS WERE NOT ANSWERED.
JUST THEN I SAW MIKE AND HIS BEST FRIEND, JUNIOR, COMING DOWN THE BLOCK TOWARD ME.
I LOOKED AT THE MAN. HE WAS MUCH BIGGER THAN MIKE OR JUNIOR. I DIDN'T LIKE THEIR ODDS.
IT WAS MIKE WHO SPOKE FIRST. HE SAW MY TEARS AND WITH TRUE CONCERN ASKED ME WHAT WAS WRONG.
I TOLD HIM THAT THE MAN TOOK HIS BALL, MY SHAME HOT ON MY FACE.
MIKE LAUGHED. CLEARLY THIS WAS JUST A MISUNDERSTANDING.
EXCUSE ME, BUT YOU HAVE MY BALL.
THAT'S *MY* BALL NOW, AND THAT'S IT.

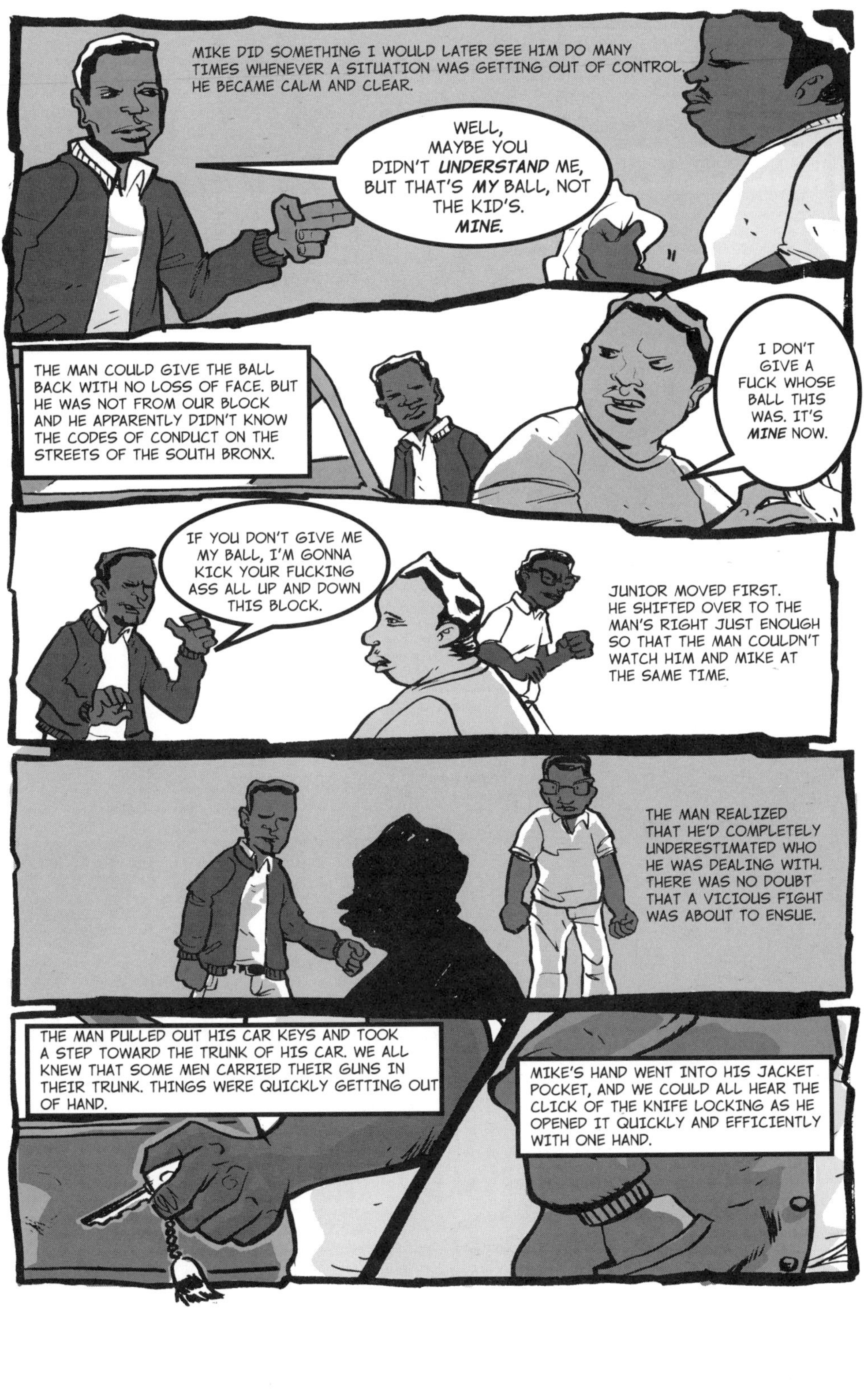
MIKE DID SOMETHING I WOULD LATER SEE HIM DO MANY TIMES WHENEVER A SITUATION WAS GETTING OUT OF CONTROL. HE BECAME CALM AND CLEAR.
WELL, MAYBE YOU DIDN'T **UNDERSTAND** ME, BUT THAT'S **MY** BALL, NOT THE KID'S. **MINE.**
THE MAN COULD GIVE THE BALL BACK WITH NO LOSS OF FACE. BUT HE WAS NOT FROM OUR BLOCK AND HE APPARENTLY DIDN'T KNOW THE CODES OF CONDUCT ON THE STREETS OF THE SOUTH BRONX.
I DON'T GIVE A FUCK WHOSE BALL THIS WAS. IT'S **MINE** NOW.
IF YOU DON'T GIVE ME MY BALL, I'M GONNA KICK YOUR FUCKING ASS ALL UP AND DOWN THIS BLOCK.
JUNIOR MOVED FIRST. HE SHIFTED OVER TO THE MAN'S RIGHT JUST ENOUGH SO THAT THE MAN COULDN'T WATCH HIM AND MIKE AT THE SAME TIME.
THE MAN REALIZED THAT HE'D COMPLETELY UNDERESTIMATED WHO HE WAS DEALING WITH. THERE WAS NO DOUBT THAT A VICIOUS FIGHT WAS ABOUT TO ENSUE.
THE MAN PULLED OUT HIS CAR KEYS AND TOOK A STEP TOWARD THE TRUNK OF HIS CAR. WE ALL KNEW THAT SOME MEN CARRIED THEIR GUNS IN THEIR TRUNK. THINGS WERE QUICKLY GETTING OUT OF HAND.
MIKE'S HAND WENT INTO HIS JACKET POCKET, AND WE COULD ALL HEAR THE CLICK OF THE KNIFE LOCKING AS HE OPENED IT QUICKLY AND EFFICIENTLY WITH ONE HAND.

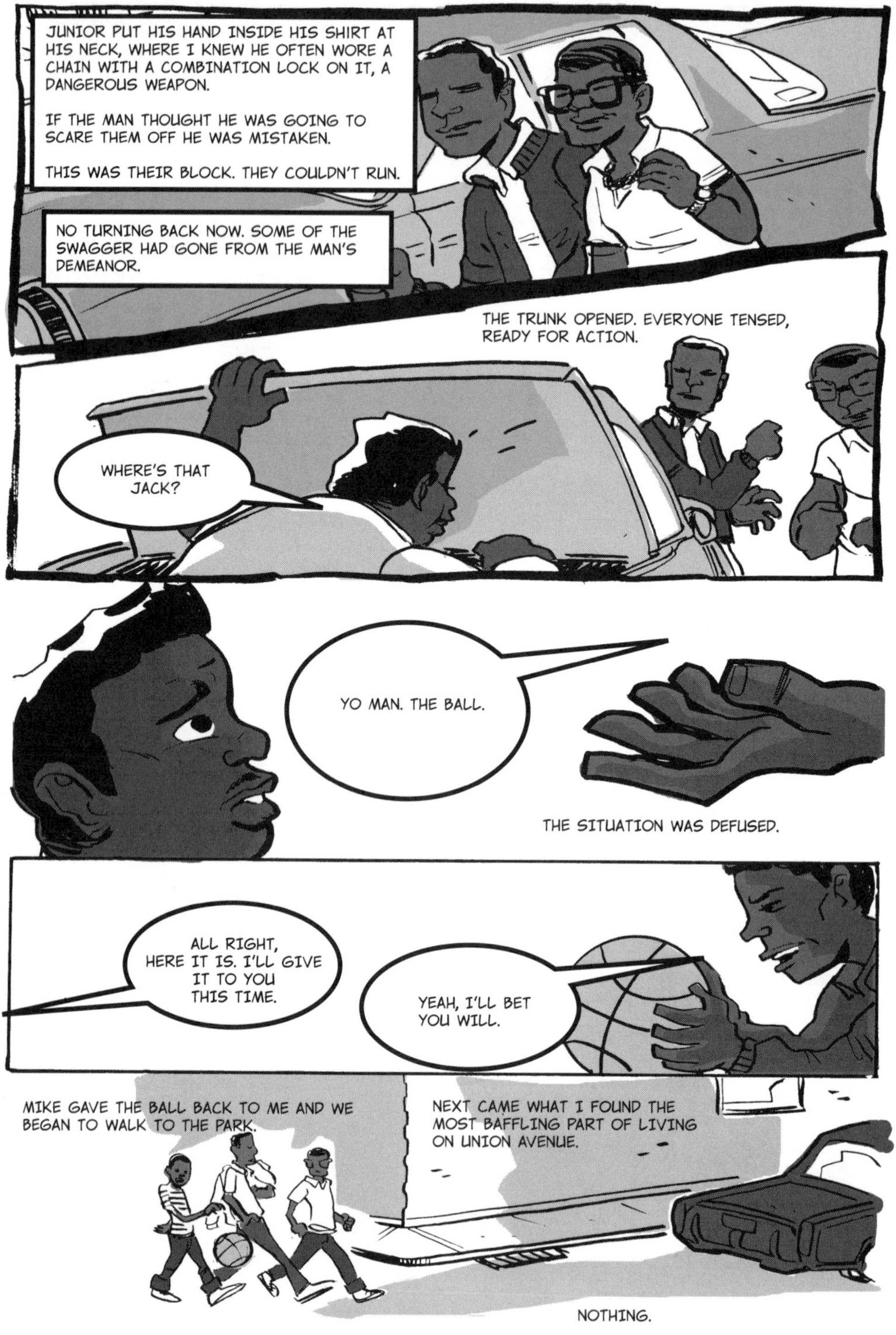
JUNIOR PUT HIS HAND INSIDE HIS SHIRT AT HIS NECK, WHERE I KNEW HE OFTEN WORE A CHAIN WITH A COMBINATION LOCK ON IT, A DANGEROUS WEAPON.
IF THE MAN THOUGHT HE WAS GOING TO SCARE THEM OFF HE WAS MISTAKEN.
THIS WAS THEIR BLOCK. THEY COULDN'T RUN.
NO TURNING BACK NOW. SOME OF THE SWAGGER HAD GONE FROM THE MAN'S DEMEANOR.
THE TRUNK OPENED. EVERYONE TENSED, READY FOR ACTION.
WHERE'S THAT JACK?
YO MAN. THE BALL.
THE SITUATION WAS DEFUSED.
ALL RIGHT, HERE IT IS. I'LL GIVE IT TO YOU THIS TIME.
YEAH, I'LL BET YOU WILL.
MIKE GAVE THE BALL BACK TO ME AND WE BEGAN TO WALK TO THE PARK.
NEXT CAME WHAT I FOUND THE MOST BAFFLING PART OF LIVING ON UNION AVENUE.
NOTHING.

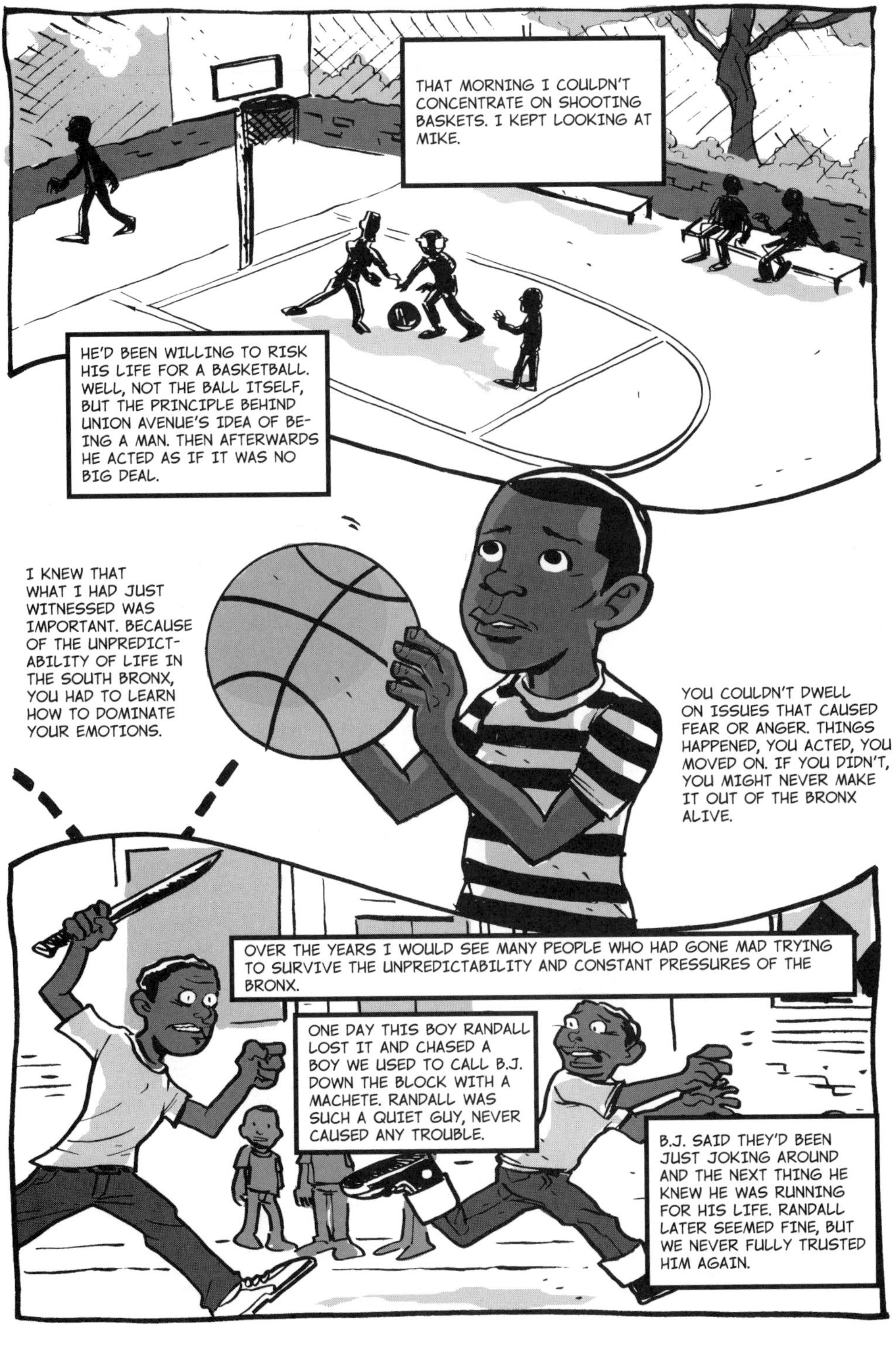

THAT MORNING I COULDN'T CONCENTRATE ON SHOOTING BASKETS. I KEPT LOOKING AT MIKE.
HE'D BEEN WILLING TO RISK HIS LIFE FOR A BASKETBALL. WELL, NOT THE BALL ITSELF, BUT THE PRINCIPLE BEHIND UNION AVENUE'S IDEA OF BE-ING A MAN. THEN AFTERWARDS HE ACTED AS IF IT WAS NO BIG DEAL.
I KNEW THAT WHAT I HAD JUST WITNESSED WAS IMPORTANT. BECAUSE OF THE UNPREDICT-ABILITY OF LIFE IN THE SOUTH BRONX, YOU HAD TO LEARN HOW TO DOMINATE YOUR EMOTIONS.
YOU COULDN'T DWELL ON ISSUES THAT CAUSED FEAR OR ANGER. THINGS HAPPENED, YOU ACTED, YOU MOVED ON. IF YOU DIDN'T, YOU MIGHT NEVER MAKE IT OUT OF THE BRONX ALIVE.
OVER THE YEARS I WOULD SEE MANY PEOPLE WHO HAD GONE MAD TRYING TO SURVIVE THE UNPREDICTABILITY AND CONSTANT PRESSURES OF THE BRONX.
ONE DAY THIS BOY RANDALL LOST IT AND CHASED A BOY WE USED TO CALL B.J. DOWN THE BLOCK WITH A MACHETE. RANDALL WAS SUCH A QUIET GUY, NEVER CAUSED ANY TROUBLE.
B.J. SAID THEY'D BEEN JUST JOKING AROUND AND THE NEXT THING HE KNEW HE WAS RUNNING FOR HIS LIFE. RANDALL LATER SEEMED FINE, BUT WE NEVER FULLY TRUSTED HIM AGAIN.

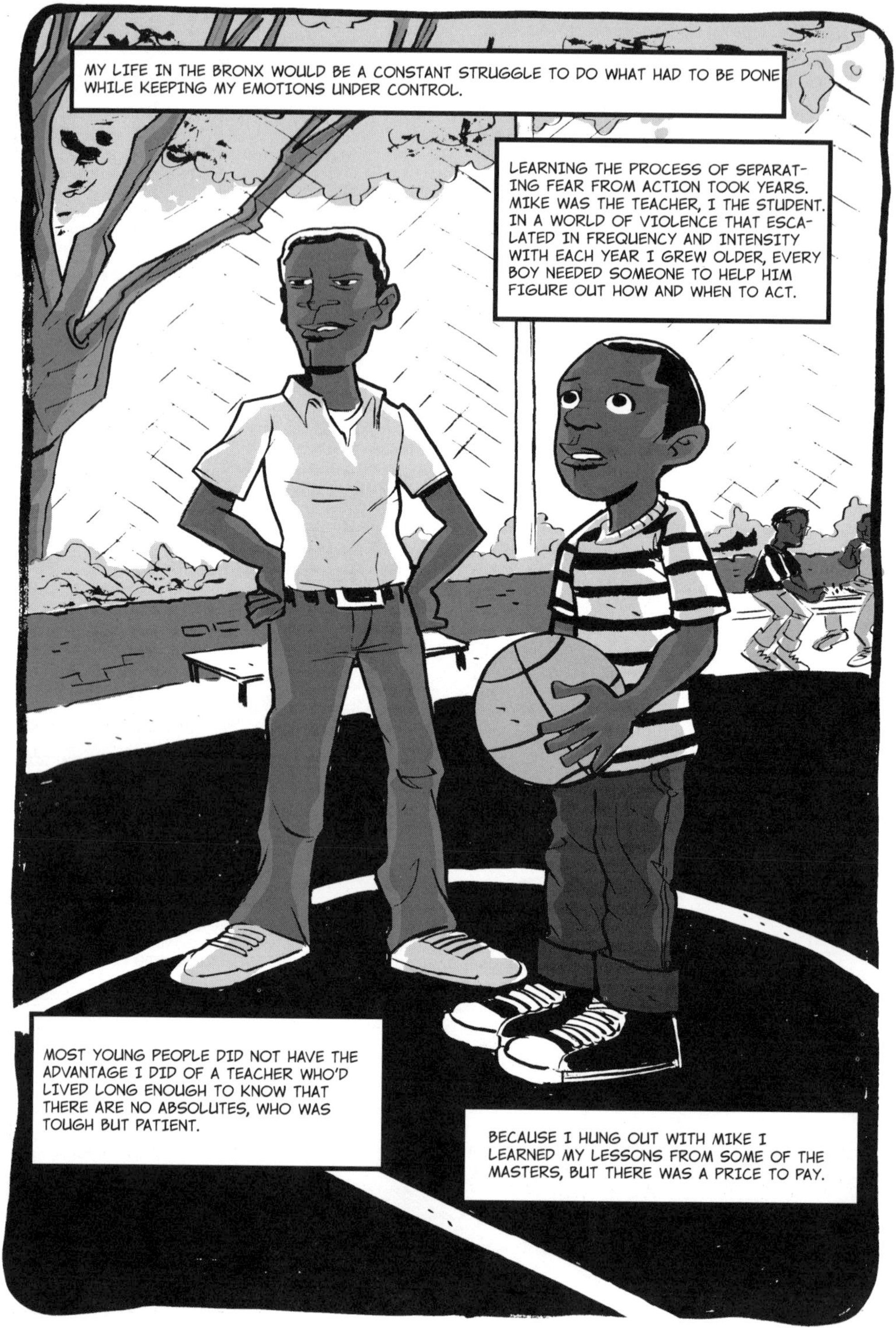
MY LIFE IN THE BRONX WOULD BE A CONSTANT STRUGGLE TO DO WHAT HAD TO BE DONE WHILE KEEPING MY EMOTIONS UNDER CONTROL.
LEARNING THE PROCESS OF SEPARATING FEAR FROM ACTION TOOK YEARS. MIKE WAS THE TEACHER, I THE STUDENT. IN A WORLD OF VIOLENCE THAT ESCALATED IN FREQUENCY AND INTENSITY WITH EACH YEAR I GREW OLDER, EVERY BOY NEEDED SOMEONE TO HELP HIM FIGURE OUT HOW AND WHEN TO ACT.
MOST YOUNG PEOPLE DID NOT HAVE THE ADVANTAGE I DID OF A TEACHER WHO'D LIVED LONG ENOUGH TO KNOW THAT THERE ARE NO ABSOLUTES, WHO WAS TOUGH BUT PATIENT.
BECAUSE I HUNG OUT WITH MIKE I LEARNED MY LESSONS FROM SOME OF THE MASTERS, BUT THERE WAS A PRICE TO PAY.

6

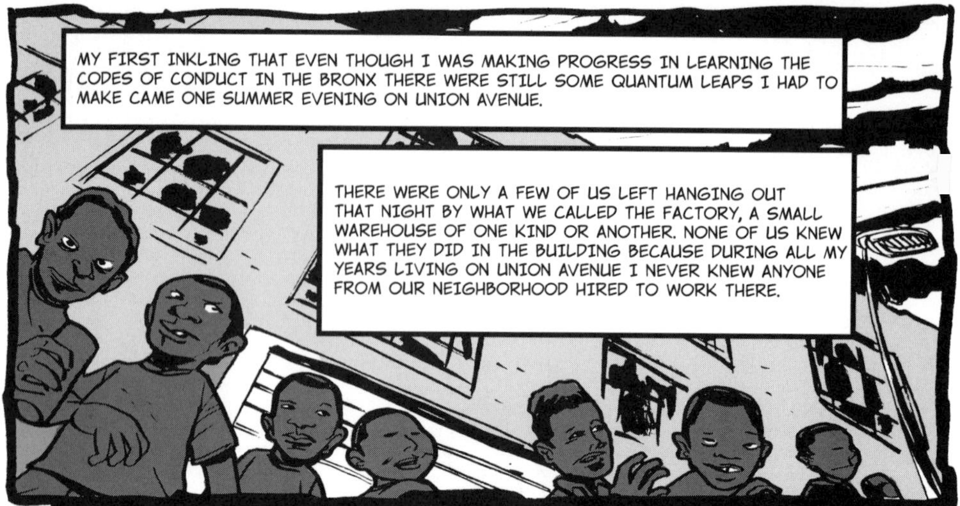
MY FIRST INKLING THAT EVEN THOUGH I WAS MAKING PROGRESS IN LEARNING THE CODES OF CONDUCT IN THE BRONX THERE WERE STILL SOME QUANTUM LEAPS I HAD TO MAKE CAME ONE SUMMER EVENING ON UNION AVENUE.
THERE WERE ONLY A FEW OF US LEFT HANGING OUT THAT NIGHT BY WHAT WE CALLED THE FACTORY, A SMALL WAREHOUSE OF ONE KIND OR ANOTHER. NONE OF US KNEW WHAT THEY DID IN THE BUILDING BECAUSE DURING ALL MY YEARS LIVING ON UNION AVENUE I NEVER KNEW ANYONE FROM OUR NEIGHBORHOOD HIRED TO WORK THERE.

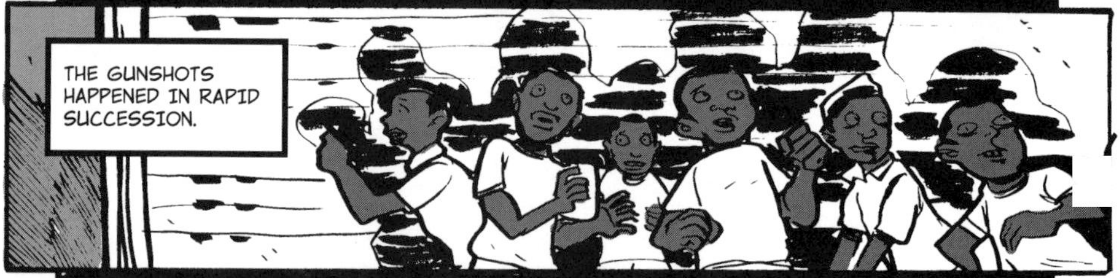
THE GUNSHOTS HAPPENED IN RAPID SUCCESSION.

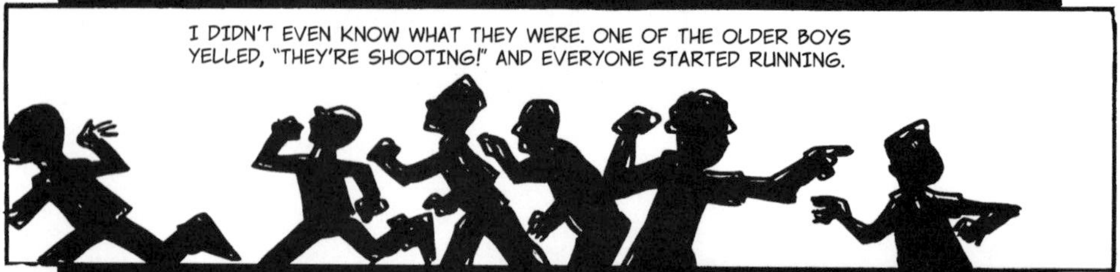
I DIDN'T EVEN KNOW WHAT THEY WERE. ONE OF THE OLDER BOYS YELLED, "THEY'RE SHOOTING!" AND EVERYONE STARTED RUNNING.

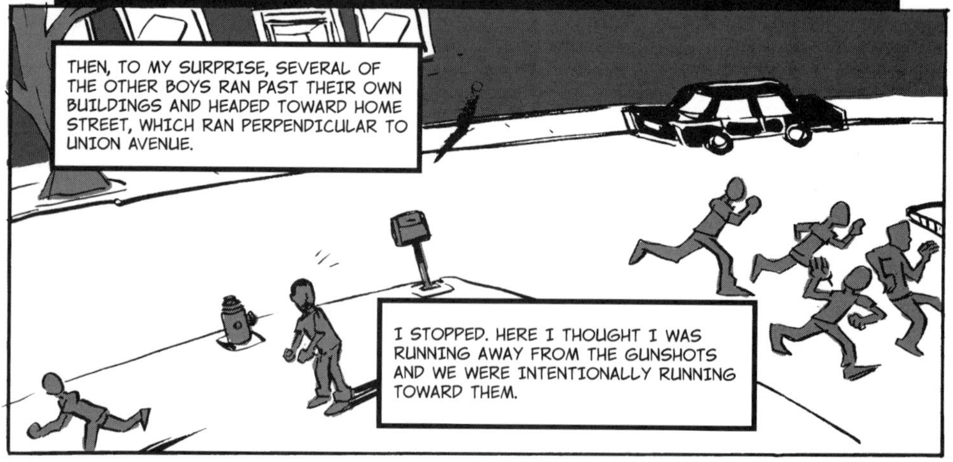
THEN, TO MY SURPRISE, SEVERAL OF THE OTHER BOYS RAN PAST THEIR OWN BUILDINGS AND HEADED TOWARD HOME STREET, WHICH RAN PERPENDICULAR TO UNION AVENUE.
I STOPPED. HERE I THOUGHT I WAS RUNNING AWAY FROM THE GUNSHOTS AND WE WERE INTENTIONALLY RUNNING TOWARD THEM.

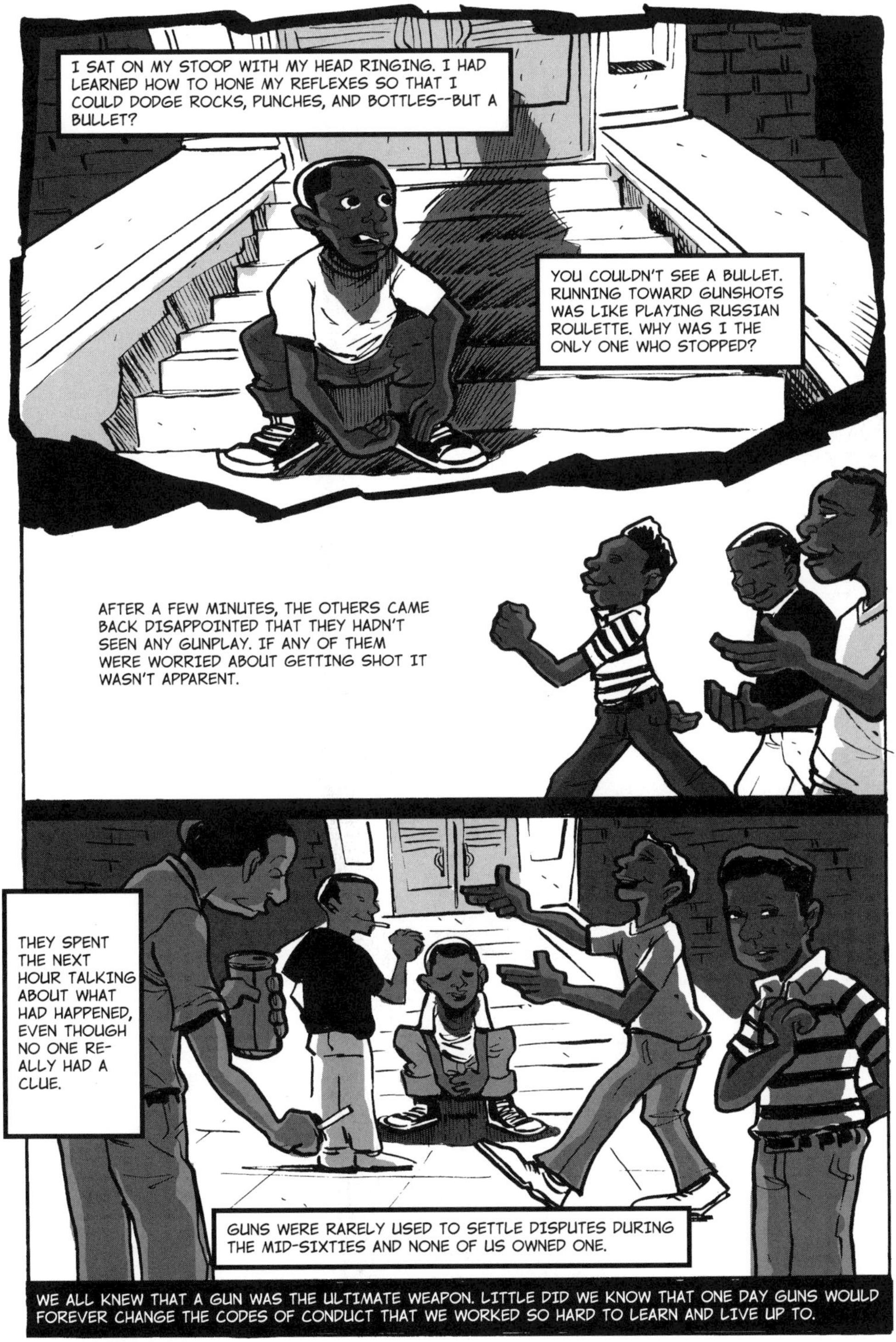
I SAT ON MY STOOP WITH MY HEAD RINGING. I HAD LEARNED HOW TO HONE MY REFLEXES SO THAT I COULD DODGE ROCKS, PUNCHES, AND BOTTLES--BUT A BULLET?
YOU COULDN'T SEE A BULLET. RUNNING TOWARD GUNSHOTS WAS LIKE PLAYING RUSSIAN ROULETTE. WHY WAS I THE ONLY ONE WHO STOPPED?
AFTER A FEW MINUTES, THE OTHERS CAME BACK DISAPPOINTED THAT THEY HADN'T SEEN ANY GUNPLAY. IF ANY OF THEM WERE WORRIED ABOUT GETTING SHOT IT WASN'T APPARENT.
THEY SPENT THE NEXT HOUR TALKING ABOUT WHAT HAD HAPPENED, EVEN THOUGH NO ONE REALLY HAD A CLUE.
GUNS WERE RARELY USED TO SETTLE DISPUTES DURING THE MID-SIXTIES AND NONE OF US OWNED ONE.
WE ALL KNEW THAT A GUN WAS THE ULTIMATE WEAPON. LITTLE DID WE KNOW THAT ONE DAY GUNS WOULD FOREVER CHANGE THE CODES OF CONDUCT THAT WE WORKED SO HARD TO LEARN AND LIVE UP TO.

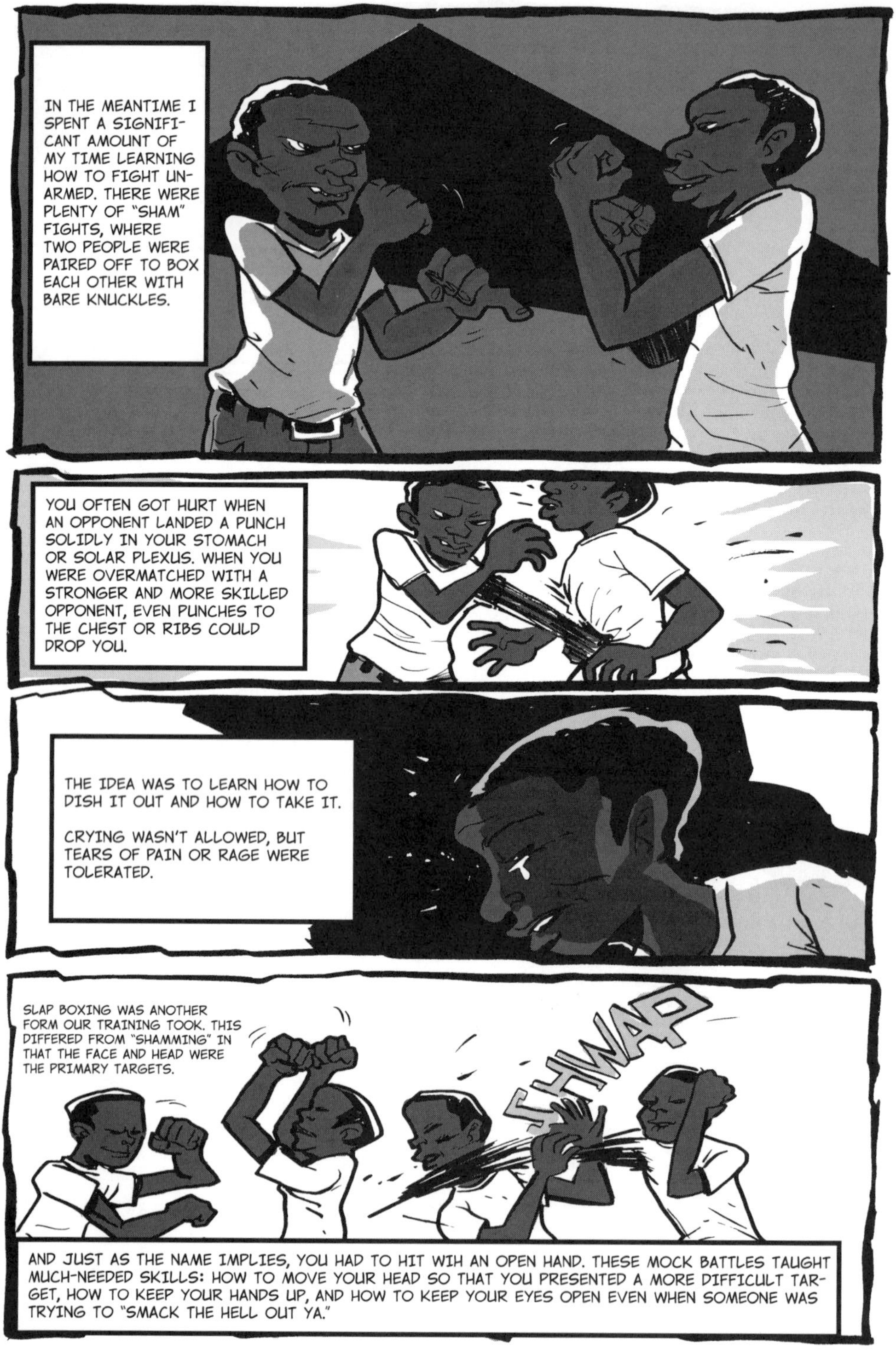
IN THE MEANTIME I SPENT A SIGNIFICANT AMOUNT OF MY TIME LEARNING HOW TO FIGHT UNARMED. THERE WERE PLENTY OF "SHAM" FIGHTS, WHERE TWO PEOPLE WERE PAIRED OFF TO BOX EACH OTHER WITH BARE KNUCKLES.
YOU OFTEN GOT HURT WHEN AN OPPONENT LANDED A PUNCH SOLIDLY IN YOUR STOMACH OR SOLAR PLEXUS. WHEN YOU WERE OVERMATCHED WITH A STRONGER AND MORE SKILLED OPPONENT, EVEN PUNCHES TO THE CHEST OR RIBS COULD DROP YOU.
THE IDEA WAS TO LEARN HOW TO DISH IT OUT AND HOW TO TAKE IT.
CRYING WASN'T ALLOWED, BUT TEARS OF PAIN OR RAGE WERE TOLERATED.
SLAP BOXING WAS ANOTHER FORM OUR TRAINING TOOK. THIS DIFFERED FROM "SHAMMING" IN THAT THE FACE AND HEAD WERE THE PRIMARY TARGETS.
SHWAP
AND JUST AS THE NAME IMPLIES, YOU HAD TO HIT WIH AN OPEN HAND. THESE MOCK BATTLES TAUGHT MUCH-NEEDED SKILLS: HOW TO MOVE YOUR HEAD SO THAT YOU PRESENTED A MORE DIFFICULT TARGET, HOW TO KEEP YOUR HANDS UP, AND HOW TO KEEP YOUR EYES OPEN EVEN WHEN SOMEONE WAS TRYING TO "SMACK THE HELL OUT YA."

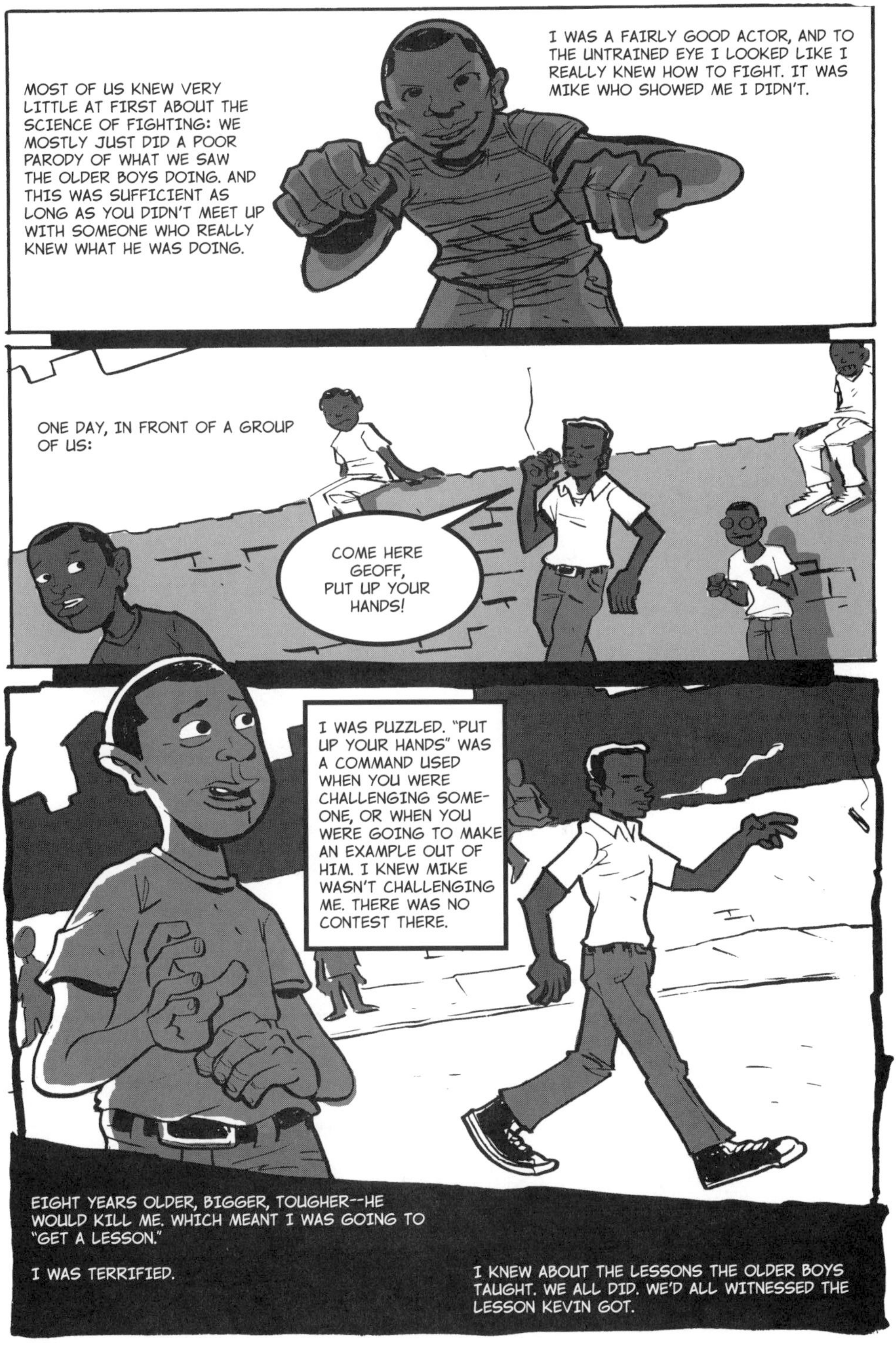
MOST OF US KNEW VERY LITTLE AT FIRST ABOUT THE SCIENCE OF FIGHTING: WE MOSTLY JUST DID A POOR PARODY OF WHAT WE SAW THE OLDER BOYS DOING. AND THIS WAS SUFFICIENT AS LONG AS YOU DIDN'T MEET UP WITH SOMEONE WHO REALLY KNEW WHAT HE WAS DOING.
I WAS A FAIRLY GOOD ACTOR, AND TO THE UNTRAINED EYE I LOOKED LIKE I REALLY KNEW HOW TO FIGHT. IT WAS MIKE WHO SHOWED ME I DIDN'T.
ONE DAY, IN FRONT OF A GROUP OF US:
COME HERE GEOFF, PUT UP YOUR HANDS!
I WAS PUZZLED. "PUT UP YOUR HANDS" WAS A COMMAND USED WHEN YOU WERE CHALLENGING SOMEONE, OR WHEN YOU WERE GOING TO MAKE AN EXAMPLE OUT OF HIM. I KNEW MIKE WASN'T CHALLENGING ME. THERE WAS NO CONTEST THERE.
EIGHT YEARS OLDER, BIGGER, TOUGHER--HE WOULD KILL ME. WHICH MEANT I WAS GOING TO "GET A LESSON."
I WAS TERRIFIED.
I KNEW ABOUT THE LESSONS THE OLDER BOYS TAUGHT. WE ALL DID. WE'D ALL WITNESSED THE LESSON KEVIN GOT.

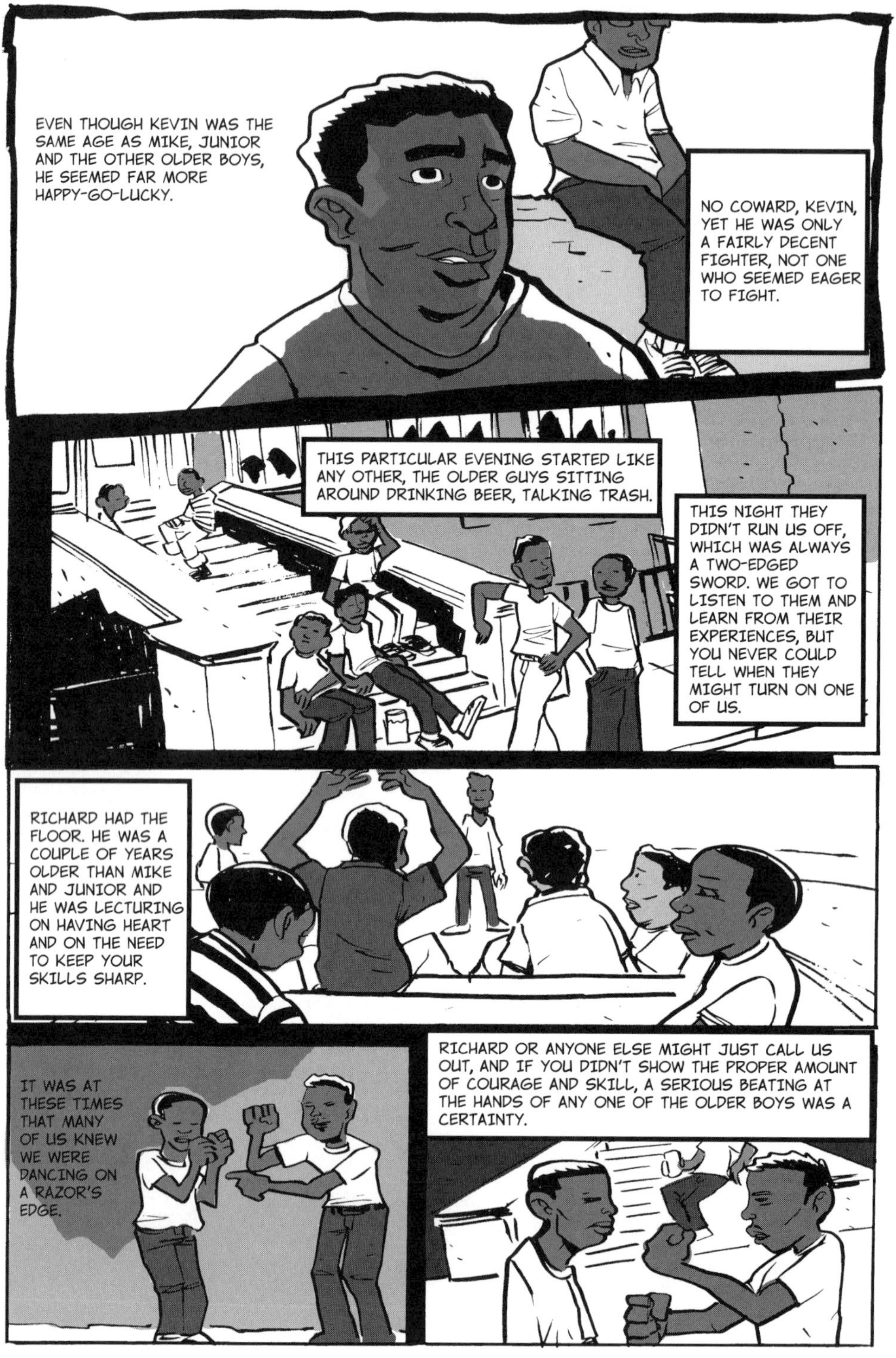
EVEN THOUGH KEVIN WAS THE SAME AGE AS MIKE, JUNIOR AND THE OTHER OLDER BOYS, HE SEEMED FAR MORE HAPPY-GO-LUCKY.
NO COWARD, KEVIN, YET HE WAS ONLY A FAIRLY DECENT FIGHTER, NOT ONE WHO SEEMED EAGER TO FIGHT.
THIS PARTICULAR EVENING STARTED LIKE ANY OTHER, THE OLDER GUYS SITTING AROUND DRINKING BEER, TALKING TRASH.
THIS NIGHT THEY DIDN'T RUN US OFF, WHICH WAS ALWAYS A TWO-EDGED SWORD. WE GOT TO LISTEN TO THEM AND LEARN FROM THEIR EXPERIENCES, BUT YOU NEVER COULD TELL WHEN THEY MIGHT TURN ON ONE OF US.
RICHARD HAD THE FLOOR. HE WAS A COUPLE OF YEARS OLDER THAN MIKE AND JUNIOR AND HE WAS LECTURING ON HAVING HEART AND ON THE NEED TO KEEP YOUR SKILLS SHARP.
IT WAS AT THESE TIMES THAT MANY OF US KNEW WE WERE DANCING ON A RAZOR'S EDGE.
RICHARD OR ANYONE ELSE MIGHT JUST CALL US OUT, AND IF YOU DIDN'T SHOW THE PROPER AMOUNT OF COURAGE AND SKILL, A SERIOUS BEATING AT THE HANDS OF ANY ONE OF THE OLDER BOYS WAS A CERTAINTY.

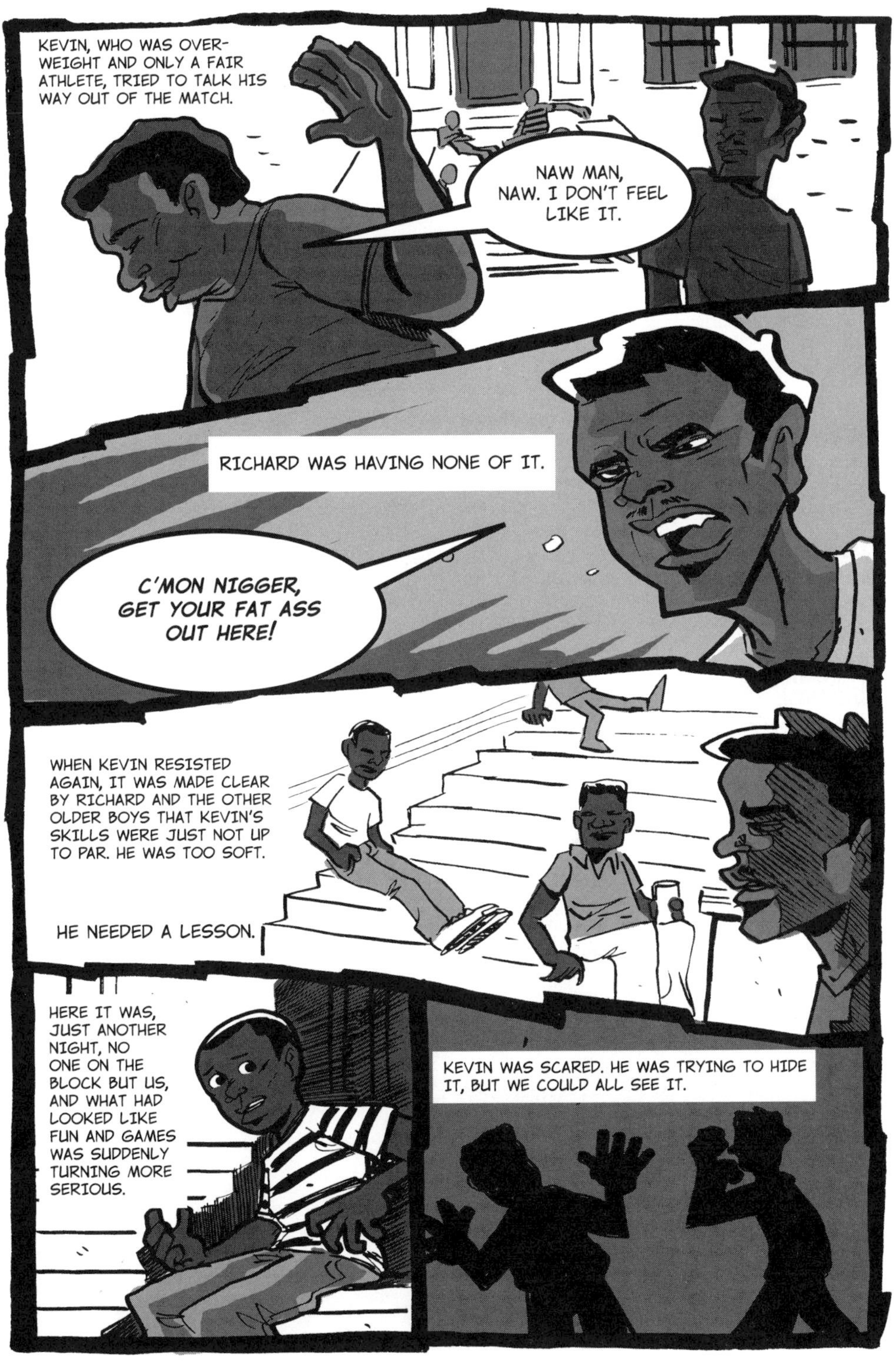
KEVIN, WHO WAS OVER-WEIGHT AND ONLY A FAIR ATHLETE, TRIED TO TALK HIS WAY OUT OF THE MATCH.
NAW MAN, NAW. I DON'T FEEL LIKE IT.
RICHARD WAS HAVING NONE OF IT.
C'MON NIGGER, GET YOUR FAT ASS OUT HERE!
WHEN KEVIN RESISTED AGAIN, IT WAS MADE CLEAR BY RICHARD AND THE OTHER OLDER BOYS THAT KEVIN'S SKILLS WERE JUST NOT UP TO PAR. HE WAS TOO SOFT.
HE NEEDED A LESSON.
HERE IT WAS, JUST ANOTHER NIGHT, NO ONE ON THE BLOCK BUT US, AND WHAT HAD LOOKED LIKE FUN AND GAMES WAS SUDDENLY TURNING MORE SERIOUS.
KEVIN WAS SCARED. HE WAS TRYING TO HIDE IT, BUT WE COULD ALL SEE IT.

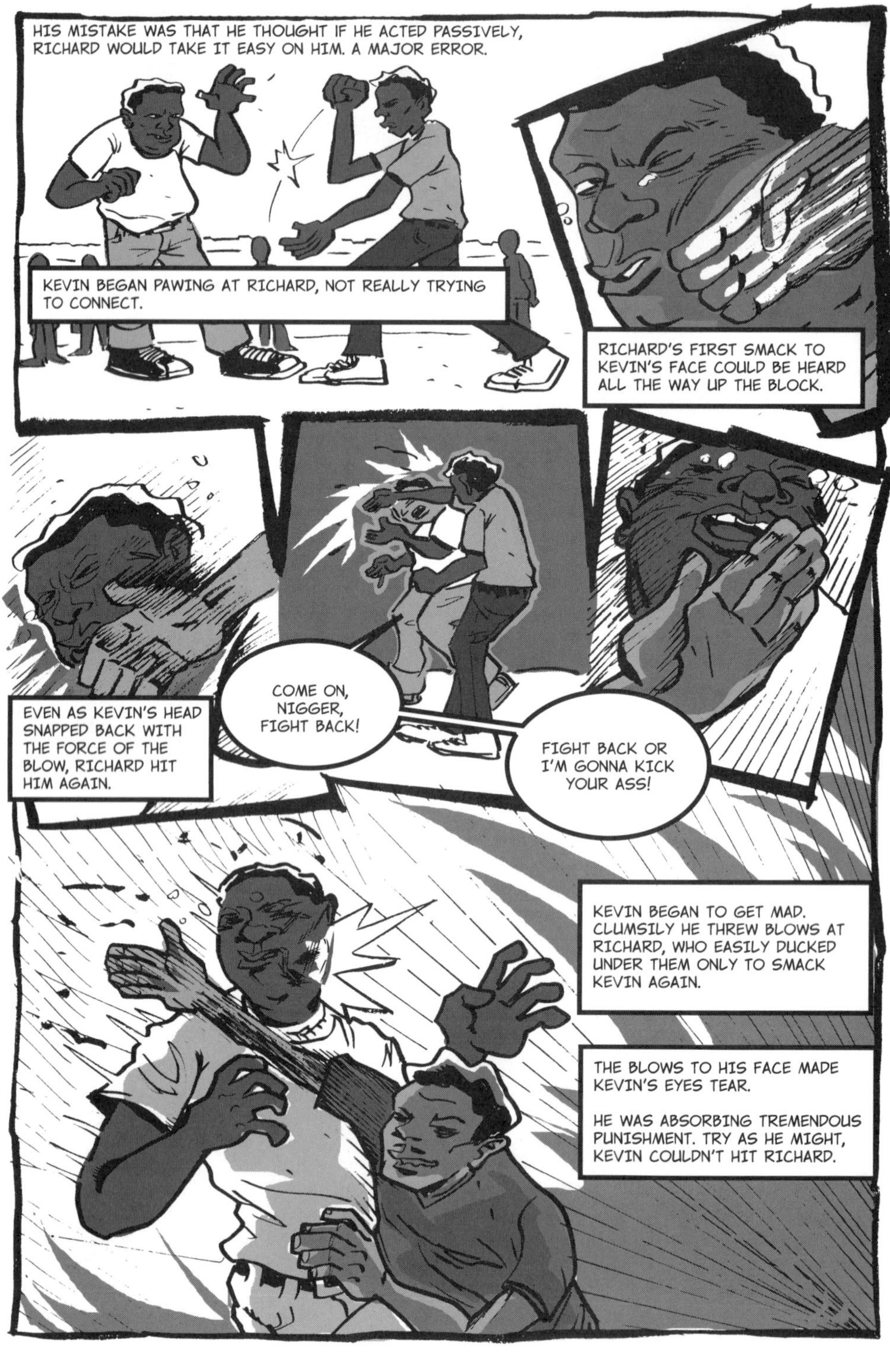
HIS MISTAKE WAS THAT HE THOUGHT IF HE ACTED PASSIVELY, RICHARD WOULD TAKE IT EASY ON HIM. A MAJOR ERROR.
KEVIN BEGAN PAWING AT RICHARD, NOT REALLY TRYING TO CONNECT.
RICHARD'S FIRST SMACK TO KEVIN'S FACE COULD BE HEARD ALL THE WAY UP THE BLOCK.
EVEN AS KEVIN'S HEAD SNAPPED BACK WITH THE FORCE OF THE BLOW, RICHARD HIT HIM AGAIN.
COME ON, NIGGER, FIGHT BACK!
FIGHT BACK OR I'M GONNA KICK YOUR ASS!
KEVIN BEGAN TO GET MAD. CLUMSILY HE THREW BLOWS AT RICHARD, WHO EASILY DUCKED UNDER THEM ONLY TO SMACK KEVIN AGAIN.
THE BLOWS TO HIS FACE MADE KEVIN'S EYES TEAR.
HE WAS ABSORBING TREMENDOUS PUNISHMENT. TRY AS HE MIGHT, KEVIN COULDN'T HIT RICHARD.

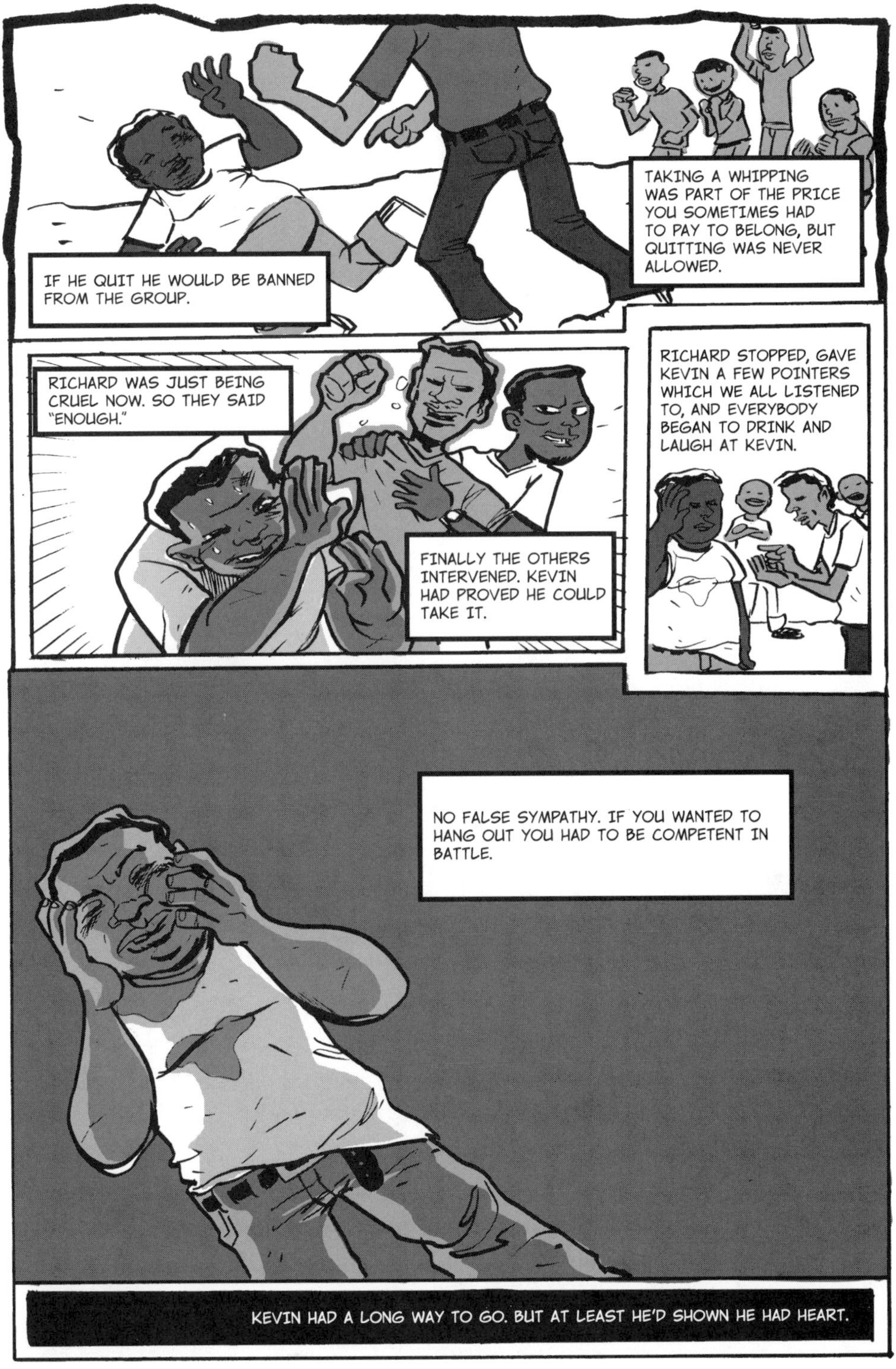
IF HE QUIT HE WOULD BE BANNED FROM THE GROUP.
TAKING A WHIPPING WAS PART OF THE PRICE YOU SOMETIMES HAD TO PAY TO BELONG, BUT QUITTING WAS NEVER ALLOWED.
RICHARD WAS JUST BEING CRUEL NOW. SO THEY SAID "ENOUGH."
FINALLY THE OTHERS INTERVENED. KEVIN HAD PROVED HE COULD TAKE IT.
RICHARD STOPPED, GAVE KEVIN A FEW POINTERS WHICH WE ALL LISTENED TO, AND EVERYBODY BEGAN TO DRINK AND LAUGH AT KEVIN.
NO FALSE SYMPATHY. IF YOU WANTED TO HANG OUT YOU HAD TO BE COMPETENT IN BATTLE.
KEVIN HAD A LONG WAY TO GO. BUT AT LEAST HE'D SHOWN HE HAD HEART.

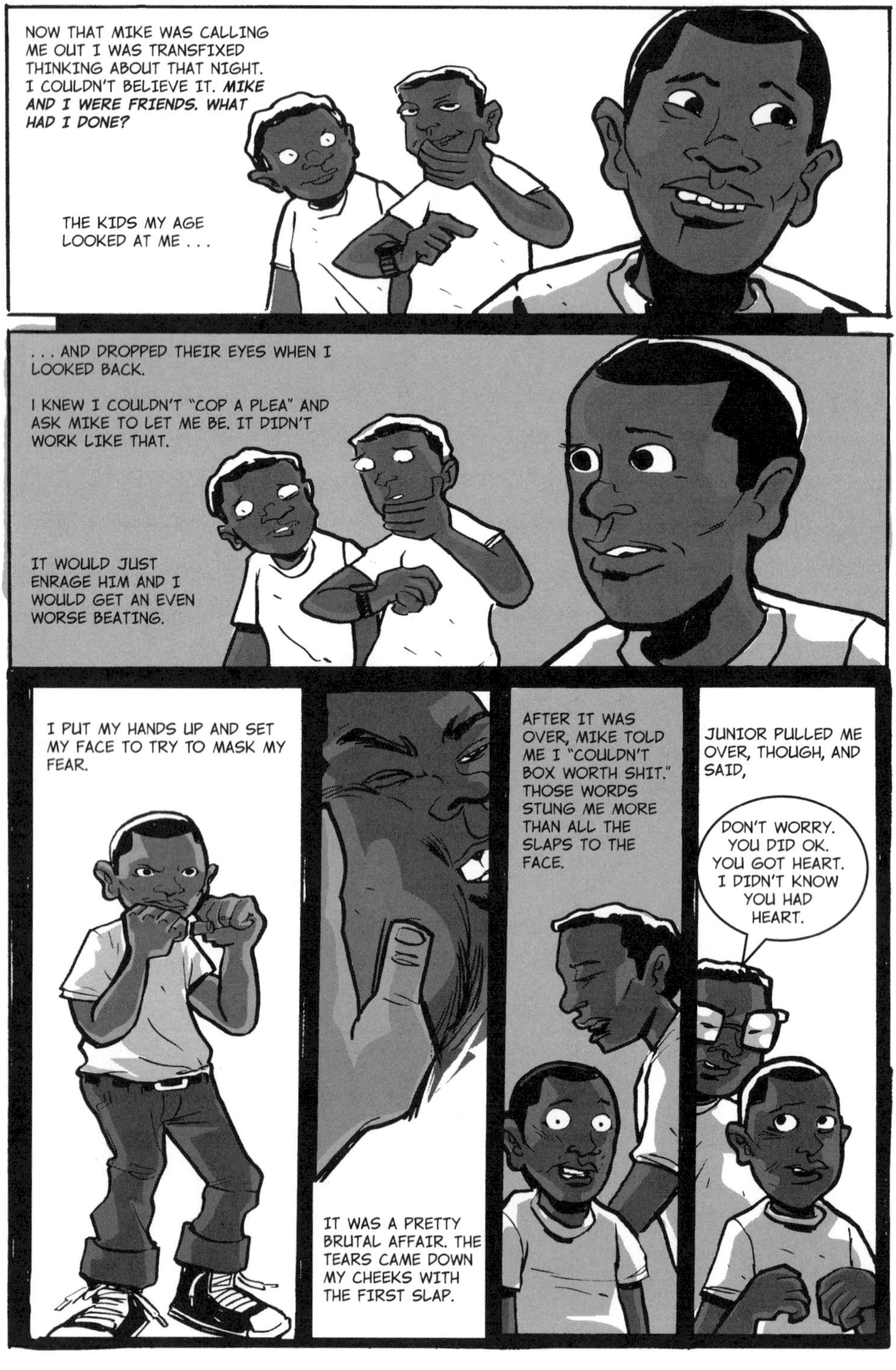
NOW THAT MIKE WAS CALLING ME OUT I WAS TRANSFIXED THINKING ABOUT THAT NIGHT. I COULDN'T BELIEVE IT. *MIKE AND I WERE FRIENDS. WHAT HAD I DONE?*
THE KIDS MY AGE LOOKED AT ME . . .
. . . AND DROPPED THEIR EYES WHEN I LOOKED BACK.
I KNEW I COULDN'T "COP A PLEA" AND ASK MIKE TO LET ME BE. IT DIDN'T WORK LIKE THAT.
IT WOULD JUST ENRAGE HIM AND I WOULD GET AN EVEN WORSE BEATING.
I PUT MY HANDS UP AND SET MY FACE TO TRY TO MASK MY FEAR.
IT WAS A PRETTY BRUTAL AFFAIR. THE TEARS CAME DOWN MY CHEEKS WITH THE FIRST SLAP.
AFTER IT WAS OVER, MIKE TOLD ME I "COULDN'T BOX WORTH SHIT." THOSE WORDS STUNG ME MORE THAN ALL THE SLAPS TO THE FACE.
JUNIOR PULLED ME OVER, THOUGH, AND SAID,
DON'T WORRY. YOU DID OK. YOU GOT HEART. I DIDN'T KNOW YOU HAD HEART.

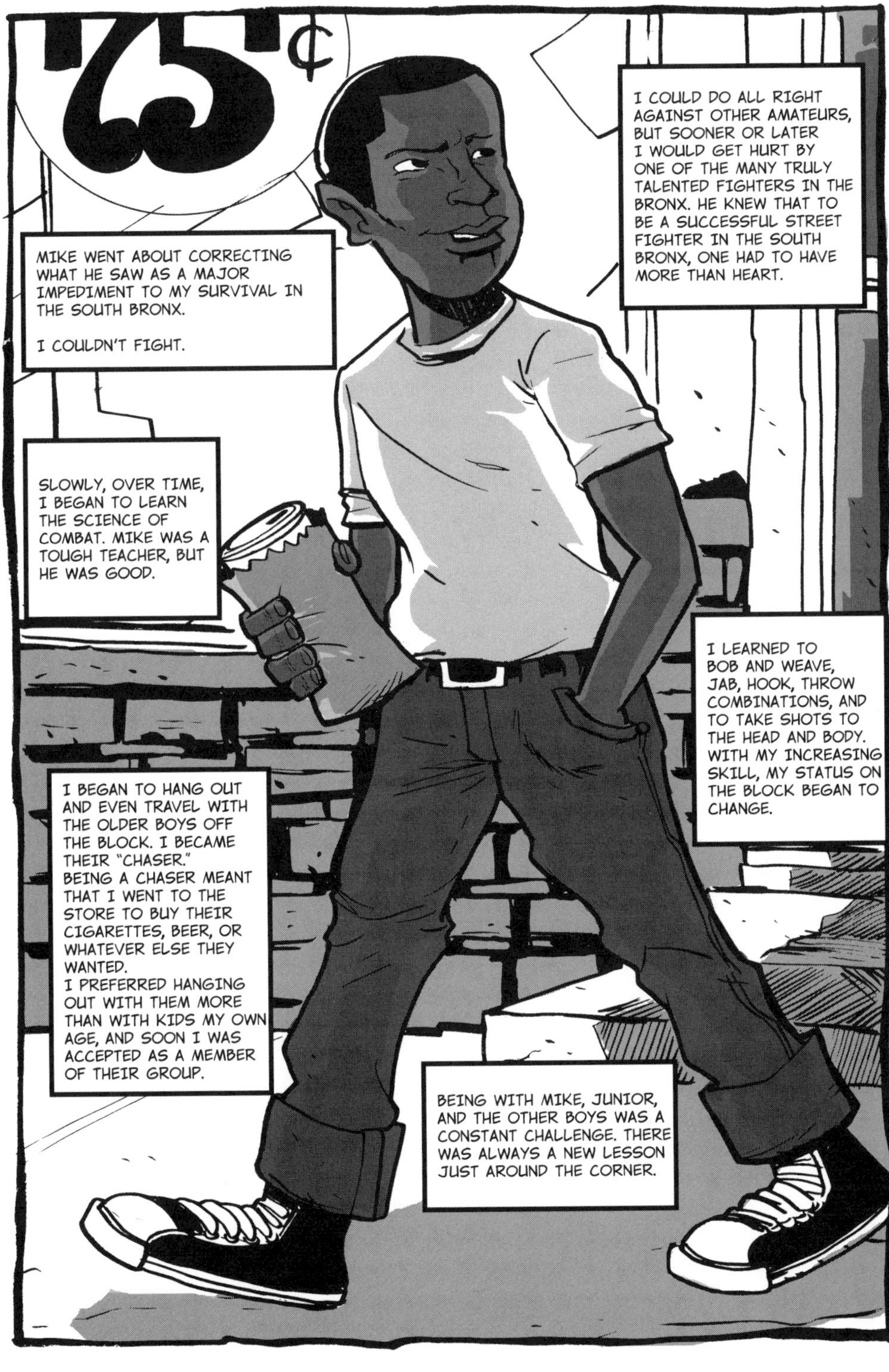
"75"¢
MIKE WENT ABOUT CORRECTING WHAT HE SAW AS A MAJOR IMPEDIMENT TO MY SURVIVAL IN THE SOUTH BRONX.
I COULDN'T FIGHT.
I COULD DO ALL RIGHT AGAINST OTHER AMATEURS, BUT SOONER OR LATER I WOULD GET HURT BY ONE OF THE MANY TRULY TALENTED FIGHTERS IN THE BRONX. HE KNEW THAT TO BE A SUCCESSFUL STREET FIGHTER IN THE SOUTH BRONX, ONE HAD TO HAVE MORE THAN HEART.
SLOWLY, OVER TIME, I BEGAN TO LEARN THE SCIENCE OF COMBAT. MIKE WAS A TOUGH TEACHER, BUT HE WAS GOOD.
I LEARNED TO BOB AND WEAVE, JAB, HOOK, THROW COMBINATIONS, AND TO TAKE SHOTS TO THE HEAD AND BODY. WITH MY INCREASING SKILL, MY STATUS ON THE BLOCK BEGAN TO CHANGE.
I BEGAN TO HANG OUT AND EVEN TRAVEL WITH THE OLDER BOYS OFF THE BLOCK. I BECAME THEIR "CHASER." BEING A CHASER MEANT THAT I WENT TO THE STORE TO BUY THEIR CIGARETTES, BEER, OR WHATEVER ELSE THEY WANTED. I PREFERRED HANGING OUT WITH THEM MORE THAN WITH KIDS MY OWN AGE, AND SOON I WAS ACCEPTED AS A MEMBER OF THEIR GROUP.
BEING WITH MIKE, JUNIOR, AND THE OTHER BOYS WAS A CONSTANT CHALLENGE. THERE WAS ALWAYS A NEW LESSON JUST AROUND THE CORNER.

7

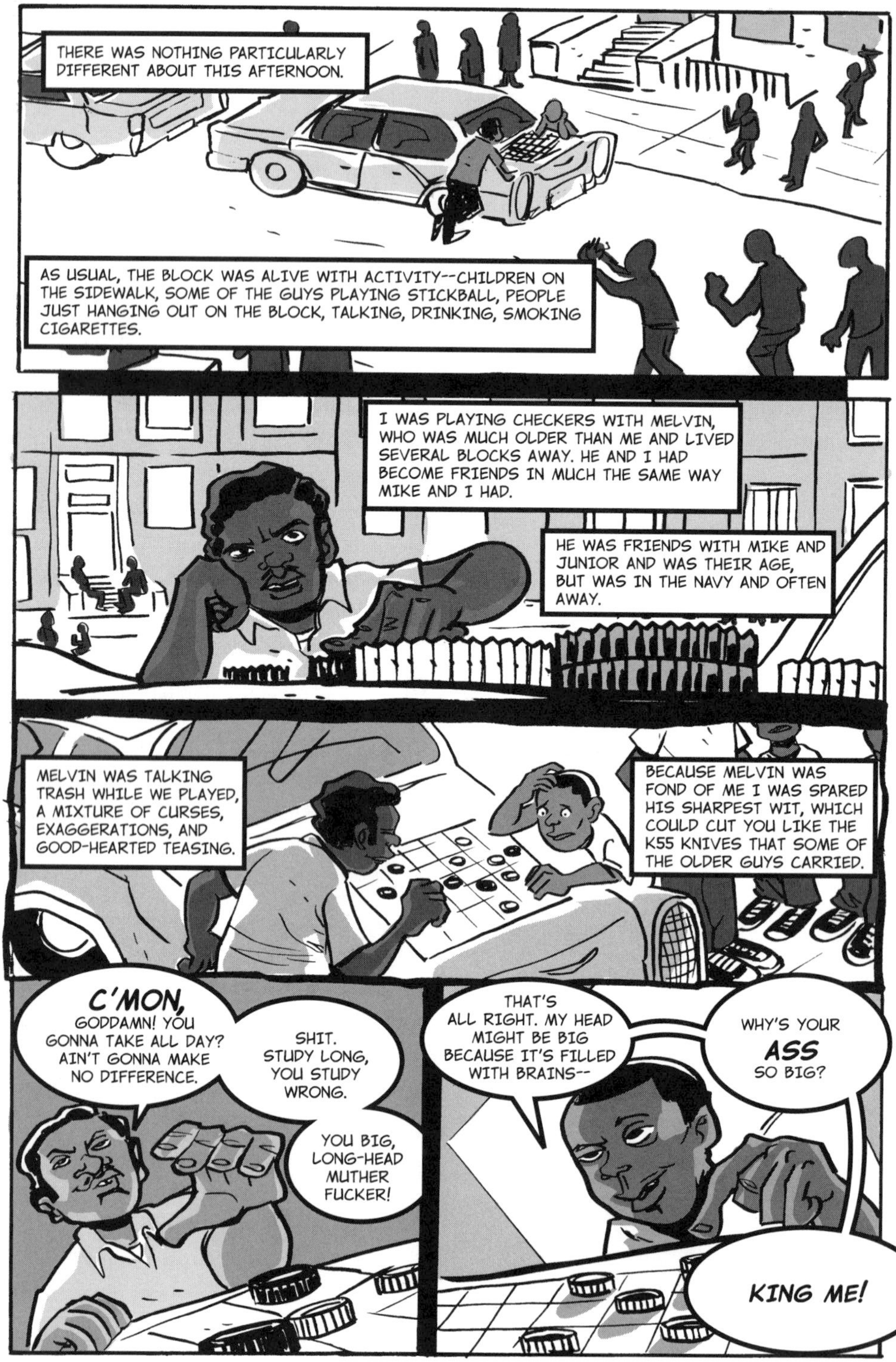

THERE WAS NOTHING PARTICULARLY DIFFERENT ABOUT THIS AFTERNOON.
AS USUAL, THE BLOCK WAS ALIVE WITH ACTIVITY--CHILDREN ON THE SIDEWALK, SOME OF THE GUYS PLAYING STICKBALL, PEOPLE JUST HANGING OUT ON THE BLOCK, TALKING, DRINKING, SMOKING CIGARETTES.
I WAS PLAYING CHECKERS WITH MELVIN, WHO WAS MUCH OLDER THAN ME AND LIVED SEVERAL BLOCKS AWAY. HE AND I HAD BECOME FRIENDS IN MUCH THE SAME WAY MIKE AND I HAD.
HE WAS FRIENDS WITH MIKE AND JUNIOR AND WAS THEIR AGE, BUT WAS IN THE NAVY AND OFTEN AWAY.
MELVIN WAS TALKING TRASH WHILE WE PLAYED, A MIXTURE OF CURSES, EXAGGERATIONS, AND GOOD-HEARTED TEASING.
BECAUSE MELVIN WAS FOND OF ME I WAS SPARED HIS SHARPEST WIT, WHICH COULD CUT YOU LIKE THE K55 KNIVES THAT SOME OF THE OLDER GUYS CARRIED.
C'MON, GODDAMN! YOU GONNA TAKE ALL DAY? AIN'T GONNA MAKE NO DIFFERENCE.
SHIT. STUDY LONG, YOU STUDY WRONG.
YOU BIG, LONG-HEAD MUTHER FUCKER!
THAT'S ALL RIGHT. MY HEAD MIGHT BE BIG BECAUSE IT'S FILLED WITH BRAINS--
WHY'S YOUR ASS SO BIG?
KING ME!

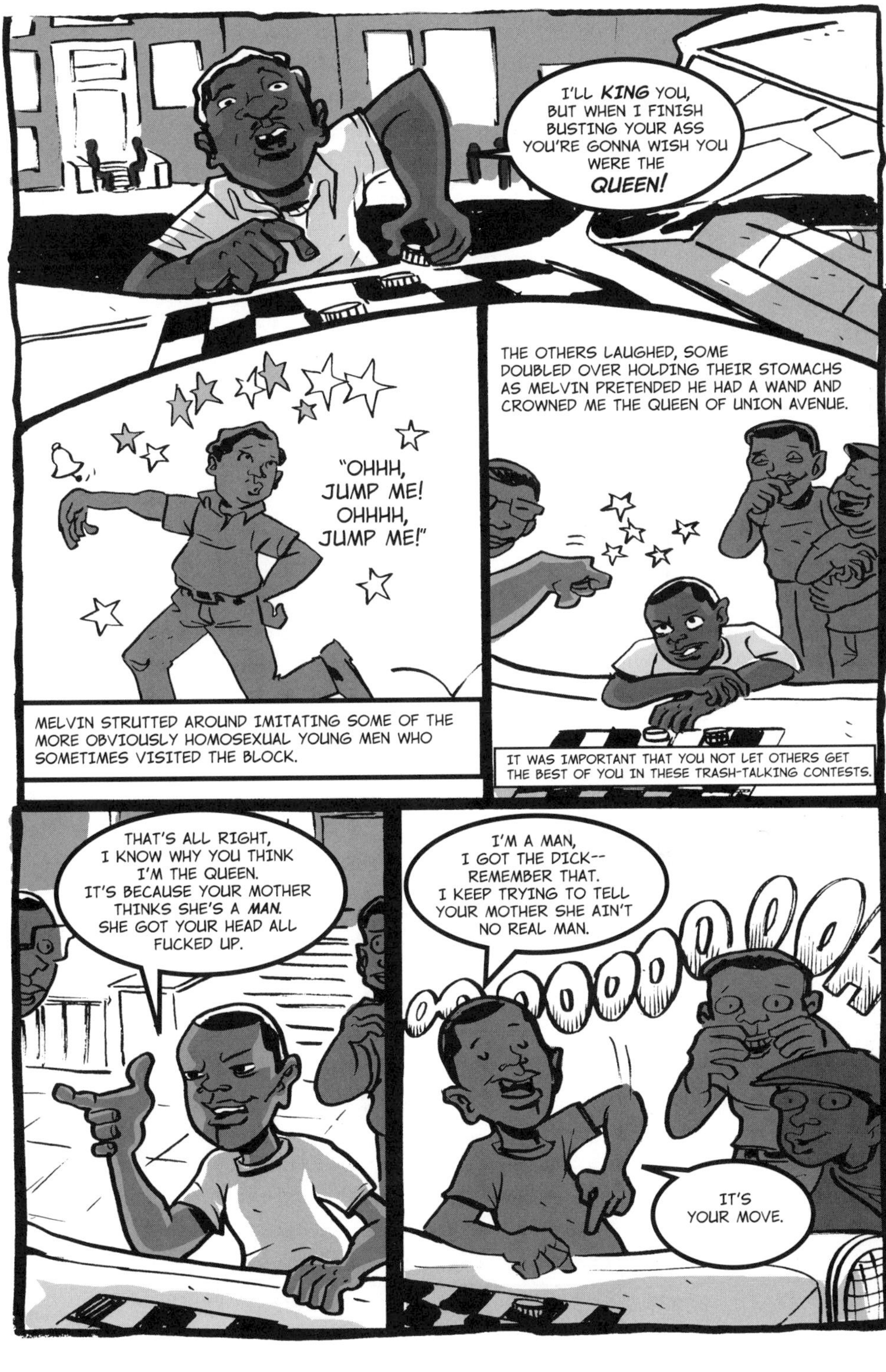
I'LL KING YOU, BUT WHEN I FINISH BUSTING YOUR ASS YOU'RE GONNA WISH YOU WERE THE QUEEN!
"OHHH, JUMP ME! OHHHH, JUMP ME!"
MELVIN STRUTTED AROUND IMITATING SOME OF THE MORE OBVIOUSLY HOMOSEXUAL YOUNG MEN WHO SOMETIMES VISITED THE BLOCK.
THE OTHERS LAUGHED, SOME DOUBLED OVER HOLDING THEIR STOMACHS AS MELVIN PRETENDED HE HAD A WAND AND CROWNED ME THE QUEEN OF UNION AVENUE.
IT WAS IMPORTANT THAT YOU NOT LET OTHERS GET THE BEST OF YOU IN THESE TRASH-TALKING CONTESTS.
THAT'S ALL RIGHT, I KNOW WHY YOU THINK I'M THE QUEEN. IT'S BECAUSE YOUR MOTHER THINKS SHE'S A MAN. SHE GOT YOUR HEAD ALL FUCKED UP.
I'M A MAN, I GOT THE DICK-- REMEMBER THAT. I KEEP TRYING TO TELL YOUR MOTHER SHE AIN'T NO REAL MAN.
OOOOOOOOOOOOK
IT'S YOUR MOVE.

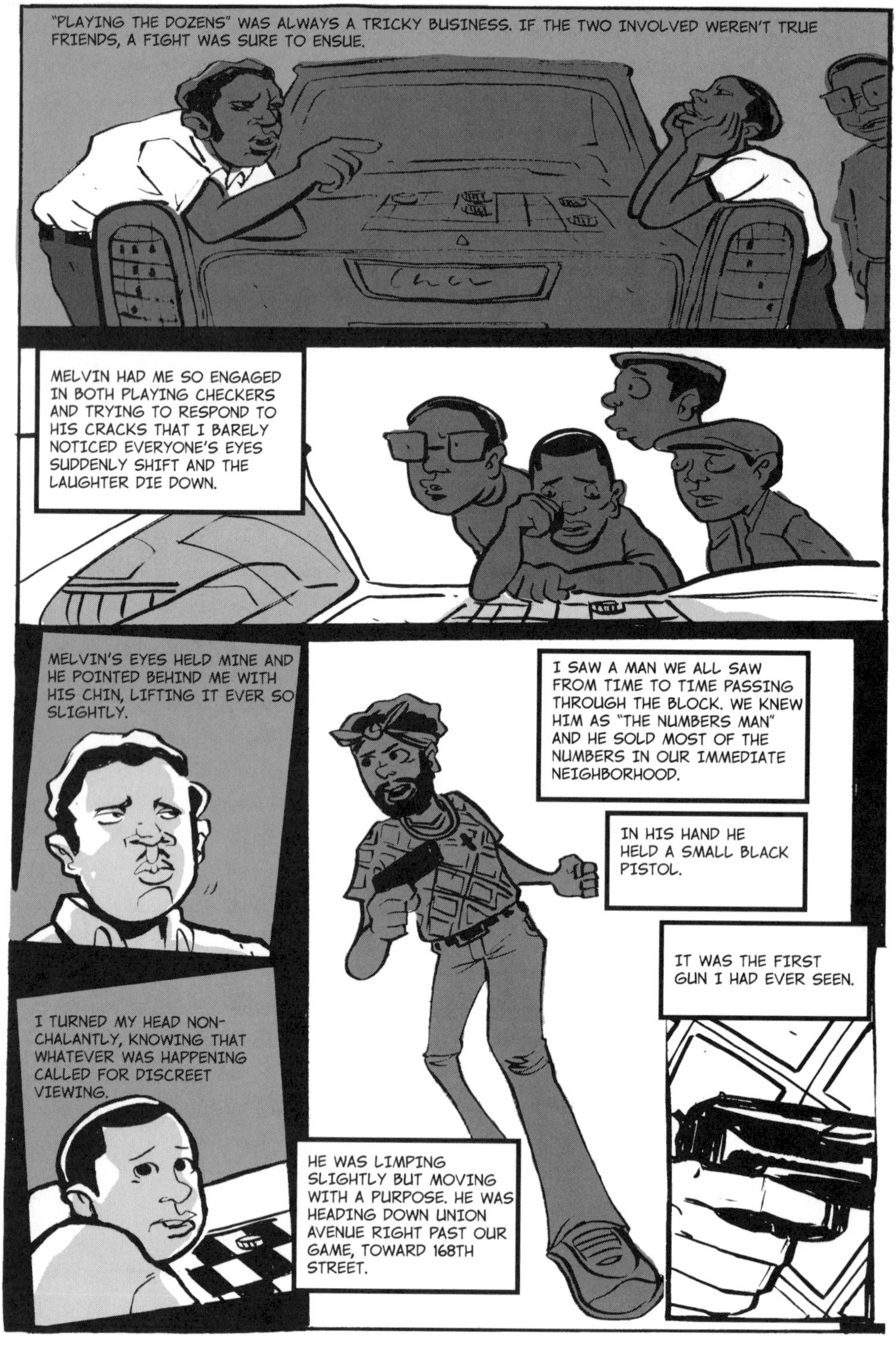
"PLAYING THE DOZENS" WAS ALWAYS A TRICKY BUSINESS. IF THE TWO INVOLVED WEREN'T TRUE FRIENDS, A FIGHT WAS SURE TO ENSUE.
MELVIN HAD ME SO ENGAGED IN BOTH PLAYING CHECKERS AND TRYING TO RESPOND TO HIS CRACKS THAT I BARELY NOTICED EVERYONE'S EYES SUDDENLY SHIFT AND THE LAUGHTER DIE DOWN.
MELVIN'S EYES HELD MINE AND HE POINTED BEHIND ME WITH HIS CHIN, LIFTING IT EVER SO SLIGHTLY.
I TURNED MY HEAD NON-CHALANTLY, KNOWING THAT WHATEVER WAS HAPPENING CALLED FOR DISCREET VIEWING.
I SAW A MAN WE ALL SAW FROM TIME TO TIME PASSING THROUGH THE BLOCK. WE KNEW HIM AS "THE NUMBERS MAN" AND HE SOLD MOST OF THE NUMBERS IN OUR IMMEDIATE NEIGHBORHOOD.
IN HIS HAND HE HELD A SMALL BLACK PISTOL.
HE WAS LIMPING SLIGHTLY BUT MOVING WITH A PURPOSE. HE WAS HEADING DOWN UNION AVENUE RIGHT PAST OUR GAME, TOWARD 168TH STREET.
IT WAS THE FIRST GUN I HAD EVER SEEN.

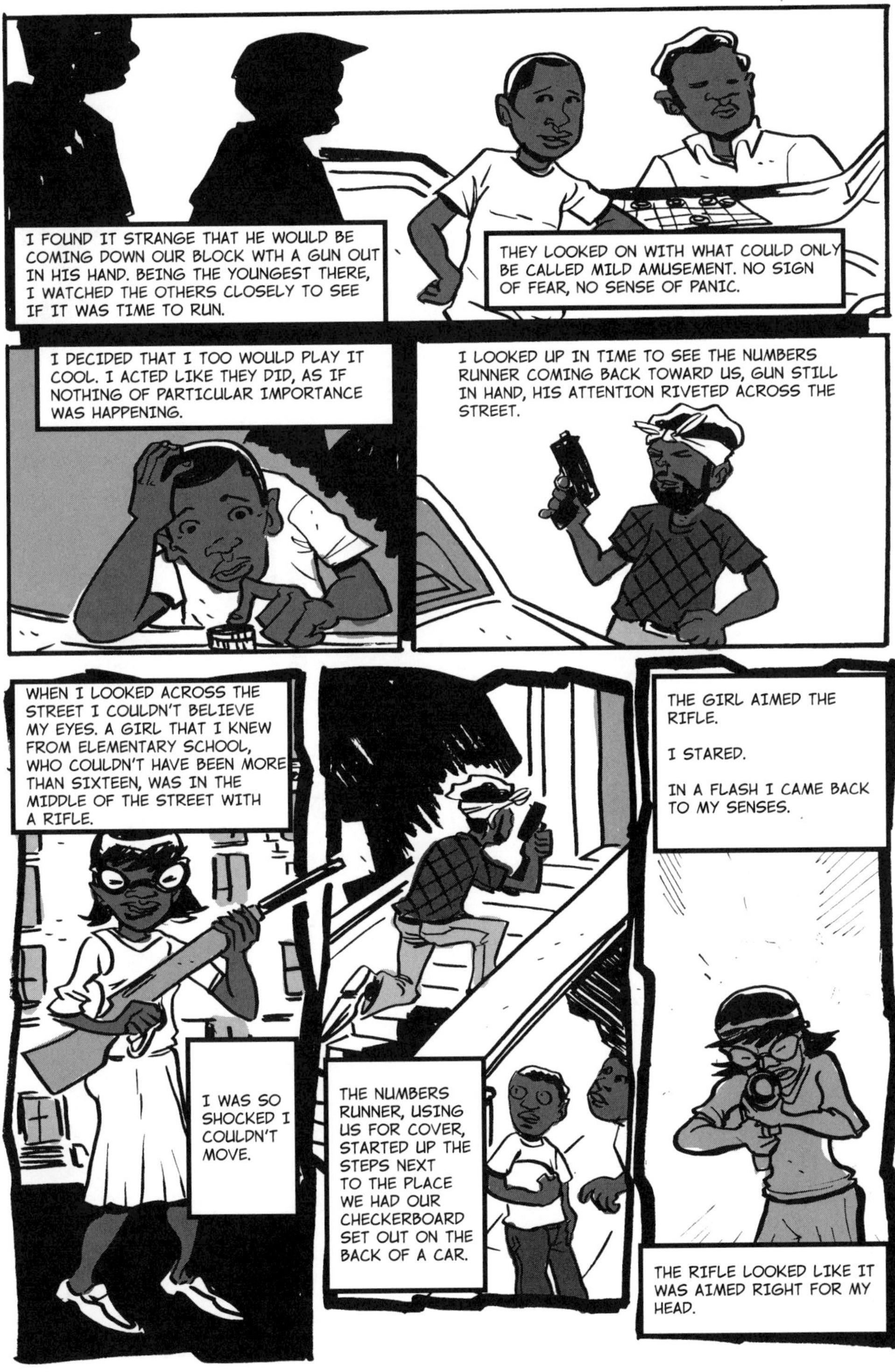
I FOUND IT STRANGE THAT HE WOULD BE COMING DOWN OUR BLOCK WTH A GUN OUT IN HIS HAND. BEING THE YOUNGEST THERE, I WATCHED THE OTHERS CLOSELY TO SEE IF IT WAS TIME TO RUN.
THEY LOOKED ON WITH WHAT COULD ONLY BE CALLED MILD AMUSEMENT. NO SIGN OF FEAR, NO SENSE OF PANIC.
I DECIDED THAT I TOO WOULD PLAY IT COOL. I ACTED LIKE THEY DID, AS IF NOTHING OF PARTICULAR IMPORTANCE WAS HAPPENING.
I LOOKED UP IN TIME TO SEE THE NUMBERS RUNNER COMING BACK TOWARD US, GUN STILL IN HAND, HIS ATTENTION RIVETED ACROSS THE STREET.
WHEN I LOOKED ACROSS THE STREET I COULDN'T BELIEVE MY EYES. A GIRL THAT I KNEW FROM ELEMENTARY SCHOOL, WHO COULDN'T HAVE BEEN MORE THAN SIXTEEN, WAS IN THE MIDDLE OF THE STREET WITH A RIFLE.
I WAS SO SHOCKED I COULDN'T MOVE.
THE NUMBERS RUNNER, USING US FOR COVER, STARTED UP THE STEPS NEXT TO THE PLACE WE HAD OUR CHECKERBOARD SET OUT ON THE BACK OF A CAR.
THE GIRL AIMED THE RIFLE.
I STARED.
IN A FLASH I CAME BACK TO MY SENSES.
THE RIFLE LOOKED LIKE IT WAS AIMED RIGHT FOR MY HEAD.

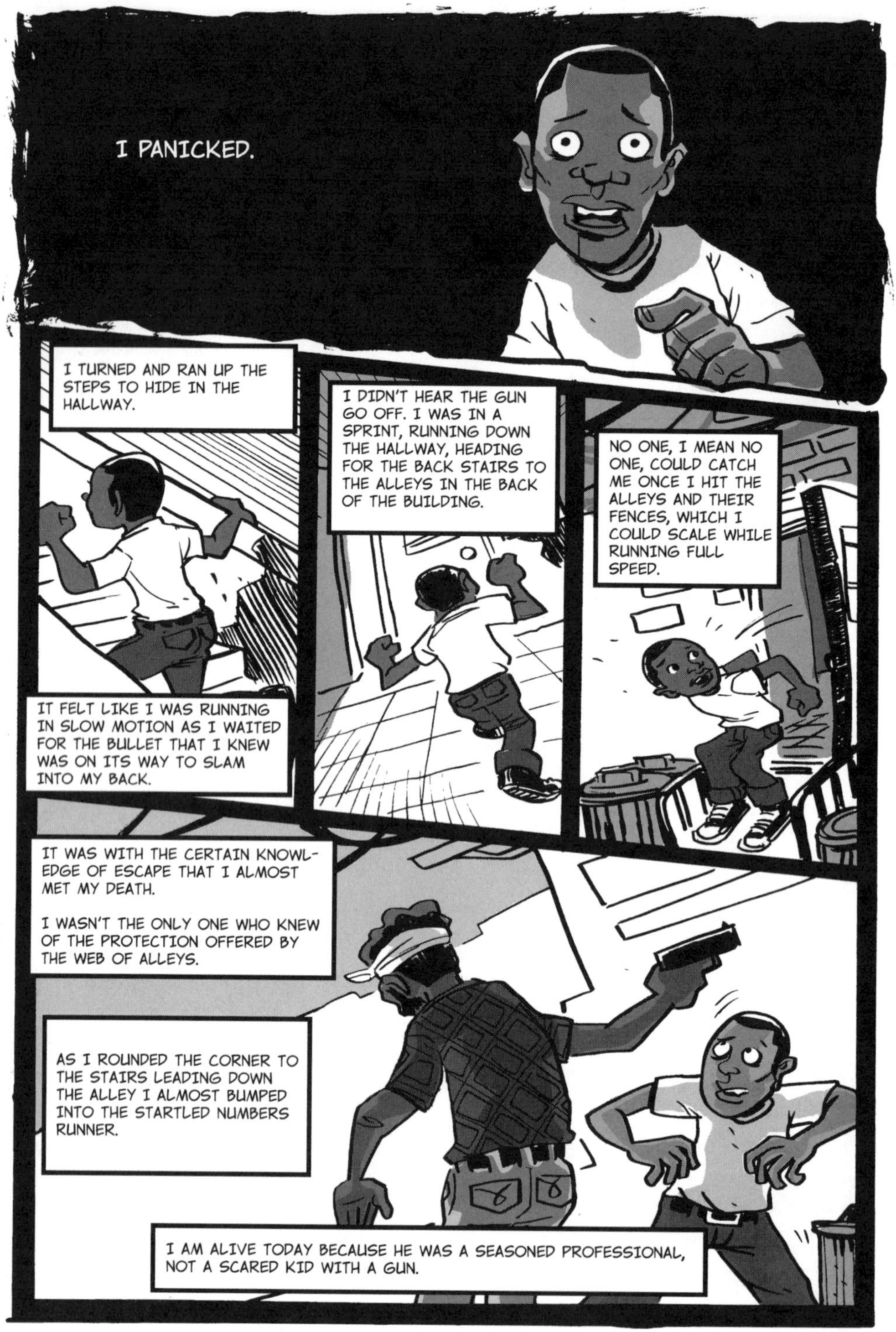
I PANICKED.
I TURNED AND RAN UP THE STEPS TO HIDE IN THE HALLWAY.
IT FELT LIKE I WAS RUNNING IN SLOW MOTION AS I WAITED FOR THE BULLET THAT I KNEW WAS ON ITS WAY TO SLAM INTO MY BACK.
I DIDN'T HEAR THE GUN GO OFF. I WAS IN A SPRINT, RUNNING DOWN THE HALLWAY, HEADING FOR THE BACK STAIRS TO THE ALLEYS IN THE BACK OF THE BUILDING.
NO ONE, I MEAN NO ONE, COULD CATCH ME ONCE I HIT THE ALLEYS AND THEIR FENCES, WHICH I COULD SCALE WHILE RUNNING FULL SPEED.
IT WAS WITH THE CERTAIN KNOWLEDGE OF ESCAPE THAT I ALMOST MET MY DEATH.
I WASN'T THE ONLY ONE WHO KNEW OF THE PROTECTION OFFERED BY THE WEB OF ALLEYS.
AS I ROUNDED THE CORNER TO THE STAIRS LEADING DOWN THE ALLEY I ALMOST BUMPED INTO THE STARTLED NUMBERS RUNNER.
I AM ALIVE TODAY BECAUSE HE WAS A SEASONED PROFESSIONAL, NOT A SCARED KID WITH A GUN.

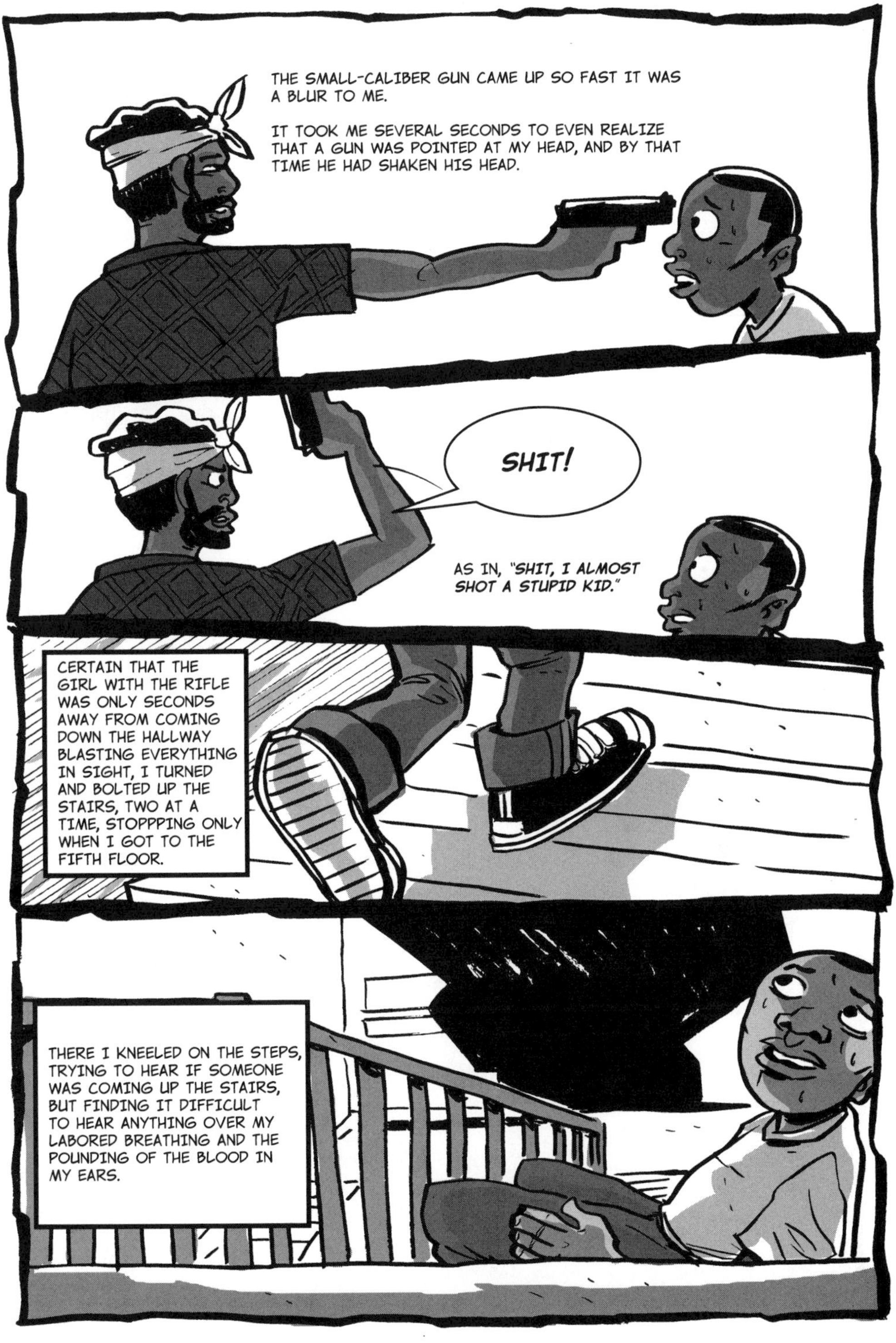
THE SMALL-CALIBER GUN CAME UP SO FAST IT WAS A BLUR TO ME.
IT TOOK ME SEVERAL SECONDS TO EVEN REALIZE THAT A GUN WAS POINTED AT MY HEAD, AND BY THAT TIME HE HAD SHAKEN HIS HEAD.
SHIT!
AS IN, "SHIT, I ALMOST SHOT A STUPID KID."
CERTAIN THAT THE GIRL WITH THE RIFLE WAS ONLY SECONDS AWAY FROM COMING DOWN THE HALLWAY BLASTING EVERYTHING IN SIGHT, I TURNED AND BOLTED UP THE STAIRS, TWO AT A TIME, STOPPPING ONLY WHEN I GOT TO THE FIFTH FLOOR.
THERE I KNEELED ON THE STEPS, TRYING TO HEAR IF SOMEONE WAS COMING UP THE STAIRS, BUT FINDING IT DIFFICULT TO HEAR ANYTHING OVER MY LABORED BREATHING AND THE POUNDING OF THE BLOOD IN MY EARS.

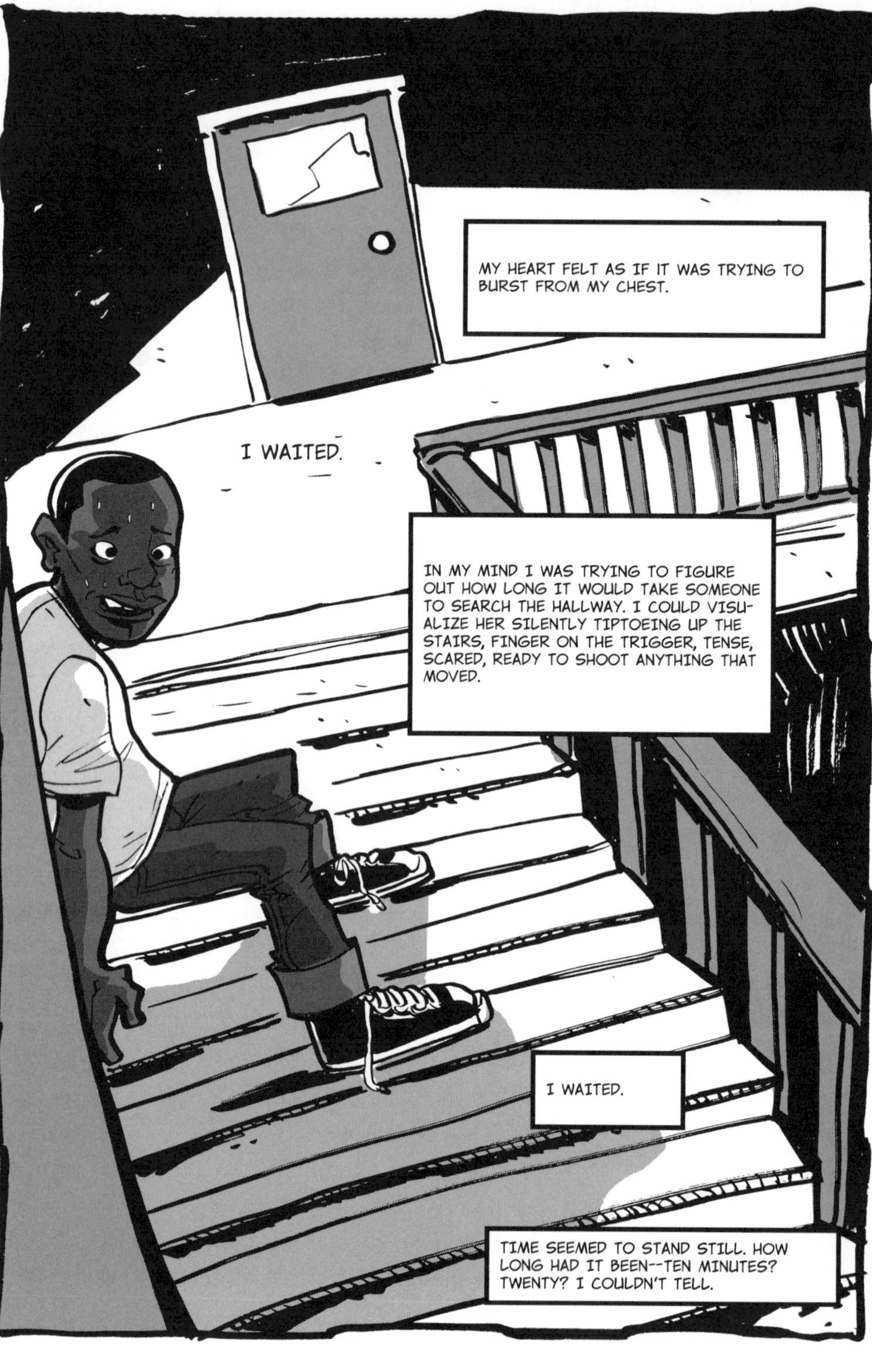

MY HEART FELT AS IF IT WAS TRYING TO BURST FROM MY CHEST.
I WAITED.
IN MY MIND I WAS TRYING TO FIGURE OUT HOW LONG IT WOULD TAKE SOMEONE TO SEARCH THE HALLWAY. I COULD VISUALIZE HER SILENTLY TIPTOEING UP THE STAIRS, FINGER ON THE TRIGGER, TENSE, SCARED, READY TO SHOOT ANYTHING THAT MOVED.
I WAITED.
TIME SEEMED TO STAND STILL. HOW LONG HAD IT BEEN--TEN MINUTES? TWENTY? I COULDN'T TELL.

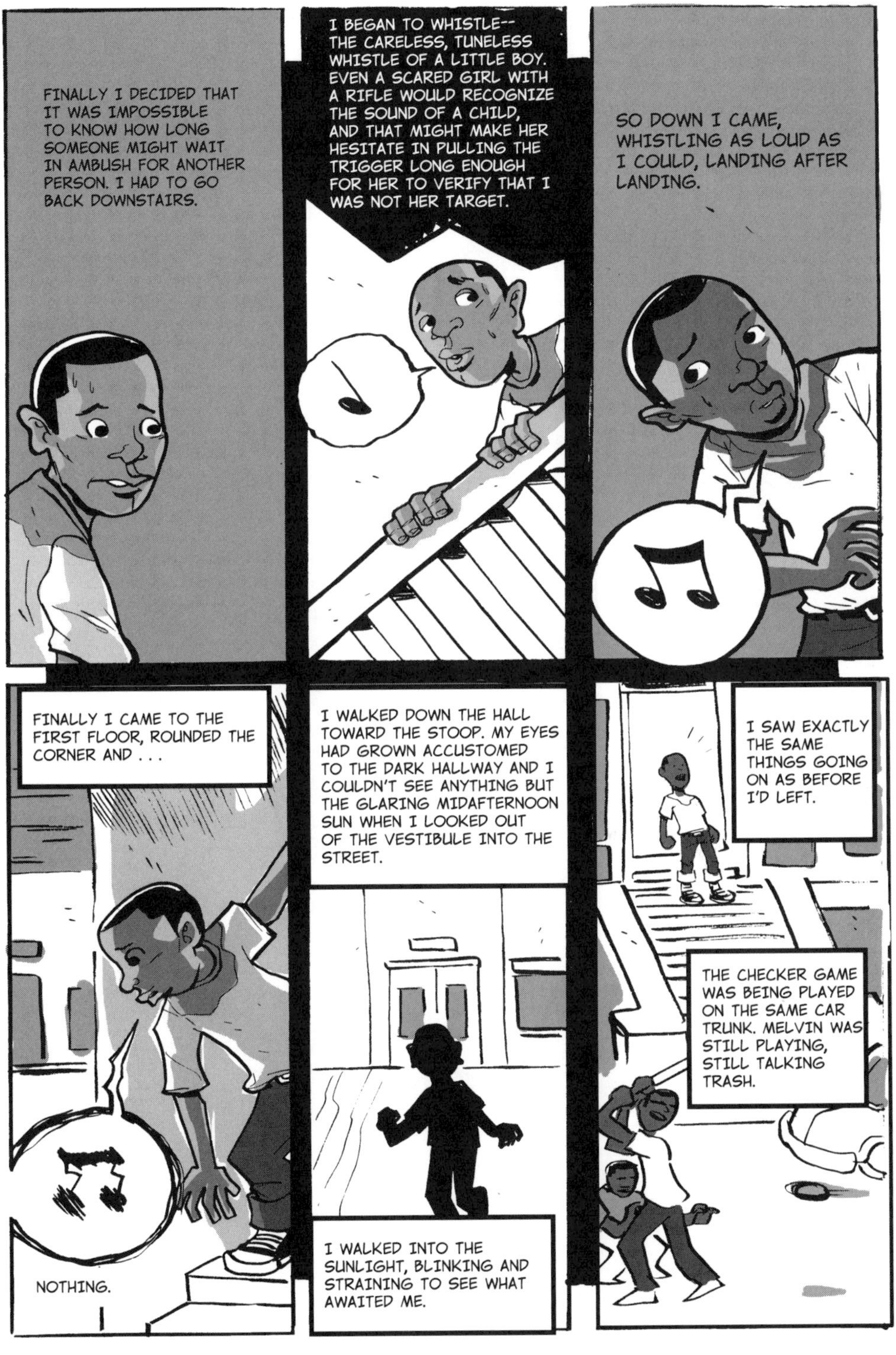
FINALLY I DECIDED THAT IT WAS IMPOSSIBLE TO KNOW HOW LONG SOMEONE MIGHT WAIT IN AMBUSH FOR ANOTHER PERSON. I HAD TO GO BACK DOWNSTAIRS.
I BEGAN TO WHISTLE-- THE CARELESS, TUNELESS WHISTLE OF A LITTLE BOY. EVEN A SCARED GIRL WITH A RIFLE WOULD RECOGNIZE THE SOUND OF A CHILD, AND THAT MIGHT MAKE HER HESITATE IN PULLING THE TRIGGER LONG ENOUGH FOR HER TO VERIFY THAT I WAS NOT HER TARGET.
SO DOWN I CAME, WHISTLING AS LOUD AS I COULD, LANDING AFTER LANDING.
FINALLY I CAME TO THE FIRST FLOOR, ROUNDED THE CORNER AND . . .
NOTHING.
I WALKED DOWN THE HALL TOWARD THE STOOP. MY EYES HAD GROWN ACCUSTOMED TO THE DARK HALLWAY AND I COULDN'T SEE ANYTHING BUT THE GLARING MIDAFTERNOON SUN WHEN I LOOKED OUT OF THE VESTIBULE INTO THE STREET.
I WALKED INTO THE SUNLIGHT, BLINKING AND STRAINING TO SEE WHAT AWAITED ME.
I SAW EXACTLY THE SAME THINGS GOING ON AS BEFORE I'D LEFT.
THE CHECKER GAME WAS BEING PLAYED ON THE SAME CAR TRUNK. MELVIN WAS STILL PLAYING, STILL TALKING TRASH.

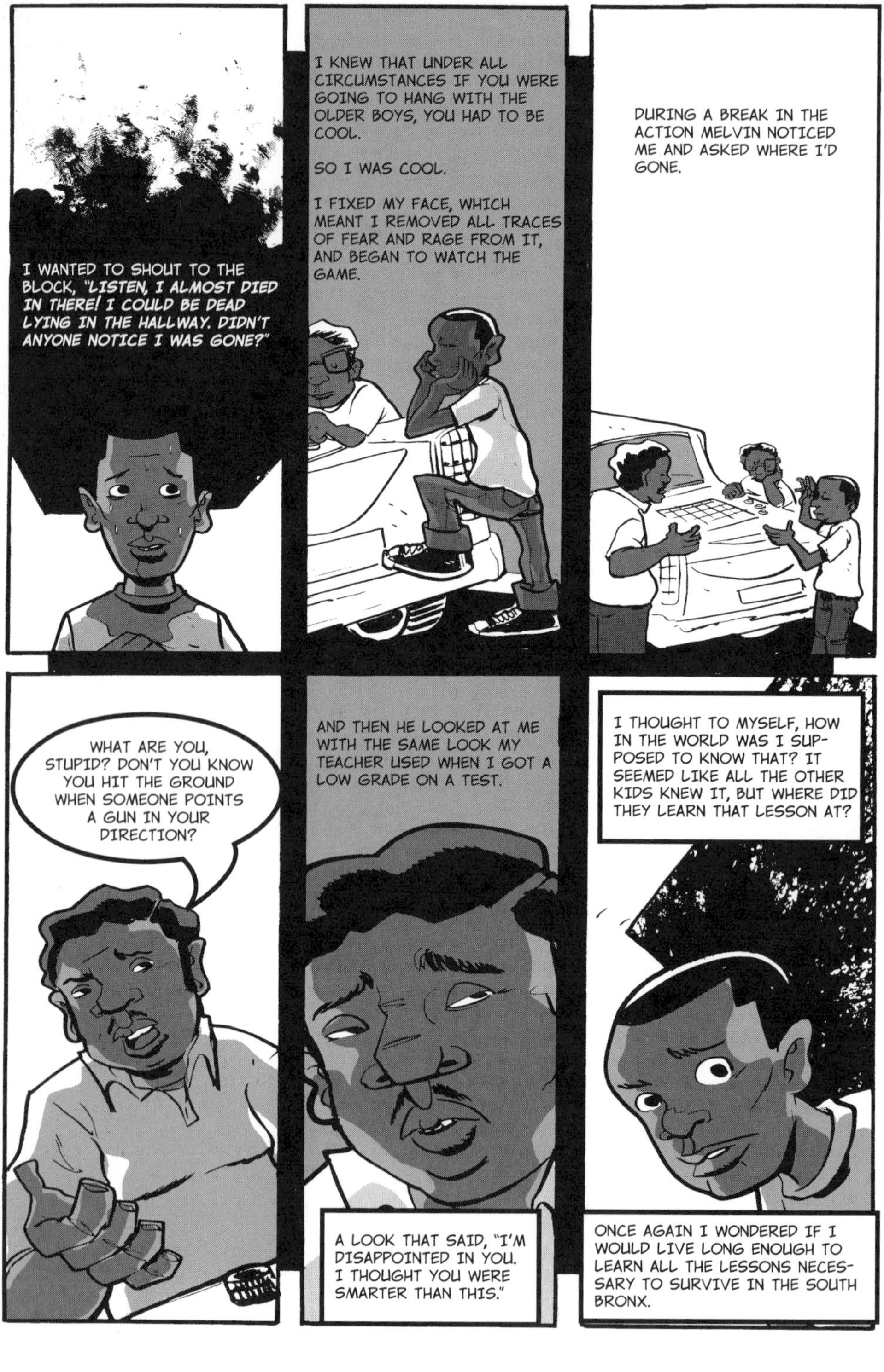
I WANTED TO SHOUT TO THE BLOCK, *"LISTEN, I ALMOST DIED IN THERE! I COULD BE DEAD LYING IN THE HALLWAY. DIDN'T ANYONE NOTICE I WAS GONE?"*
I KNEW THAT UNDER ALL CIRCUMSTANCES IF YOU WERE GOING TO HANG WITH THE OLDER BOYS, YOU HAD TO BE COOL.
SO I WAS COOL.
I FIXED MY FACE, WHICH MEANT I REMOVED ALL TRACES OF FEAR AND RAGE FROM IT, AND BEGAN TO WATCH THE GAME.
DURING A BREAK IN THE ACTION MELVIN NOTICED ME AND ASKED WHERE I'D GONE.
WHAT ARE YOU, STUPID? DON'T YOU KNOW YOU HIT THE GROUND WHEN SOMEONE POINTS A GUN IN YOUR DIRECTION?
AND THEN HE LOOKED AT ME WITH THE SAME LOOK MY TEACHER USED WHEN I GOT A LOW GRADE ON A TEST.
A LOOK THAT SAID, "I'M DISAPPOINTED IN YOU. I THOUGHT YOU WERE SMARTER THAN THIS."
I THOUGHT TO MYSELF, HOW IN THE WORLD WAS I SUPPOSED TO KNOW THAT? IT SEEMED LIKE ALL THE OTHER KIDS KNEW IT, BUT WHERE DID THEY LEARN THAT LESSON AT?
ONCE AGAIN I WONDERED IF I WOULD LIVE LONG ENOUGH TO LEARN ALL THE LESSONS NECESSARY TO SURVIVE IN THE SOUTH BRONX.

HIT THE GROUND--SOUND ADVICE WHEN SOMEONE IS POINTING A GUN IN YOUR DIRECTION BUT YOU ARE NOT THE PRIMARY TARGET. HIT THE GROUND, AS ALL SOLDIERS ARE TAUGHT TO DO WHEN THEY COME UNDER FIRE.

NOT A BAD TEST QUESTION TO USE IN OUR URBAN SCHOOLS:

WHEN SOMEONE POINTS A GUN IN YOUR DIRECTION BUT DOESN'T WANT TO SHOOT YOU IN PARTICULAR, YOU SHOULD

A.   RUN INTO THE NEAREST BUILDING.
B.   YELL AND SCREAM WHILE YOU RUN AWAY.
C.   STAND STILL.
D.   HIT THE GROUND.

MOST KIDS THAT I KNOW GET THIS QUESTION WRONG. THEY USUALLY CHOOSE B OR C. I LEARNED THE RIGHT ANSWER FROM MELVIN: HIT THE GROUND.

IT WAS ONLY A FEW YEARS LATER THAT MELVIN WAS SHOT. HE WAS TRYING TO STOP ANOTHER MAN FROM BEATING ONE OF HIS FEMALE RELATIVES.

THE MAN PULLED A GUN.
MELVIN TRIED TO RUN.
HE WAS SHOT IN THE BACK.

HE LIVED THE NEXT TWENTY YEARS IN A WHEELCHAIR, PARALYZED FROM THE WAIST DOWN. HE WAS NEVER THE SAME.

THE BULLET DESTROYED MORE THAN HIS ABILITY TO WALK. BEING CRIPPLED AT SUCH A YOUNG AGE ROBBED HIM OF HIS YOUTH, AND FINALLY OF HIS WILL TO LIVE.

HE DIED TWO YEARS AGO, ANOTHER CASUALTY OF UNION AVENUE.

8

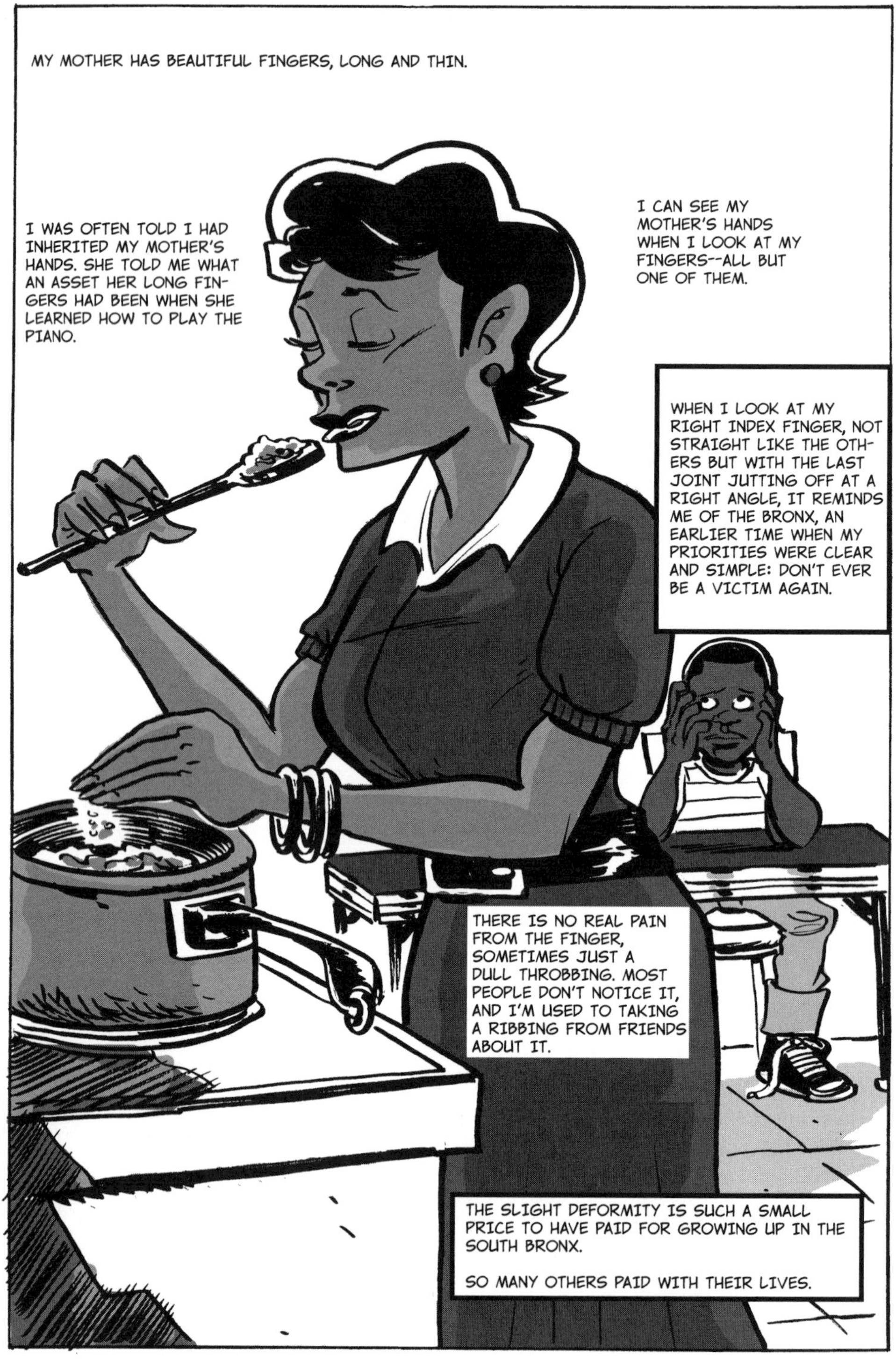
MY MOTHER HAS BEAUTIFUL FINGERS, LONG AND THIN.
I WAS OFTEN TOLD I HAD INHERITED MY MOTHER'S HANDS. SHE TOLD ME WHAT AN ASSET HER LONG FINGERS HAD BEEN WHEN SHE LEARNED HOW TO PLAY THE PIANO.
I CAN SEE MY MOTHER'S HANDS WHEN I LOOK AT MY FINGERS--ALL BUT ONE OF THEM.
WHEN I LOOK AT MY RIGHT INDEX FINGER, NOT STRAIGHT LIKE THE OTHERS BUT WITH THE LAST JOINT JUTTING OFF AT A RIGHT ANGLE, IT REMINDS ME OF THE BRONX, AN EARLIER TIME WHEN MY PRIORITIES WERE CLEAR AND SIMPLE: DON'T EVER BE A VICTIM AGAIN.
THERE IS NO REAL PAIN FROM THE FINGER, SOMETIMES JUST A DULL THROBBING. MOST PEOPLE DON'T NOTICE IT, AND I'M USED TO TAKING A RIBBING FROM FRIENDS ABOUT IT.
THE SLIGHT DEFORMITY IS SUCH A SMALL PRICE TO HAVE PAID FOR GROWING UP IN THE SOUTH BRONX.
SO MANY OTHERS PAID WITH THEIR LIVES.

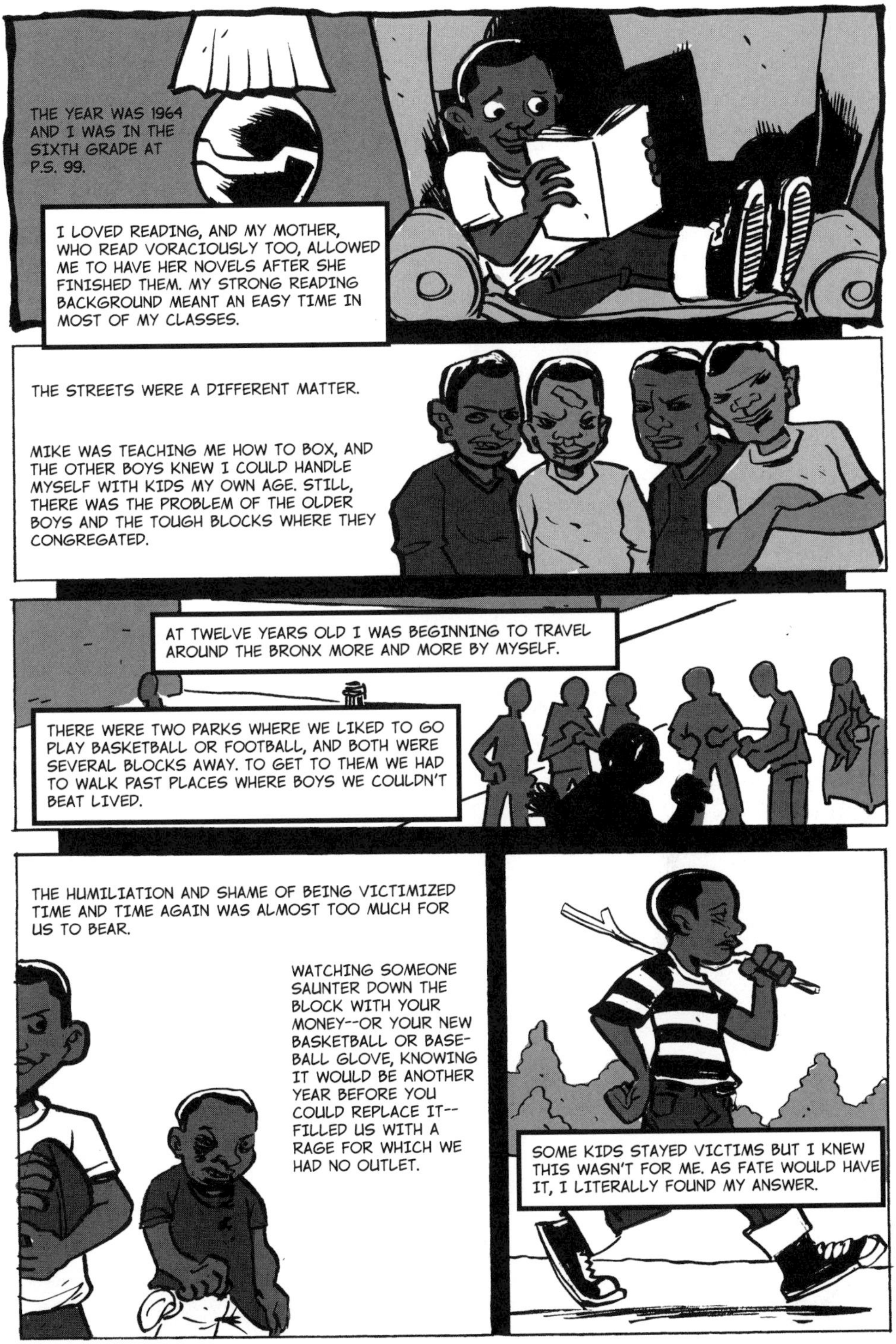
THE YEAR WAS 1964 AND I WAS IN THE SIXTH GRADE AT P.S. 99.
I LOVED READING, AND MY MOTHER, WHO READ VORACIOUSLY TOO, ALLOWED ME TO HAVE HER NOVELS AFTER SHE FINISHED THEM. MY STRONG READING BACKGROUND MEANT AN EASY TIME IN MOST OF MY CLASSES.
THE STREETS WERE A DIFFERENT MATTER.
MIKE WAS TEACHING ME HOW TO BOX, AND THE OTHER BOYS KNEW I COULD HANDLE MYSELF WITH KIDS MY OWN AGE. STILL, THERE WAS THE PROBLEM OF THE OLDER BOYS AND THE TOUGH BLOCKS WHERE THEY CONGREGATED.
AT TWELVE YEARS OLD I WAS BEGINNING TO TRAVEL AROUND THE BRONX MORE AND MORE BY MYSELF.
THERE WERE TWO PARKS WHERE WE LIKED TO GO PLAY BASKETBALL OR FOOTBALL, AND BOTH WERE SEVERAL BLOCKS AWAY. TO GET TO THEM WE HAD TO WALK PAST PLACES WHERE BOYS WE COULDN'T BEAT LIVED.
THE HUMILIATION AND SHAME OF BEING VICTIMIZED TIME AND TIME AGAIN WAS ALMOST TOO MUCH FOR US TO BEAR.
WATCHING SOMEONE SAUNTER DOWN THE BLOCK WITH YOUR MONEY--OR YOUR NEW BASKETBALL OR BASE-BALL GLOVE, KNOWING IT WOULD BE ANOTHER YEAR BEFORE YOU COULD REPLACE IT--FILLED US WITH A RAGE FOR WHICH WE HAD NO OUTLET.
SOME KIDS STAYED VICTIMS BUT I KNEW THIS WASN'T FOR ME. AS FATE WOULD HAVE IT, I LITERALLY FOUND MY ANSWER.

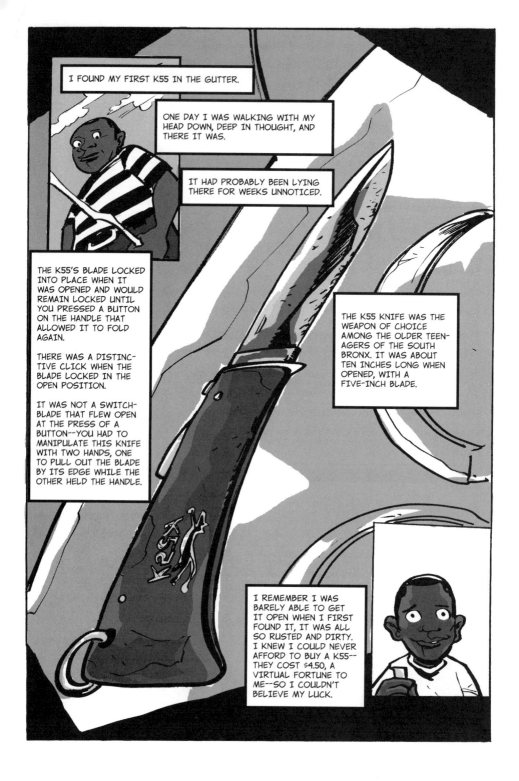

I FOUND MY FIRST K55 IN THE GUTTER.

ONE DAY I WAS WALKING WITH MY HEAD DOWN, DEEP IN THOUGHT, AND THERE IT WAS.

IT HAD PROBABLY BEEN LYING THERE FOR WEEKS UNNOTICED.

THE K55'S BLADE LOCKED INTO PLACE WHEN IT WAS OPENED AND WOULD REMAIN LOCKED UNTIL YOU PRESSED A BUTTON ON THE HANDLE THAT ALLOWED IT TO FOLD AGAIN.

THERE WAS A DISTINC-TIVE CLICK WHEN THE BLADE LOCKED IN THE OPEN POSITION.

IT WAS NOT A SWITCH-BLADE THAT FLEW OPEN AT THE PRESS OF A BUTTON--YOU HAD TO MANIPULATE THIS KNIFE WITH TWO HANDS, ONE TO PULL OUT THE BLADE BY ITS EDGE WHILE THE OTHER HELD THE HANDLE.

THE K55 KNIFE WAS THE WEAPON OF CHOICE AMONG THE OLDER TEEN-AGERS OF THE SOUTH BRONX. IT WAS ABOUT TEN INCHES LONG WHEN OPENED, WITH A FIVE-INCH BLADE.

I REMEMBER I WAS BARELY ABLE TO GET IT OPEN WHEN I FIRST FOUND IT, IT WAS ALL SO RUSTED AND DIRTY. I KNEW I COULD NEVER AFFORD TO BUY A K55-- THEY COST $4.50, A VIRTUAL FORTUNE TO ME--SO I COULDN'T BELIEVE MY LUCK.

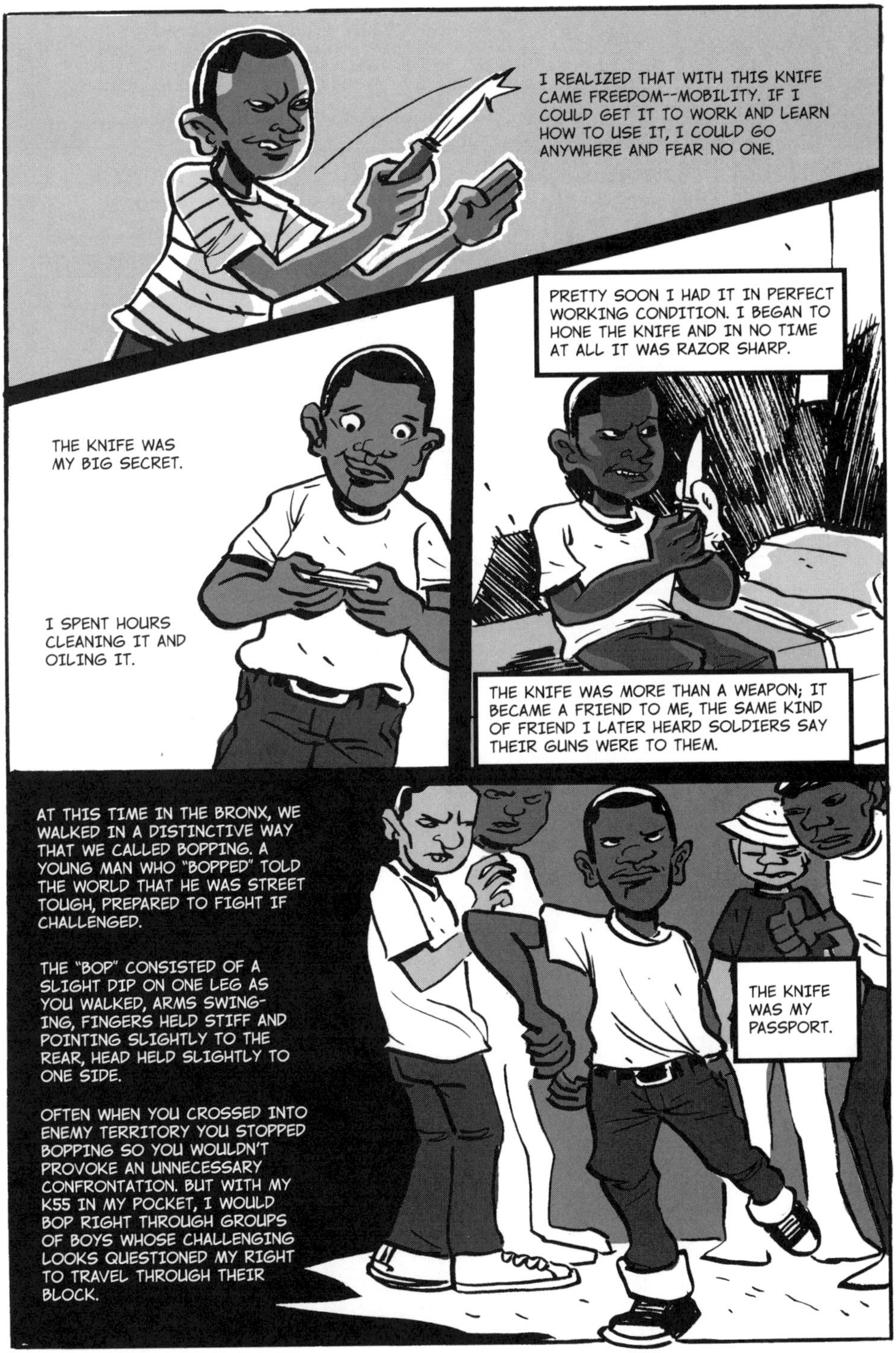
I REALIZED THAT WITH THIS KNIFE CAME FREEDOM--MOBILITY. IF I COULD GET IT TO WORK AND LEARN HOW TO USE IT, I COULD GO ANYWHERE AND FEAR NO ONE.
THE KNIFE WAS MY BIG SECRET.
I SPENT HOURS CLEANING IT AND OILING IT.
PRETTY SOON I HAD IT IN PERFECT WORKING CONDITION. I BEGAN TO HONE THE KNIFE AND IN NO TIME AT ALL IT WAS RAZOR SHARP.
THE KNIFE WAS MORE THAN A WEAPON; IT BECAME A FRIEND TO ME, THE SAME KIND OF FRIEND I LATER HEARD SOLDIERS SAY THEIR GUNS WERE TO THEM.
AT THIS TIME IN THE BRONX, WE WALKED IN A DISTINCTIVE WAY THAT WE CALLED BOPPING. A YOUNG MAN WHO "BOPPED" TOLD THE WORLD THAT HE WAS STREET TOUGH, PREPARED TO FIGHT IF CHALLENGED.
THE "BOP" CONSISTED OF A SLIGHT DIP ON ONE LEG AS YOU WALKED, ARMS SWINGING, FINGERS HELD STIFF AND POINTING SLIGHTLY TO THE REAR, HEAD HELD SLIGHTLY TO ONE SIDE.
OFTEN WHEN YOU CROSSED INTO ENEMY TERRITORY YOU STOPPED BOPPING SO YOU WOULDN'T PROVOKE AN UNNECESSARY CONFRONTATION. BUT WITH MY K55 IN MY POCKET, I WOULD BOP RIGHT THROUGH GROUPS OF BOYS WHOSE CHALLENGING LOOKS QUESTIONED MY RIGHT TO TRAVEL THROUGH THEIR BLOCK.
THE KNIFE WAS MY PASSPORT.

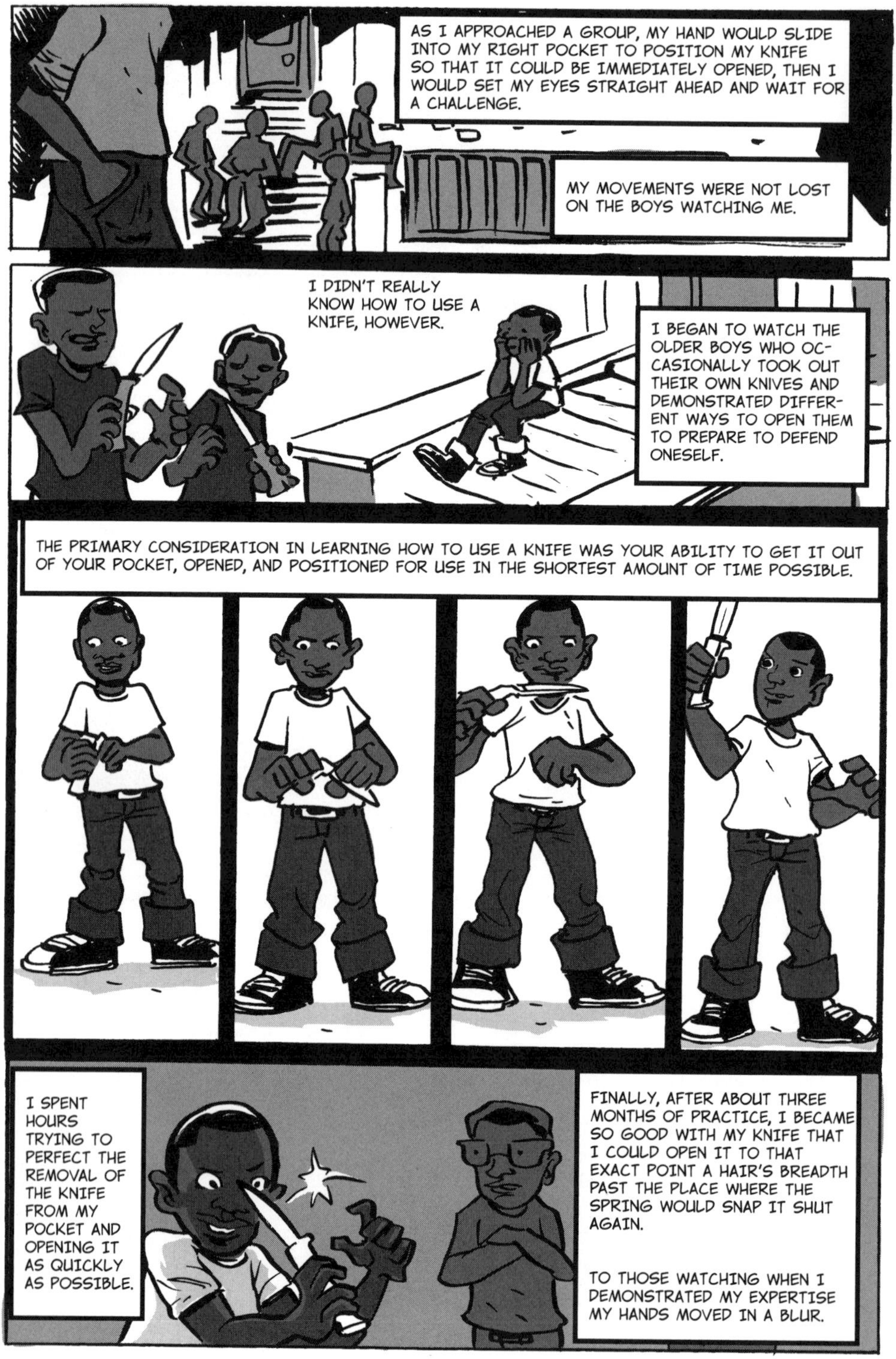
AS I APPROACHED A GROUP, MY HAND WOULD SLIDE INTO MY RIGHT POCKET TO POSITION MY KNIFE SO THAT IT COULD BE IMMEDIATELY OPENED, THEN I WOULD SET MY EYES STRAIGHT AHEAD AND WAIT FOR A CHALLENGE.
MY MOVEMENTS WERE NOT LOST ON THE BOYS WATCHING ME.
I DIDN'T REALLY KNOW HOW TO USE A KNIFE, HOWEVER.
I BEGAN TO WATCH THE OLDER BOYS WHO OCCASIONALLY TOOK OUT THEIR OWN KNIVES AND DEMONSTRATED DIFFERENT WAYS TO OPEN THEM TO PREPARE TO DEFEND ONESELF.
THE PRIMARY CONSIDERATION IN LEARNING HOW TO USE A KNIFE WAS YOUR ABILITY TO GET IT OUT OF YOUR POCKET, OPENED, AND POSITIONED FOR USE IN THE SHORTEST AMOUNT OF TIME POSSIBLE.
I SPENT HOURS TRYING TO PERFECT THE REMOVAL OF THE KNIFE FROM MY POCKET AND OPENING IT AS QUICKLY AS POSSIBLE.
FINALLY, AFTER ABOUT THREE MONTHS OF PRACTICE, I BECAME SO GOOD WITH MY KNIFE THAT I COULD OPEN IT TO THAT EXACT POINT A HAIR'S BREADTH PAST THE PLACE WHERE THE SPRING WOULD SNAP IT SHUT AGAIN.
TO THOSE WATCHING WHEN I DEMONSTRATED MY EXPERTISE MY HANDS MOVED IN A BLUR.

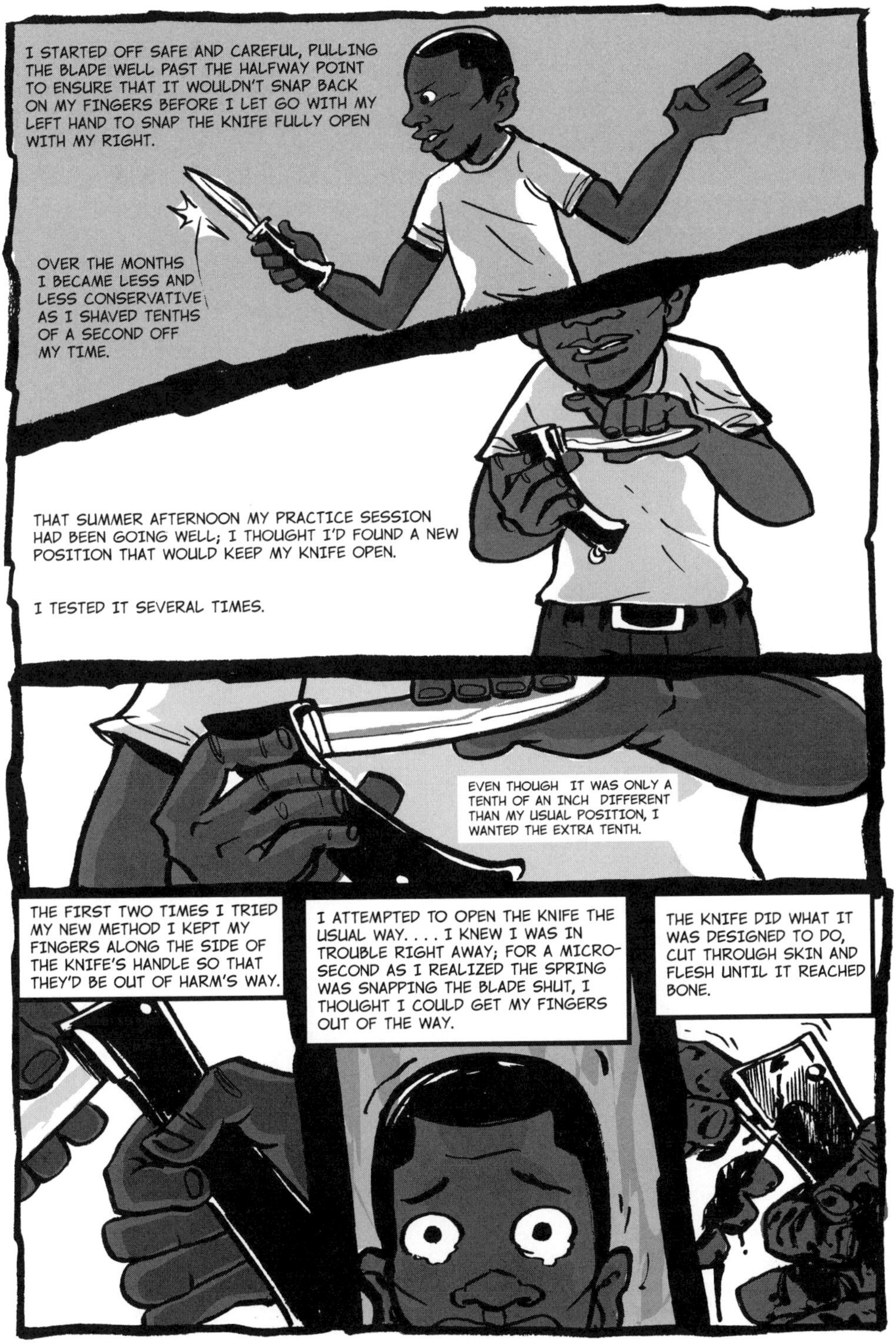

I STARTED OFF SAFE AND CAREFUL, PULLING THE BLADE WELL PAST THE HALFWAY POINT TO ENSURE THAT IT WOULDN'T SNAP BACK ON MY FINGERS BEFORE I LET GO WITH MY LEFT HAND TO SNAP THE KNIFE FULLY OPEN WITH MY RIGHT.
OVER THE MONTHS I BECAME LESS AND LESS CONSERVATIVE AS I SHAVED TENTHS OF A SECOND OFF MY TIME.
THAT SUMMER AFTERNOON MY PRACTICE SESSION HAD BEEN GOING WELL; I THOUGHT I'D FOUND A NEW POSITION THAT WOULD KEEP MY KNIFE OPEN.
I TESTED IT SEVERAL TIMES.
EVEN THOUGH IT WAS ONLY A TENTH OF AN INCH DIFFERENT THAN MY USUAL POSITION, I WANTED THE EXTRA TENTH.
THE FIRST TWO TIMES I TRIED MY NEW METHOD I KEPT MY FINGERS ALONG THE SIDE OF THE KNIFE'S HANDLE SO THAT THEY'D BE OUT OF HARM'S WAY.
I ATTEMPTED TO OPEN THE KNIFE THE USUAL WAY. . . . I KNEW I WAS IN TROUBLE RIGHT AWAY; FOR A MICRO-SECOND AS I REALIZED THE SPRING WAS SNAPPING THE BLADE SHUT, I THOUGHT I COULD GET MY FINGERS OUT OF THE WAY.
THE KNIFE DID WHAT IT WAS DESIGNED TO DO, CUT THROUGH SKIN AND FLESH UNTIL IT REACHED BONE.

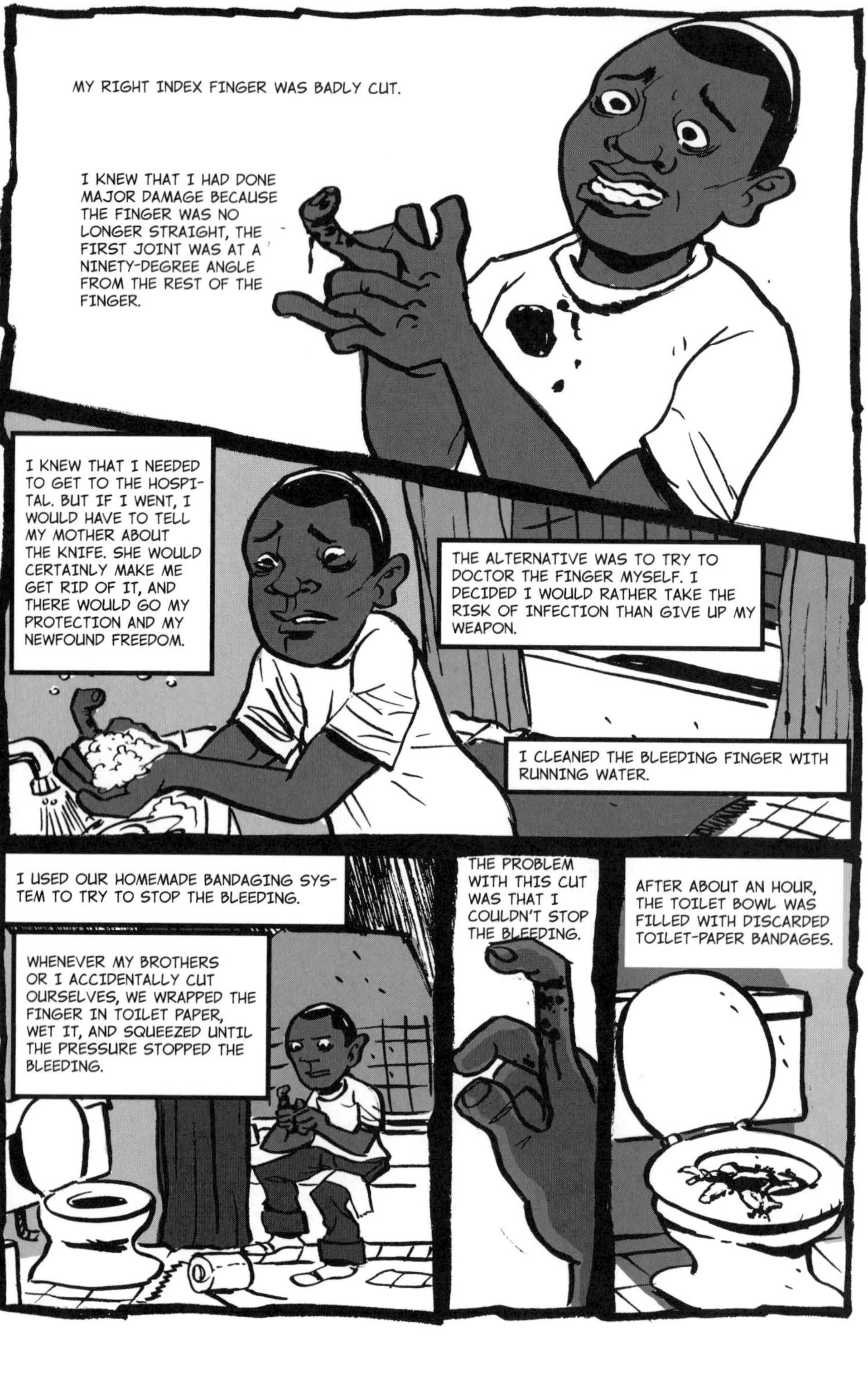
MY RIGHT INDEX FINGER WAS BADLY CUT.
I KNEW THAT I HAD DONE MAJOR DAMAGE BECAUSE THE FINGER WAS NO LONGER STRAIGHT, THE FIRST JOINT WAS AT A NINETY-DEGREE ANGLE FROM THE REST OF THE FINGER.
I KNEW THAT I NEEDED TO GET TO THE HOSPITAL. BUT IF I WENT, I WOULD HAVE TO TELL MY MOTHER ABOUT THE KNIFE. SHE WOULD CERTAINLY MAKE ME GET RID OF IT, AND THERE WOULD GO MY PROTECTION AND MY NEWFOUND FREEDOM.
THE ALTERNATIVE WAS TO TRY TO DOCTOR THE FINGER MYSELF. I DECIDED I WOULD RATHER TAKE THE RISK OF INFECTION THAN GIVE UP MY WEAPON.
I CLEANED THE BLEEDING FINGER WITH RUNNING WATER.
I USED OUR HOMEMADE BANDAGING SYSTEM TO TRY TO STOP THE BLEEDING.
WHENEVER MY BROTHERS OR I ACCIDENTALLY CUT OURSELVES, WE WRAPPED THE FINGER IN TOILET PAPER, WET IT, AND SQUEEZED UNTIL THE PRESSURE STOPPED THE BLEEDING.
THE PROBLEM WITH THIS CUT WAS THAT I COULDN'T STOP THE BLEEDING.
AFTER ABOUT AN HOUR, THE TOILET BOWL WAS FILLED WITH DISCARDED TOILET-PAPER BANDAGES.

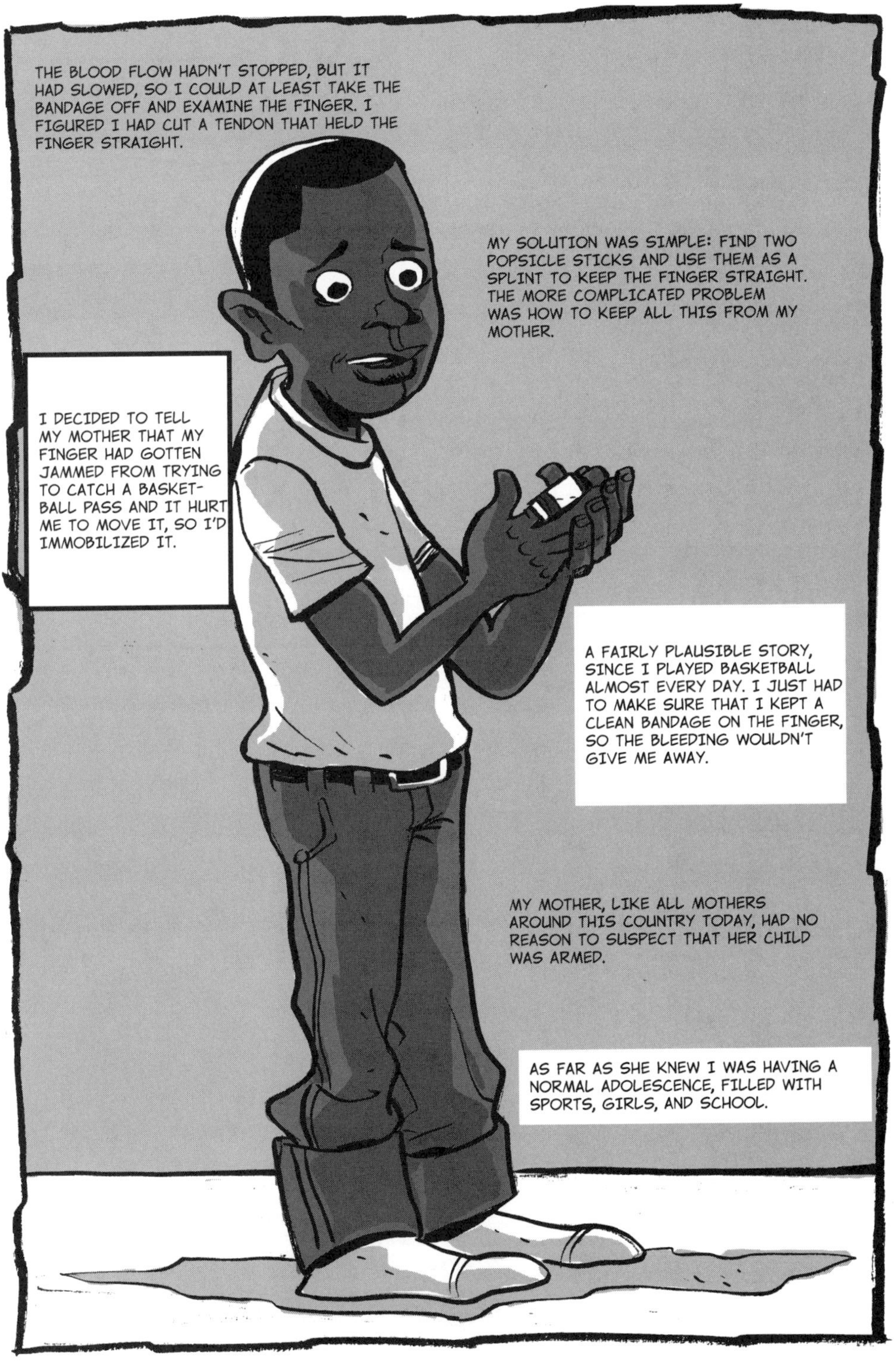
THE BLOOD FLOW HADN'T STOPPED, BUT IT HAD SLOWED, SO I COULD AT LEAST TAKE THE BANDAGE OFF AND EXAMINE THE FINGER. I FIGURED I HAD CUT A TENDON THAT HELD THE FINGER STRAIGHT.
MY SOLUTION WAS SIMPLE: FIND TWO POPSICLE STICKS AND USE THEM AS A SPLINT TO KEEP THE FINGER STRAIGHT. THE MORE COMPLICATED PROBLEM WAS HOW TO KEEP ALL THIS FROM MY MOTHER.
I DECIDED TO TELL MY MOTHER THAT MY FINGER HAD GOTTEN JAMMED FROM TRYING TO CATCH A BASKET-BALL PASS AND IT HURT ME TO MOVE IT, SO I'D IMMOBILIZED IT.
A FAIRLY PLAUSIBLE STORY, SINCE I PLAYED BASKETBALL ALMOST EVERY DAY. I JUST HAD TO MAKE SURE THAT I KEPT A CLEAN BANDAGE ON THE FINGER, SO THE BLEEDING WOULDN'T GIVE ME AWAY.
MY MOTHER, LIKE ALL MOTHERS AROUND THIS COUNTRY TODAY, HAD NO REASON TO SUSPECT THAT HER CHILD WAS ARMED.
AS FAR AS SHE KNEW I WAS HAVING A NORMAL ADOLESCENCE, FILLED WITH SPORTS, GIRLS, AND SCHOOL.

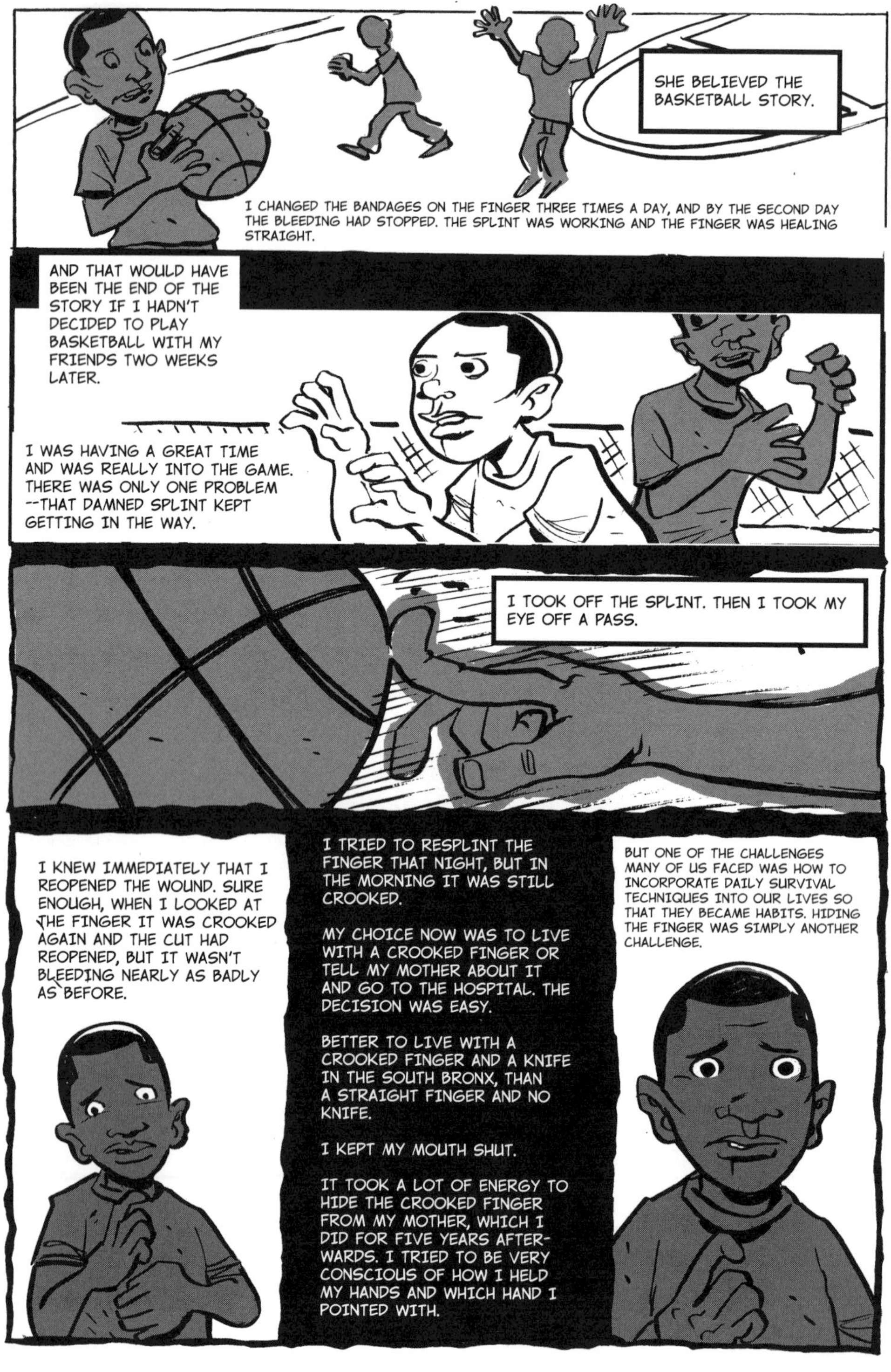
SHE BELIEVED THE BASKETBALL STORY.
I CHANGED THE BANDAGES ON THE FINGER THREE TIMES A DAY, AND BY THE SECOND DAY THE BLEEDING HAD STOPPED. THE SPLINT WAS WORKING AND THE FINGER WAS HEALING STRAIGHT.
AND THAT WOULD HAVE BEEN THE END OF THE STORY IF I HADN'T DECIDED TO PLAY BASKETBALL WITH MY FRIENDS TWO WEEKS LATER.
I WAS HAVING A GREAT TIME AND WAS REALLY INTO THE GAME. THERE WAS ONLY ONE PROBLEM --THAT DAMNED SPLINT KEPT GETTING IN THE WAY.
I TOOK OFF THE SPLINT. THEN I TOOK MY EYE OFF A PASS.
I KNEW IMMEDIATELY THAT I REOPENED THE WOUND. SURE ENOUGH, WHEN I LOOKED AT THE FINGER IT WAS CROOKED AGAIN AND THE CUT HAD REOPENED, BUT IT WASN'T BLEEDING NEARLY AS BADLY AS BEFORE.
I TRIED TO RESPLINT THE FINGER THAT NIGHT, BUT IN THE MORNING IT WAS STILL CROOKED.
MY CHOICE NOW WAS TO LIVE WITH A CROOKED FINGER OR TELL MY MOTHER ABOUT IT AND GO TO THE HOSPITAL. THE DECISION WAS EASY.
BETTER TO LIVE WITH A CROOKED FINGER AND A KNIFE IN THE SOUTH BRONX, THAN A STRAIGHT FINGER AND NO KNIFE.
I KEPT MY MOUTH SHUT.
IT TOOK A LOT OF ENERGY TO HIDE THE CROOKED FINGER FROM MY MOTHER, WHICH I DID FOR FIVE YEARS AFTER-WARDS. I TRIED TO BE VERY CONSCIOUS OF HOW I HELD MY HANDS AND WHICH HAND I POINTED WITH.
BUT ONE OF THE CHALLENGES MANY OF US FACED WAS HOW TO INCORPORATE DAILY SURVIVAL TECHNIQUES INTO OUR LIVES SO THAT THEY BECAME HABITS. HIDING THE FINGER WAS SIMPLY ANOTHER CHALLENGE.

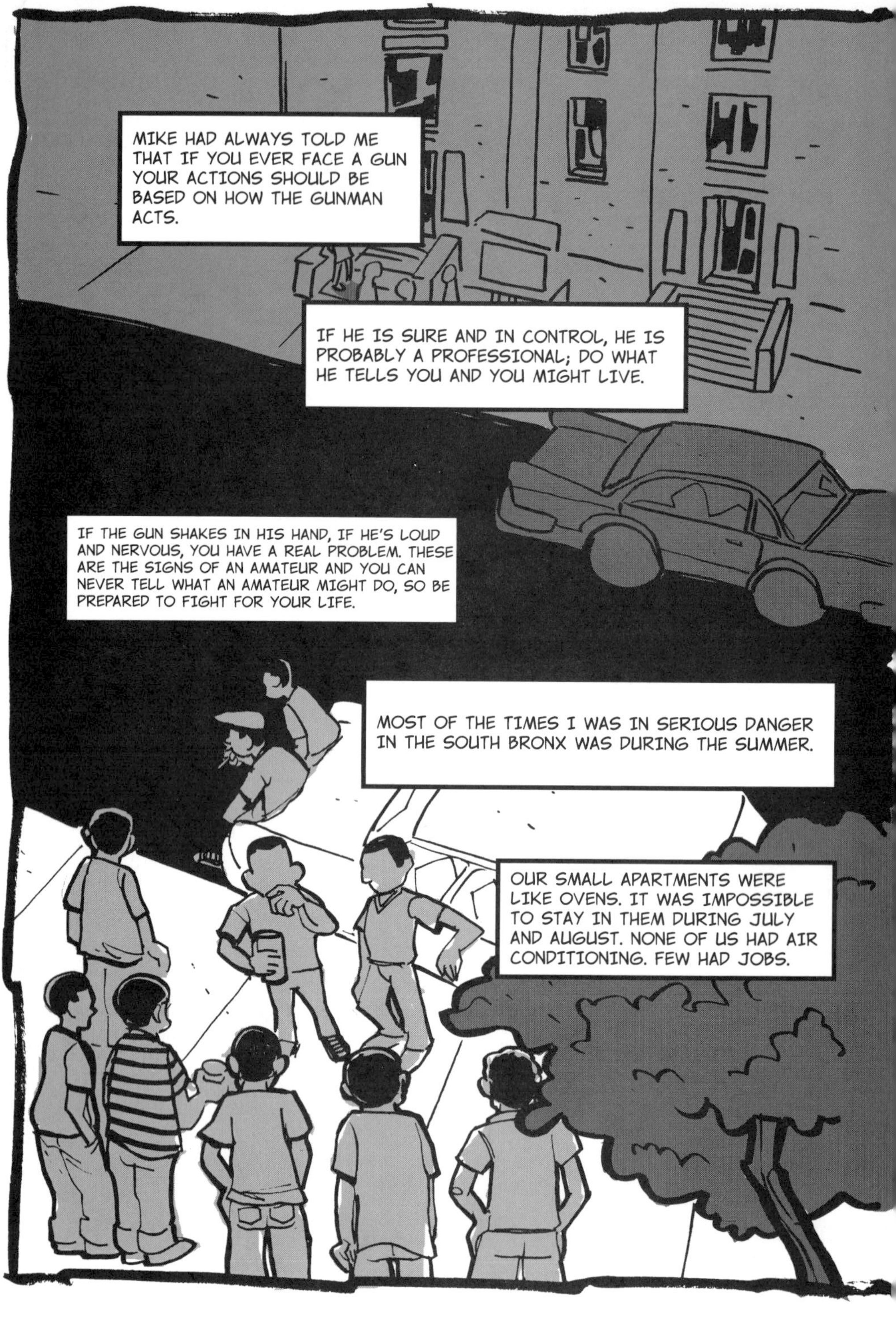
MIKE HAD ALWAYS TOLD ME THAT IF YOU EVER FACE A GUN YOUR ACTIONS SHOULD BE BASED ON HOW THE GUNMAN ACTS.
IF HE IS SURE AND IN CONTROL, HE IS PROBABLY A PROFESSIONAL; DO WHAT HE TELLS YOU AND YOU MIGHT LIVE.
IF THE GUN SHAKES IN HIS HAND, IF HE'S LOUD AND NERVOUS, YOU HAVE A REAL PROBLEM. THESE ARE THE SIGNS OF AN AMATEUR AND YOU CAN NEVER TELL WHAT AN AMATEUR MIGHT DO, SO BE PREPARED TO FIGHT FOR YOUR LIFE.
MOST OF THE TIMES I WAS IN SERIOUS DANGER IN THE SOUTH BRONX WAS DURING THE SUMMER.
OUR SMALL APARTMENTS WERE LIKE OVENS. IT WAS IMPOSSIBLE TO STAY IN THEM DURING JULY AND AUGUST. NONE OF US HAD AIR CONDITIONING. FEW HAD JOBS.

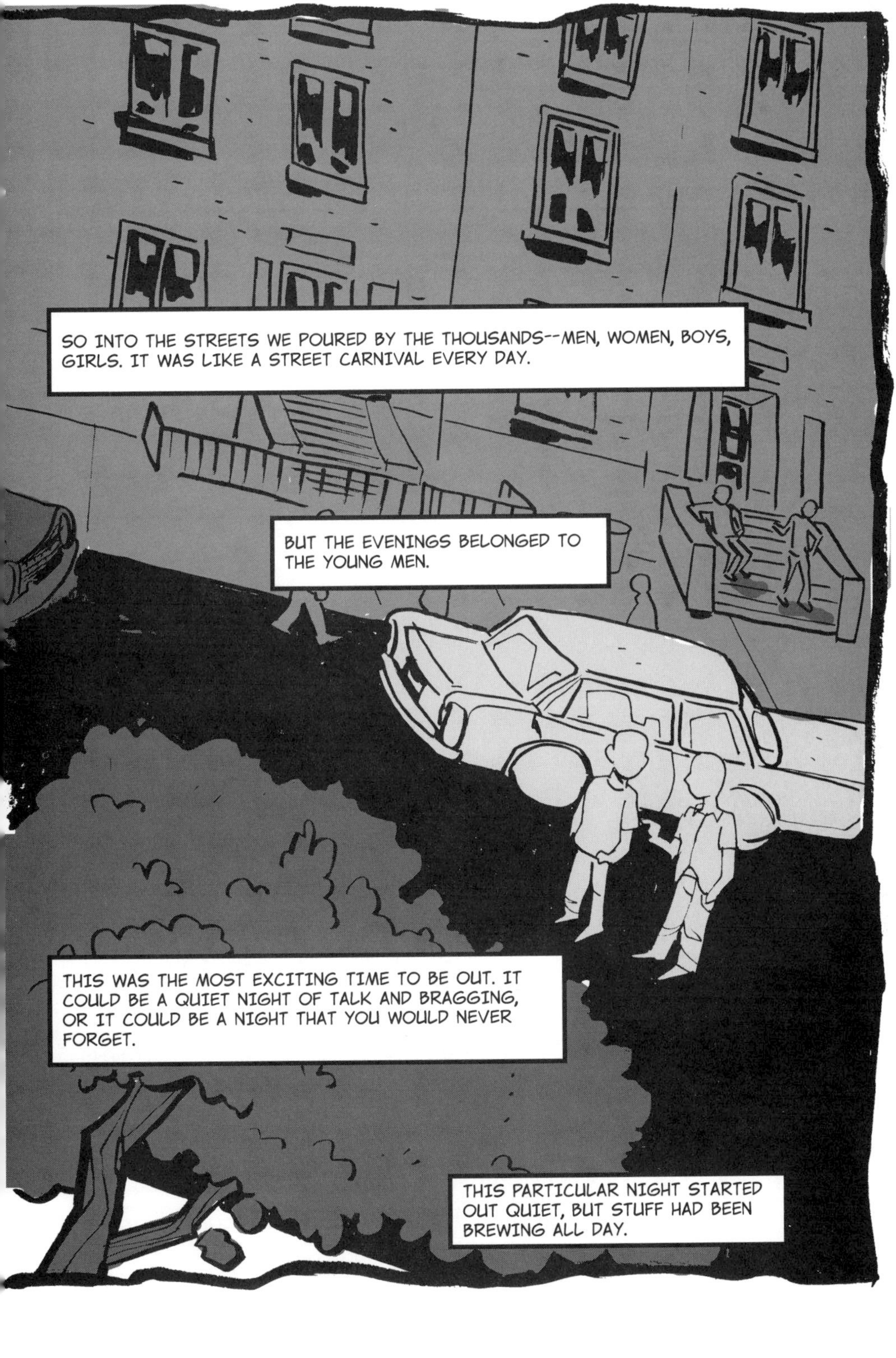
SO INTO THE STREETS WE POURED BY THE THOUSANDS--MEN, WOMEN, BOYS, GIRLS. IT WAS LIKE A STREET CARNIVAL EVERY DAY.
BUT THE EVENINGS BELONGED TO THE YOUNG MEN.
THIS WAS THE MOST EXCITING TIME TO BE OUT. IT COULD BE A QUIET NIGHT OF TALK AND BRAGGING, OR IT COULD BE A NIGHT THAT YOU WOULD NEVER FORGET.
THIS PARTICULAR NIGHT STARTED OUT QUIET, BUT STUFF HAD BEEN BREWING ALL DAY.

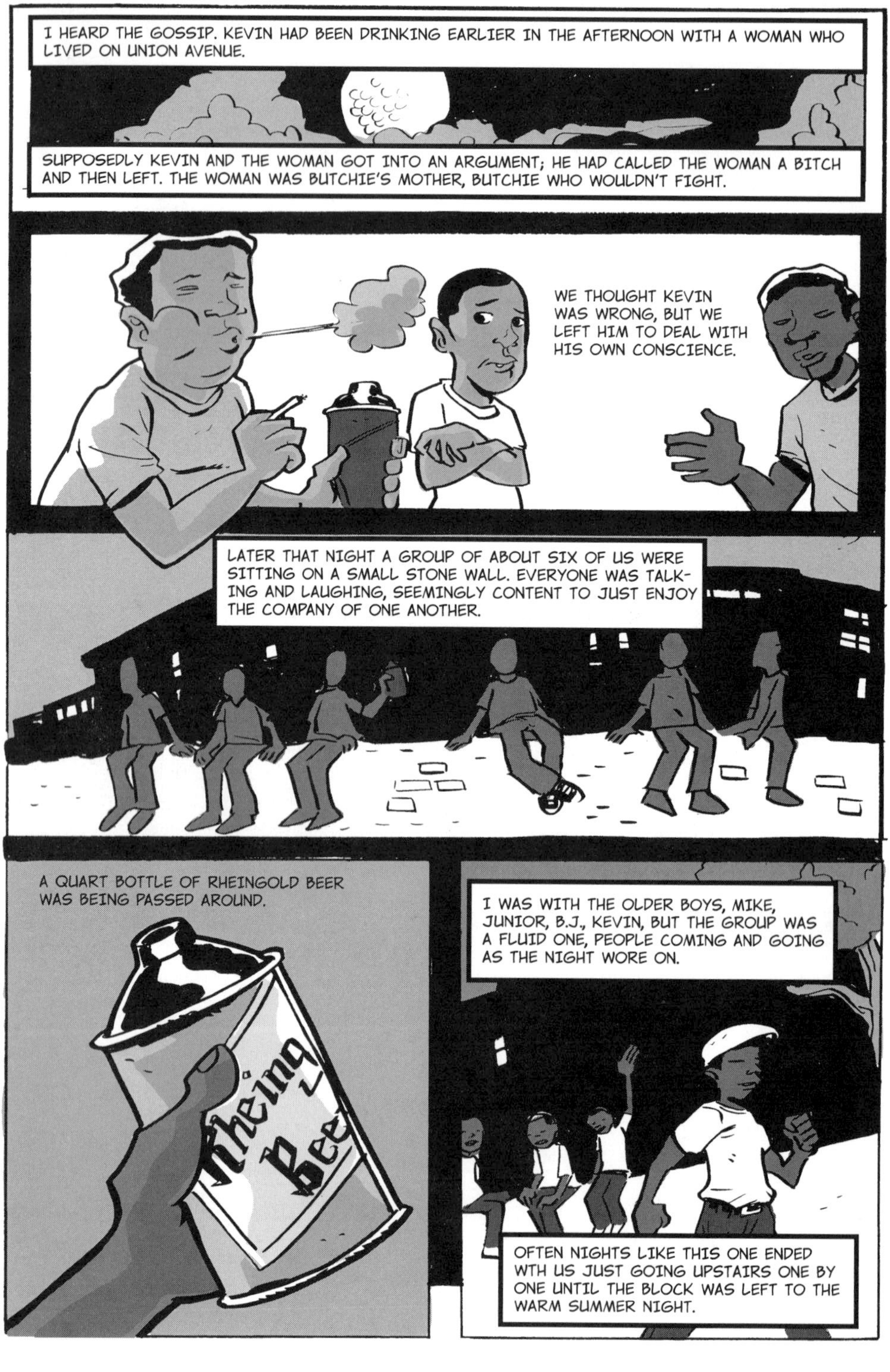
I HEARD THE GOSSIP. KEVIN HAD BEEN DRINKING EARLIER IN THE AFTERNOON WITH A WOMAN WHO LIVED ON UNION AVENUE.
SUPPOSEDLY KEVIN AND THE WOMAN GOT INTO AN ARGUMENT; HE HAD CALLED THE WOMAN A BITCH AND THEN LEFT. THE WOMAN WAS BUTCHIE'S MOTHER, BUTCHIE WHO WOULDN'T FIGHT.
WE THOUGHT KEVIN WAS WRONG, BUT WE LEFT HIM TO DEAL WITH HIS OWN CONSCIENCE.
LATER THAT NIGHT A GROUP OF ABOUT SIX OF US WERE SITTING ON A SMALL STONE WALL. EVERYONE WAS TALKING AND LAUGHING, SEEMINGLY CONTENT TO JUST ENJOY THE COMPANY OF ONE ANOTHER.
A QUART BOTTLE OF RHEINGOLD BEER WAS BEING PASSED AROUND.
I WAS WITH THE OLDER BOYS, MIKE, JUNIOR, B.J., KEVIN, BUT THE GROUP WAS A FLUID ONE, PEOPLE COMING AND GOING AS THE NIGHT WORE ON.
OFTEN NIGHTS LIKE THIS ONE ENDED WTH US JUST GOING UPSTAIRS ONE BY ONE UNTIL THE BLOCK WAS LEFT TO THE WARM SUMMER NIGHT.

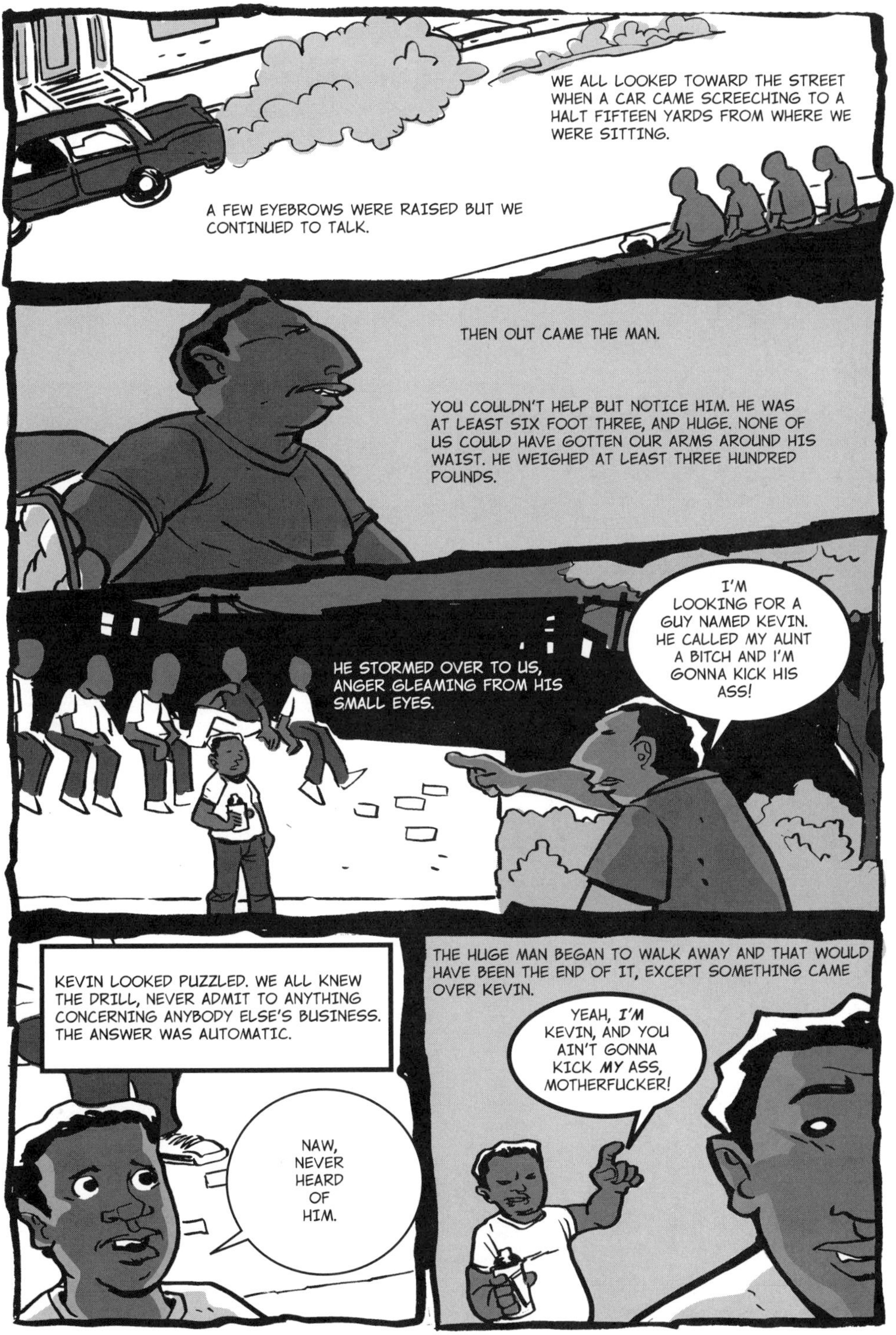
WE ALL LOOKED TOWARD THE STREET WHEN A CAR CAME SCREECHING TO A HALT FIFTEEN YARDS FROM WHERE WE WERE SITTING.
A FEW EYEBROWS WERE RAISED BUT WE CONTINUED TO TALK.
THEN OUT CAME THE MAN.
YOU COULDN'T HELP BUT NOTICE HIM. HE WAS AT LEAST SIX FOOT THREE, AND HUGE. NONE OF US COULD HAVE GOTTEN OUR ARMS AROUND HIS WAIST. HE WEIGHED AT LEAST THREE HUNDRED POUNDS.
HE STORMED OVER TO US, ANGER GLEAMING FROM HIS SMALL EYES.
I'M LOOKING FOR A GUY NAMED KEVIN. HE CALLED MY AUNT A BITCH AND I'M GONNA KICK HIS ASS!
KEVIN LOOKED PUZZLED. WE ALL KNEW THE DRILL, NEVER ADMIT TO ANYTHING CONCERNING ANYBODY ELSE'S BUSINESS. THE ANSWER WAS AUTOMATIC.
NAW, NEVER HEARD OF HIM.
THE HUGE MAN BEGAN TO WALK AWAY AND THAT WOULD HAVE BEEN THE END OF IT, EXCEPT SOMETHING CAME OVER KEVIN.
YEAH, *I'M* KEVIN, AND YOU AIN'T GONNA KICK *MY* ASS, MOTHERFUCKER!

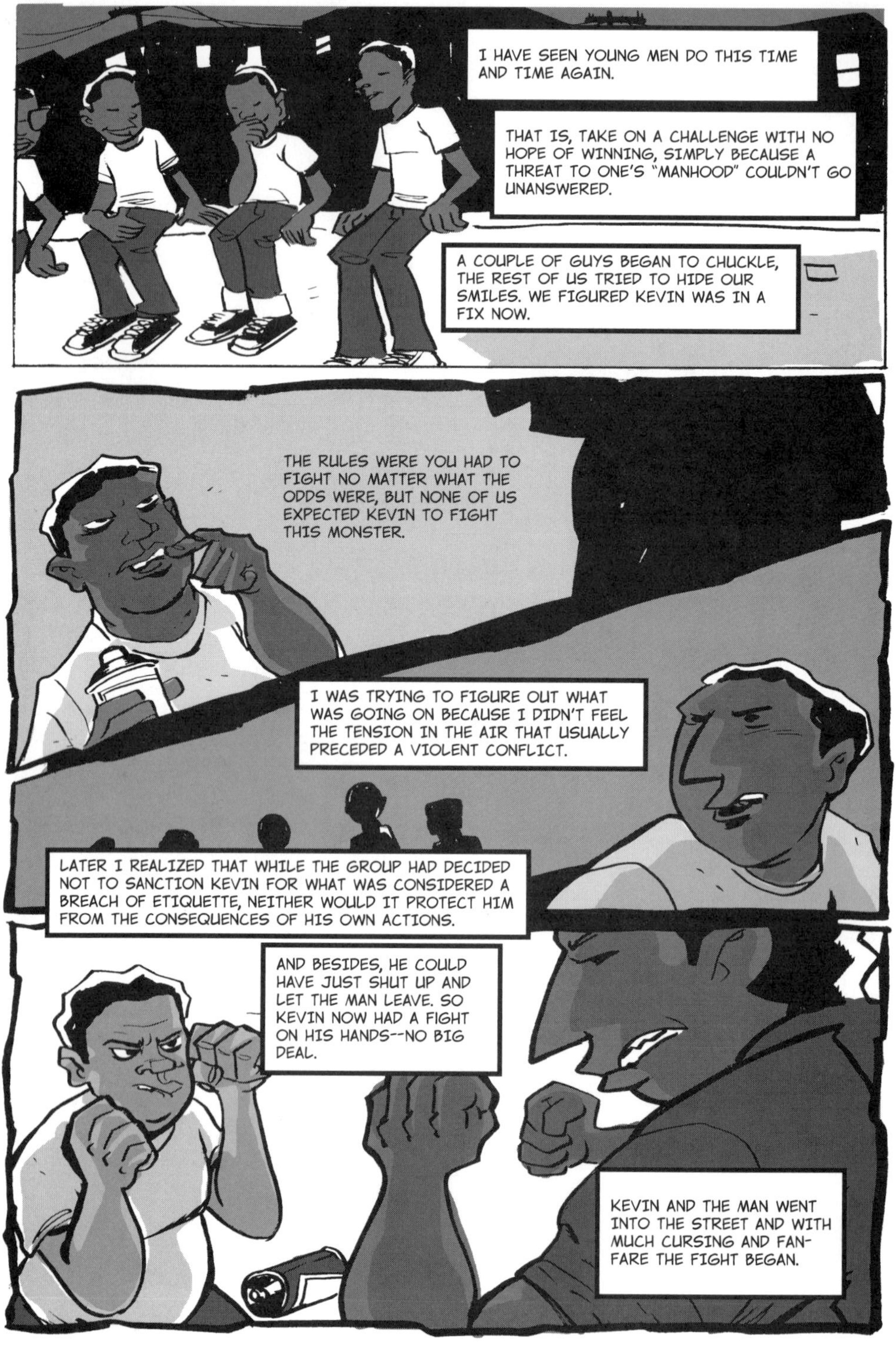
I HAVE SEEN YOUNG MEN DO THIS TIME AND TIME AGAIN.
THAT IS, TAKE ON A CHALLENGE WITH NO HOPE OF WINNING, SIMPLY BECAUSE A THREAT TO ONE'S "MANHOOD" COULDN'T GO UNANSWERED.
A COUPLE OF GUYS BEGAN TO CHUCKLE, THE REST OF US TRIED TO HIDE OUR SMILES. WE FIGURED KEVIN WAS IN A FIX NOW.
THE RULES WERE YOU HAD TO FIGHT NO MATTER WHAT THE ODDS WERE, BUT NONE OF US EXPECTED KEVIN TO FIGHT THIS MONSTER.
I WAS TRYING TO FIGURE OUT WHAT WAS GOING ON BECAUSE I DIDN'T FEEL THE TENSION IN THE AIR THAT USUALLY PRECEDED A VIOLENT CONFLICT.
LATER I REALIZED THAT WHILE THE GROUP HAD DECIDED NOT TO SANCTION KEVIN FOR WHAT WAS CONSIDERED A BREACH OF ETIQUETTE, NEITHER WOULD IT PROTECT HIM FROM THE CONSEQUENCES OF HIS OWN ACTIONS.
AND BESIDES, HE COULD HAVE JUST SHUT UP AND LET THE MAN LEAVE. SO KEVIN NOW HAD A FIGHT ON HIS HANDS--NO BIG DEAL.
KEVIN AND THE MAN WENT INTO THE STREET AND WITH MUCH CURSING AND FAN-FARE THE FIGHT BEGAN.

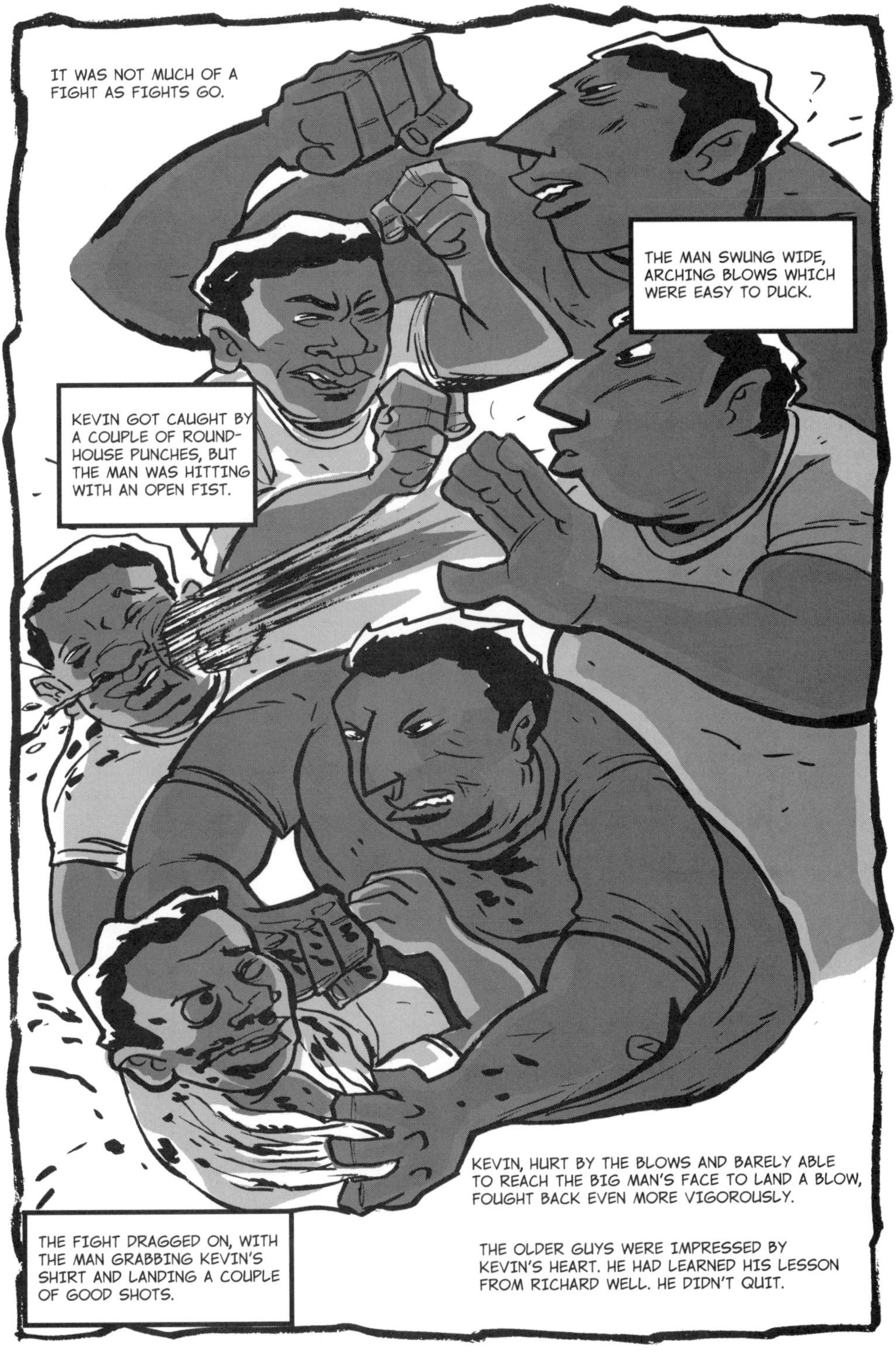

IT WAS NOT MUCH OF A FIGHT AS FIGHTS GO.
THE MAN SWUNG WIDE, ARCHING BLOWS WHICH WERE EASY TO DUCK.
KEVIN GOT CAUGHT BY A COUPLE OF ROUND-HOUSE PUNCHES, BUT THE MAN WAS HITTING WITH AN OPEN FIST.
KEVIN, HURT BY THE BLOWS AND BARELY ABLE TO REACH THE BIG MAN'S FACE TO LAND A BLOW, FOUGHT BACK EVEN MORE VIGOROUSLY.
THE FIGHT DRAGGED ON, WITH THE MAN GRABBING KEVIN'S SHIRT AND LANDING A COUPLE OF GOOD SHOTS.
THE OLDER GUYS WERE IMPRESSED BY KEVIN'S HEART. HE HAD LEARNED HIS LESSON FROM RICHARD WELL. HE DIDN'T QUIT.

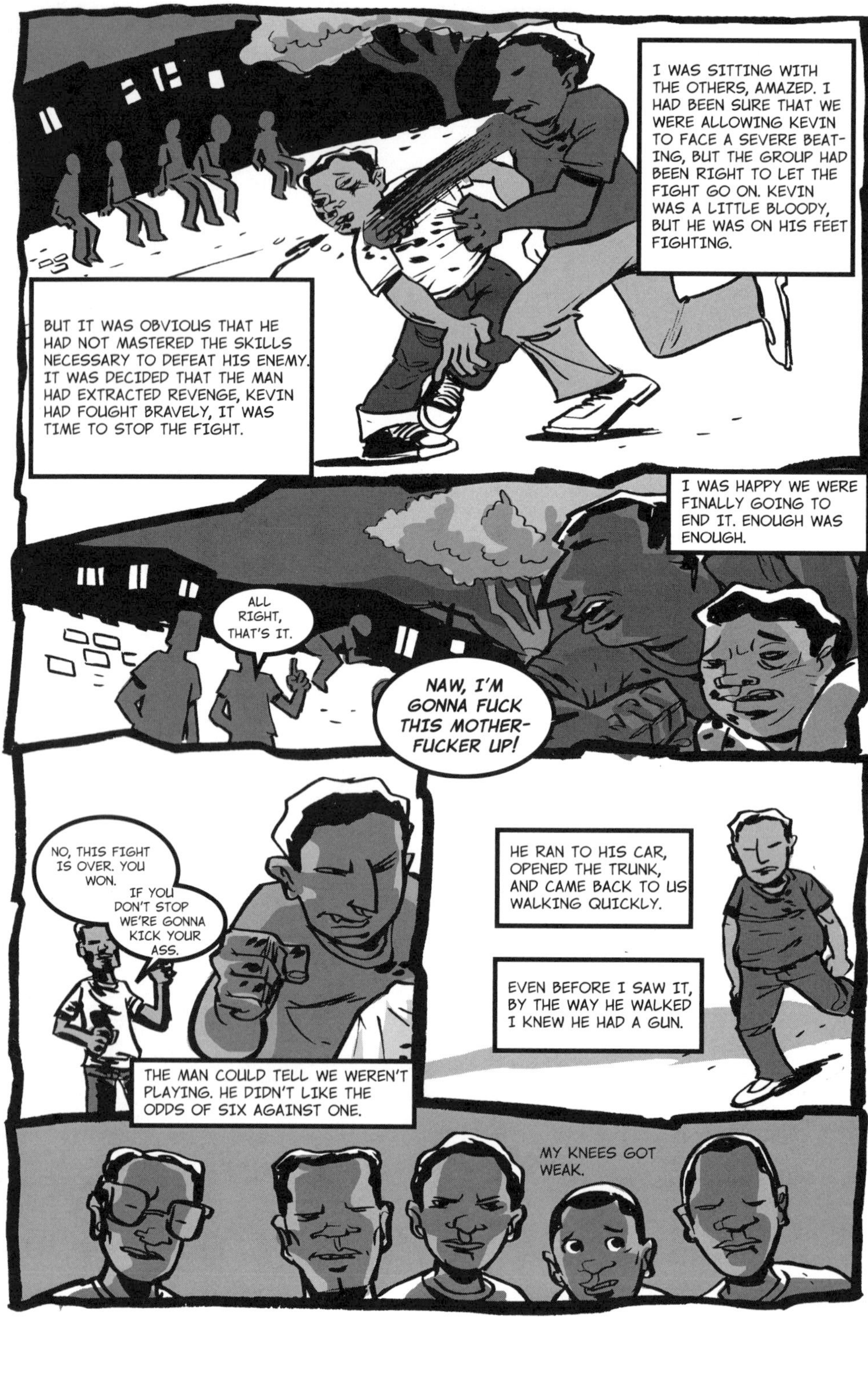

I WAS SITTING WITH THE OTHERS, AMAZED. I HAD BEEN SURE THAT WE WERE ALLOWING KEVIN TO FACE A SEVERE BEAT-ING, BUT THE GROUP HAD BEEN RIGHT TO LET THE FIGHT GO ON. KEVIN WAS A LITTLE BLOODY, BUT HE WAS ON HIS FEET FIGHTING.
BUT IT WAS OBVIOUS THAT HE HAD NOT MASTERED THE SKILLS NECESSARY TO DEFEAT HIS ENEMY. IT WAS DECIDED THAT THE MAN HAD EXTRACTED REVENGE, KEVIN HAD FOUGHT BRAVELY, IT WAS TIME TO STOP THE FIGHT.
I WAS HAPPY WE WERE FINALLY GOING TO END IT. ENOUGH WAS ENOUGH.
ALL RIGHT, THAT'S IT.
NAW, I'M GONNA FUCK THIS MOTHER-FUCKER UP!
NO, THIS FIGHT IS OVER. YOU WON.
IF YOU DON'T STOP WE'RE GONNA KICK YOUR ASS.
THE MAN COULD TELL WE WEREN'T PLAYING. HE DIDN'T LIKE THE ODDS OF SIX AGAINST ONE.
HE RAN TO HIS CAR, OPENED THE TRUNK, AND CAME BACK TO US WALKING QUICKLY.
EVEN BEFORE I SAW IT, BY THE WAY HE WALKED I KNEW HE HAD A GUN.
MY KNEES GOT WEAK.

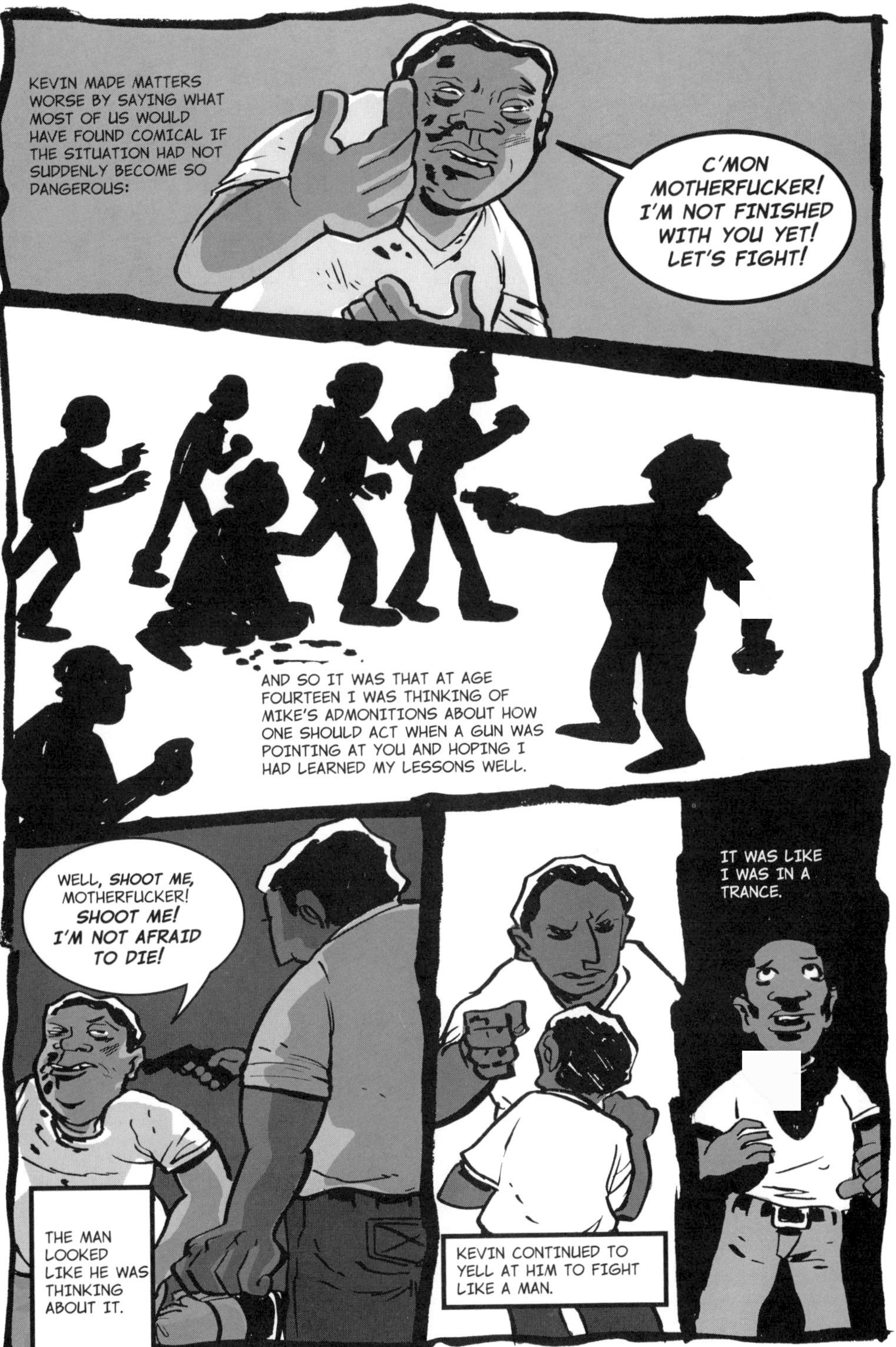
KEVIN MADE MATTERS WORSE BY SAYING WHAT MOST OF US WOULD HAVE FOUND COMICAL IF THE SITUATION HAD NOT SUDDENLY BECOME SO DANGEROUS:
C'MON MOTHERFUCKER! I'M NOT FINISHED WITH YOU YET! LET'S FIGHT!
AND SO IT WAS THAT AT AGE FOURTEEN I WAS THINKING OF MIKE'S ADMONITIONS ABOUT HOW ONE SHOULD ACT WHEN A GUN WAS POINTING AT YOU AND HOPING I HAD LEARNED MY LESSONS WELL.
WELL, SHOOT ME, MOTHERFUCKER! SHOOT ME! I'M NOT AFRAID TO DIE!
THE MAN LOOKED LIKE HE WAS THINKING ABOUT IT.
KEVIN CONTINUED TO YELL AT HIM TO FIGHT LIKE A MAN.
IT WAS LIKE I WAS IN A TRANCE.

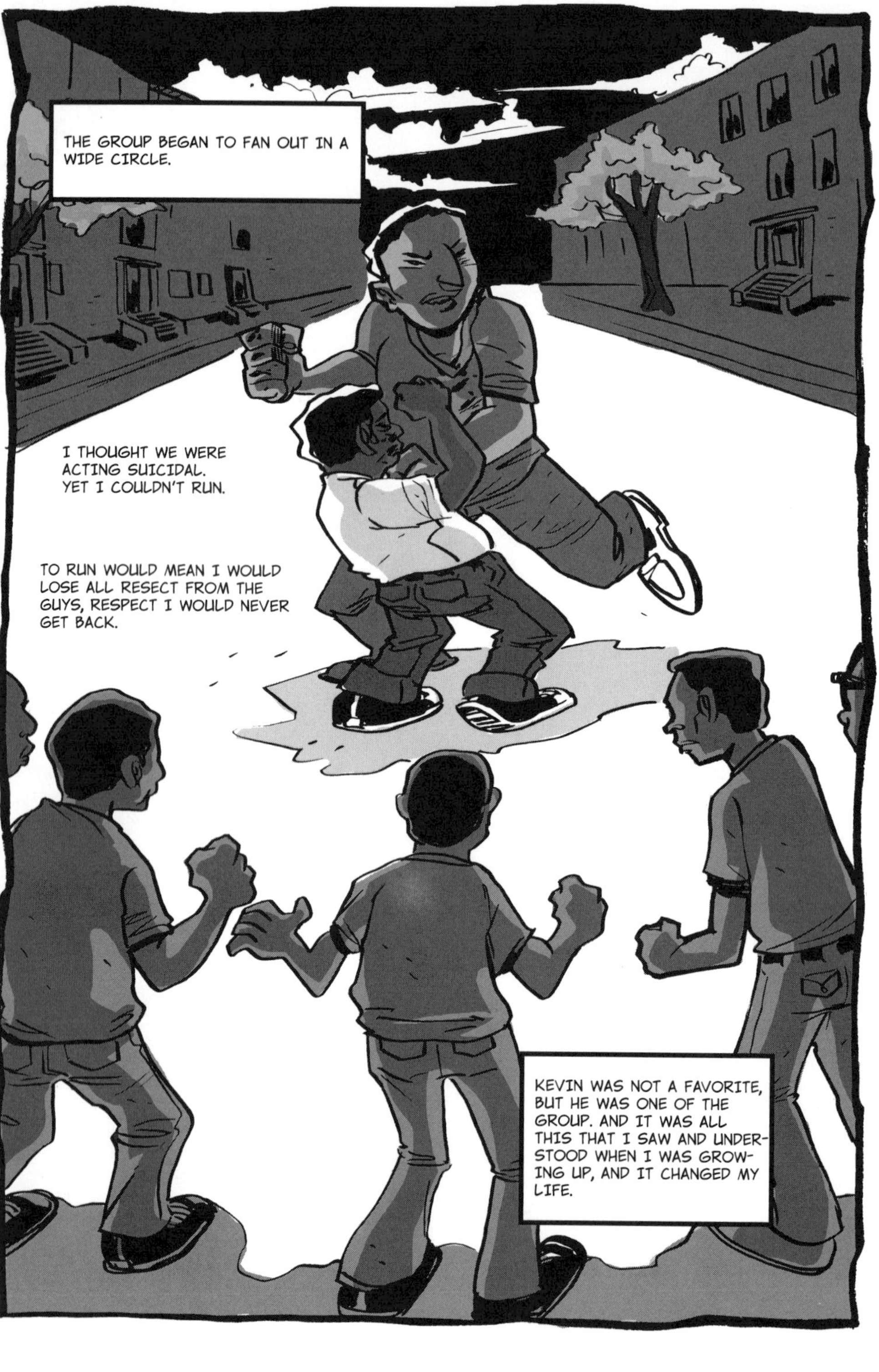
THE GROUP BEGAN TO FAN OUT IN A WIDE CIRCLE.
I THOUGHT WE WERE ACTING SUICIDAL. YET I COULDN'T RUN.
TO RUN WOULD MEAN I WOULD LOSE ALL RESECT FROM THE GUYS, RESPECT I WOULD NEVER GET BACK.
KEVIN WAS NOT A FAVORITE, BUT HE WAS ONE OF THE GROUP. AND IT WAS ALL THIS THAT I SAW AND UNDERSTOOD WHEN I WAS GROWING UP, AND IT CHANGED MY LIFE.

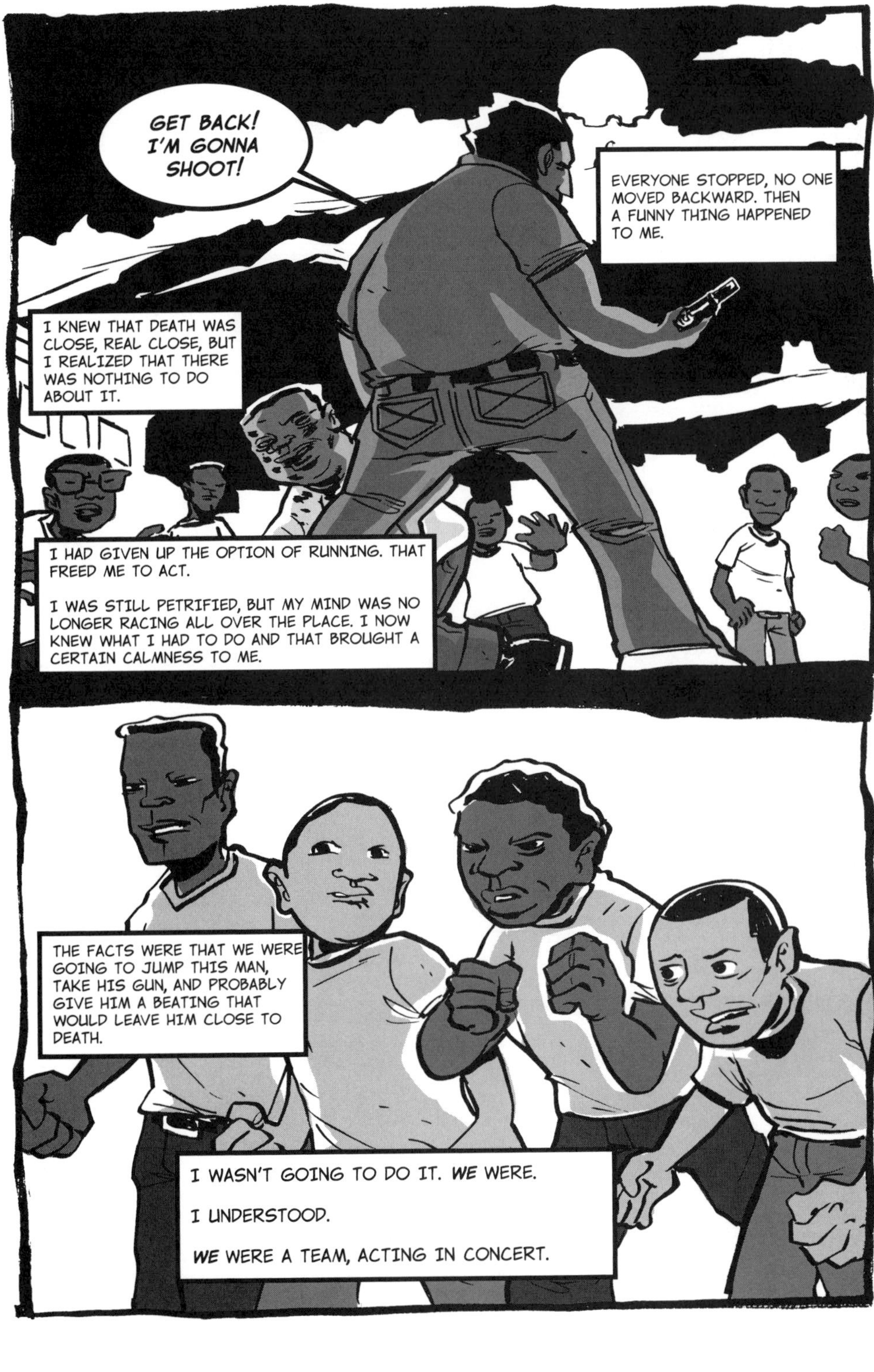
GET BACK! I'M GONNA SHOOT!
EVERYONE STOPPED, NO ONE MOVED BACKWARD. THEN A FUNNY THING HAPPENED TO ME.
I KNEW THAT DEATH WAS CLOSE, REAL CLOSE, BUT I REALIZED THAT THERE WAS NOTHING TO DO ABOUT IT.
I HAD GIVEN UP THE OPTION OF RUNNING. THAT FREED ME TO ACT.
I WAS STILL PETRIFIED, BUT MY MIND WAS NO LONGER RACING ALL OVER THE PLACE. I NOW KNEW WHAT I HAD TO DO AND THAT BROUGHT A CERTAIN CALMNESS TO ME.
THE FACTS WERE THAT WE WERE GOING TO JUMP THIS MAN, TAKE HIS GUN, AND PROBABLY GIVE HIM A BEATING THAT WOULD LEAVE HIM CLOSE TO DEATH.
I WASN'T GOING TO DO IT. *WE* WERE.
I UNDERSTOOD.
WE WERE A TEAM, ACTING IN CONCERT.

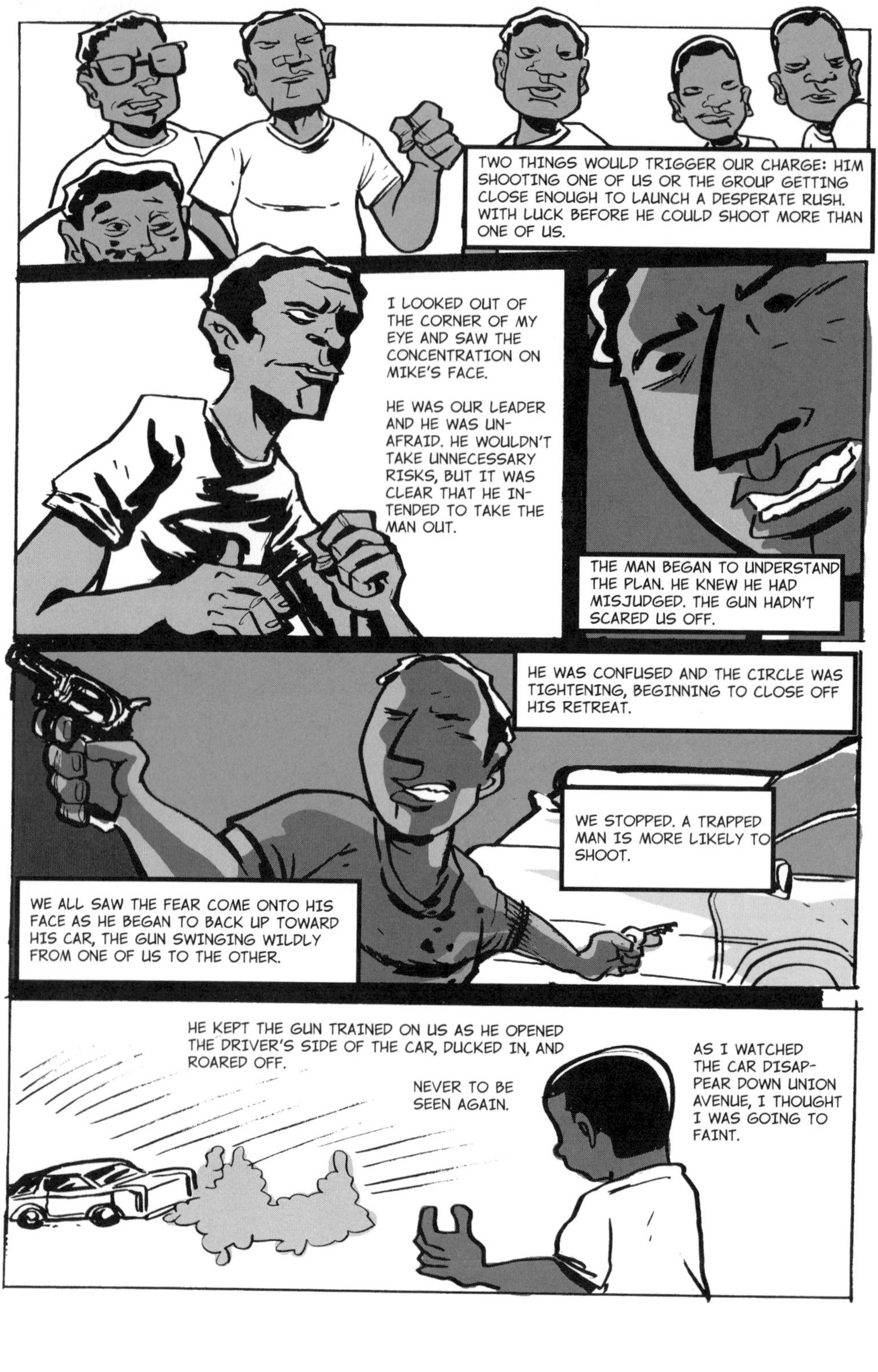
TWO THINGS WOULD TRIGGER OUR CHARGE: HIM SHOOTING ONE OF US OR THE GROUP GETTING CLOSE ENOUGH TO LAUNCH A DESPERATE RUSH. WITH LUCK BEFORE HE COULD SHOOT MORE THAN ONE OF US.
I LOOKED OUT OF THE CORNER OF MY EYE AND SAW THE CONCENTRATION ON MIKE'S FACE.
HE WAS OUR LEADER AND HE WAS UNAFRAID. HE WOULDN'T TAKE UNNECESSARY RISKS, BUT IT WAS CLEAR THAT HE INTENDED TO TAKE THE MAN OUT.
THE MAN BEGAN TO UNDERSTAND THE PLAN. HE KNEW HE HAD MISJUDGED. THE GUN HADN'T SCARED US OFF.
HE WAS CONFUSED AND THE CIRCLE WAS TIGHTENING, BEGINNING TO CLOSE OFF HIS RETREAT.
WE STOPPED. A TRAPPED MAN IS MORE LIKELY TO SHOOT.
WE ALL SAW THE FEAR COME ONTO HIS FACE AS HE BEGAN TO BACK UP TOWARD HIS CAR, THE GUN SWINGING WILDLY FROM ONE OF US TO THE OTHER.
HE KEPT THE GUN TRAINED ON US AS HE OPENED THE DRIVER'S SIDE OF THE CAR, DUCKED IN, AND ROARED OFF.
NEVER TO BE SEEN AGAIN.
AS I WATCHED THE CAR DISAPPEAR DOWN UNION AVENUE, I THOUGHT I WAS GOING TO FAINT.

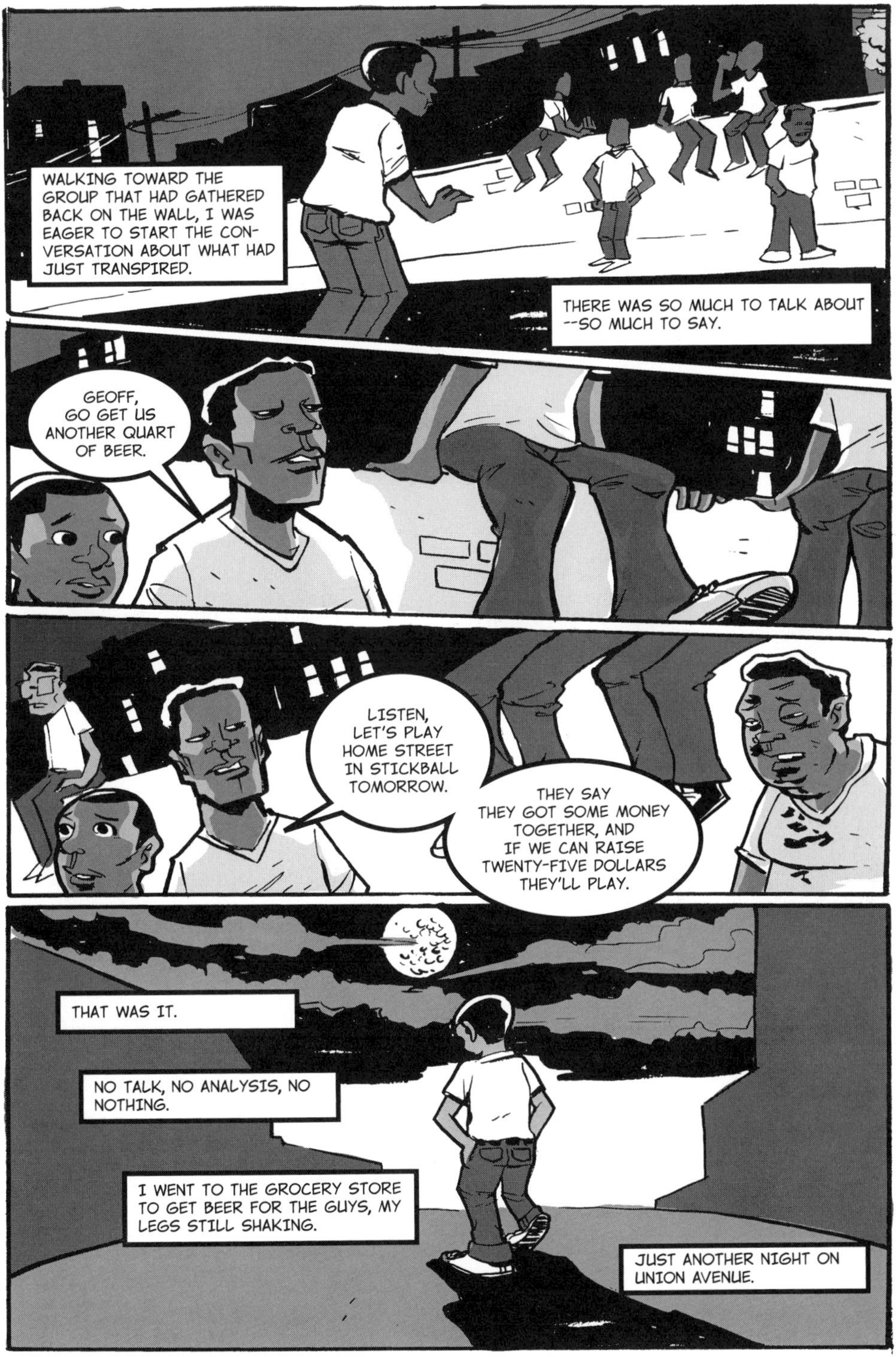
WALKING TOWARD THE GROUP THAT HAD GATHERED BACK ON THE WALL, I WAS EAGER TO START THE CON-VERSATION ABOUT WHAT HAD JUST TRANSPIRED.
THERE WAS SO MUCH TO TALK ABOUT --SO MUCH TO SAY.
GEOFF, GO GET US ANOTHER QUART OF BEER.
LISTEN, LET'S PLAY HOME STREET IN STICKBALL TOMORROW.
THEY SAY THEY GOT SOME MONEY TOGETHER, AND IF WE CAN RAISE TWENTY-FIVE DOLLARS THEY'LL PLAY.
THAT WAS IT.
NO TALK, NO ANALYSIS, NO NOTHING.
I WENT TO THE GROCERY STORE TO GET BEER FOR THE GUYS, MY LEGS STILL SHAKING.
JUST ANOTHER NIGHT ON UNION AVENUE.

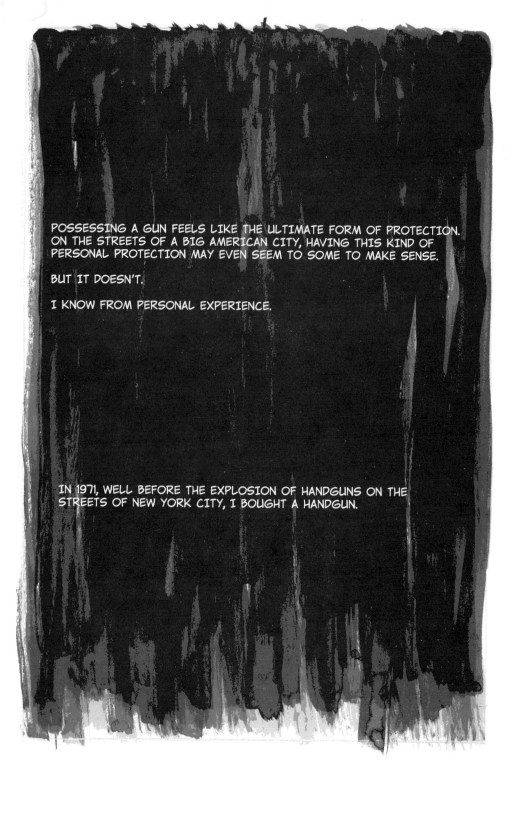

POSSESSING A GUN FEELS LIKE THE ULTIMATE FORM OF PROTECTION.
ON THE STREETS OF A BIG AMERICAN CITY, HAVING THIS KIND OF
PERSONAL PROTECTION MAY EVEN SEEM TO SOME TO MAKE SENSE.

BUT IT DOESN'T.

I KNOW FROM PERSONAL EXPERIENCE.

IN 1971, WELL BEFORE THE EXPLOSION OF HANDGUNS ON THE
STREETS OF NEW YORK CITY, I BOUGHT A HANDGUN.

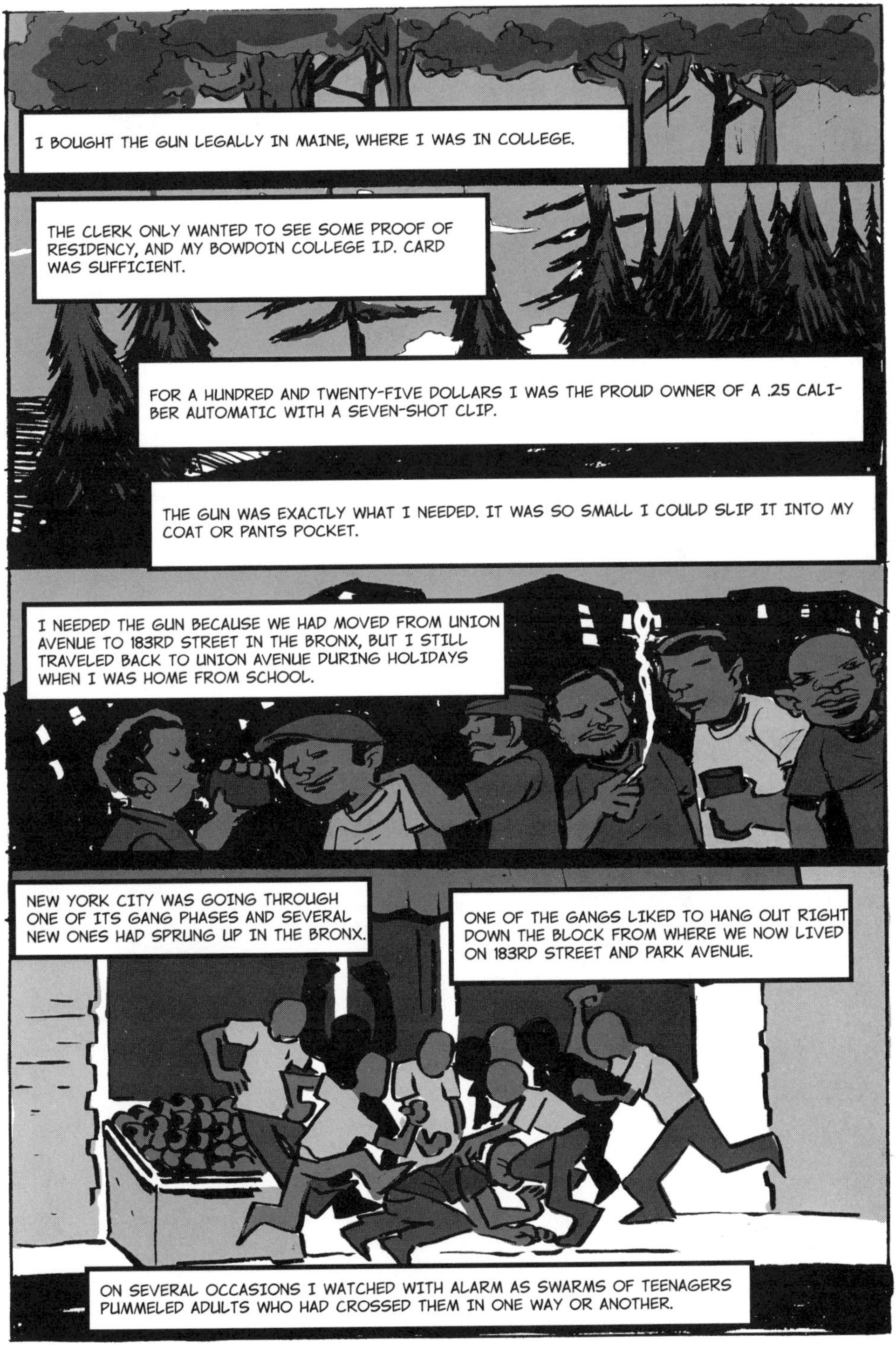
I BOUGHT THE GUN LEGALLY IN MAINE, WHERE I WAS IN COLLEGE.
THE CLERK ONLY WANTED TO SEE SOME PROOF OF RESIDENCY, AND MY BOWDOIN COLLEGE I.D. CARD WAS SUFFICIENT.
FOR A HUNDRED AND TWENTY-FIVE DOLLARS I WAS THE PROUD OWNER OF A .25 CALIBER AUTOMATIC WITH A SEVEN-SHOT CLIP.
THE GUN WAS EXACTLY WHAT I NEEDED. IT WAS SO SMALL I COULD SLIP IT INTO MY COAT OR PANTS POCKET.
I NEEDED THE GUN BECAUSE WE HAD MOVED FROM UNION AVENUE TO 183RD STREET IN THE BRONX, BUT I STILL TRAVELED BACK TO UNION AVENUE DURING HOLIDAYS WHEN I WAS HOME FROM SCHOOL.
NEW YORK CITY WAS GOING THROUGH ONE OF ITS GANG PHASES AND SEVERAL NEW ONES HAD SPRUNG UP IN THE BRONX.
ONE OF THE GANGS LIKED TO HANG OUT RIGHT DOWN THE BLOCK FROM WHERE WE NOW LIVED ON 183RD STREET AND PARK AVENUE.
ON SEVERAL OCCASIONS I WATCHED WITH ALARM AS SWARMS OF TEENAGERS PUMMELED ADULTS WHO HAD CROSSED THEM IN ONE WAY OR ANOTHER.

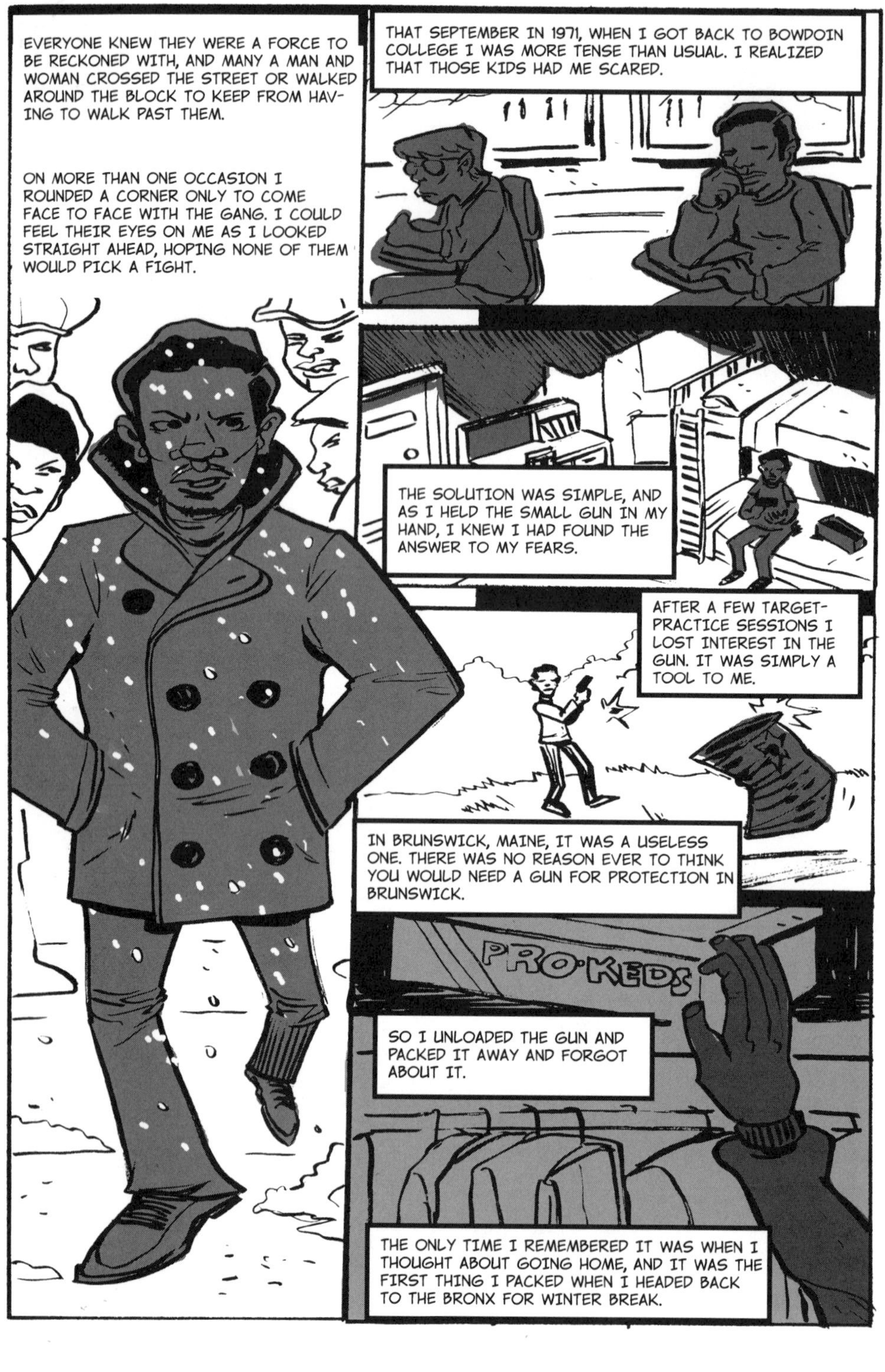
EVERYONE KNEW THEY WERE A FORCE TO BE RECKONED WITH, AND MANY A MAN AND WOMAN CROSSED THE STREET OR WALKED AROUND THE BLOCK TO KEEP FROM HAVING TO WALK PAST THEM.
ON MORE THAN ONE OCCASION I ROUNDED A CORNER ONLY TO COME FACE TO FACE WITH THE GANG. I COULD FEEL THEIR EYES ON ME AS I LOOKED STRAIGHT AHEAD, HOPING NONE OF THEM WOULD PICK A FIGHT.
THAT SEPTEMBER IN 1971, WHEN I GOT BACK TO BOWDOIN COLLEGE I WAS MORE TENSE THAN USUAL. I REALIZED THAT THOSE KIDS HAD ME SCARED.
THE SOLUTION WAS SIMPLE, AND AS I HELD THE SMALL GUN IN MY HAND, I KNEW I HAD FOUND THE ANSWER TO MY FEARS.
AFTER A FEW TARGET-PRACTICE SESSIONS I LOST INTEREST IN THE GUN. IT WAS SIMPLY A TOOL TO ME.
IN BRUNSWICK, MAINE, IT WAS A USELESS ONE. THERE WAS NO REASON EVER TO THINK YOU WOULD NEED A GUN FOR PROTECTION IN BRUNSWICK.
PRO-KEDS
SO I UNLOADED THE GUN AND PACKED IT AWAY AND FORGOT ABOUT IT.
THE ONLY TIME I REMEMBERED IT WAS WHEN I THOUGHT ABOUT GOING HOME, AND IT WAS THE FIRST THING I PACKED WHEN I HEADED BACK TO THE BRONX FOR WINTER BREAK.

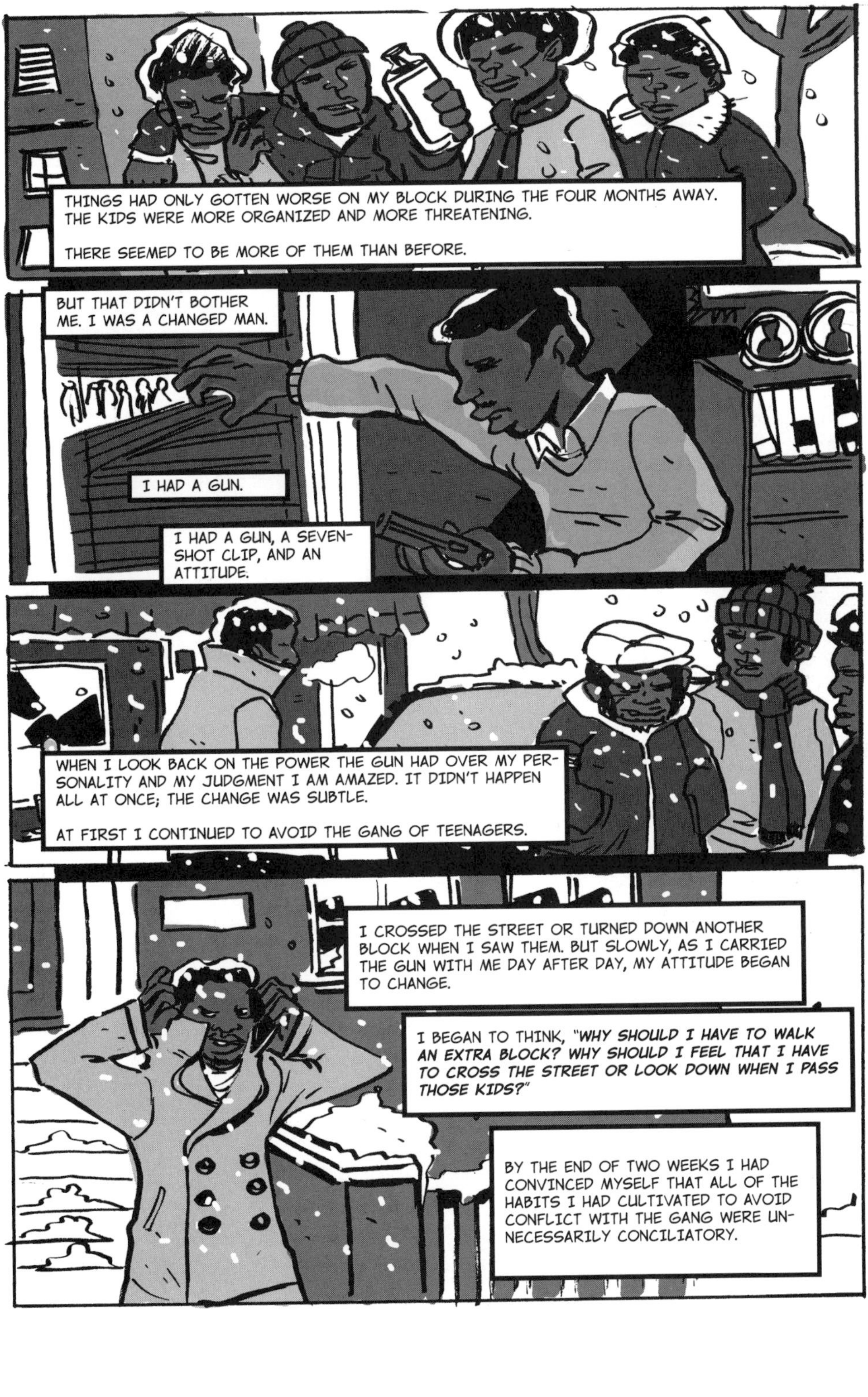
THINGS HAD ONLY GOTTEN WORSE ON MY BLOCK DURING THE FOUR MONTHS AWAY. THE KIDS WERE MORE ORGANIZED AND MORE THREATENING.
THERE SEEMED TO BE MORE OF THEM THAN BEFORE.
BUT THAT DIDN'T BOTHER ME. I WAS A CHANGED MAN.
I HAD A GUN.
I HAD A GUN, A SEVEN-SHOT CLIP, AND AN ATTITUDE.
WHEN I LOOK BACK ON THE POWER THE GUN HAD OVER MY PERSONALITY AND MY JUDGMENT I AM AMAZED. IT DIDN'T HAPPEN ALL AT ONCE; THE CHANGE WAS SUBTLE.
AT FIRST I CONTINUED TO AVOID THE GANG OF TEENAGERS.
I CROSSED THE STREET OR TURNED DOWN ANOTHER BLOCK WHEN I SAW THEM. BUT SLOWLY, AS I CARRIED THE GUN WITH ME DAY AFTER DAY, MY ATTITUDE BEGAN TO CHANGE.
I BEGAN TO THINK, ***"WHY SHOULD I HAVE TO WALK AN EXTRA BLOCK? WHY SHOULD I FEEL THAT I HAVE TO CROSS THE STREET OR LOOK DOWN WHEN I PASS THOSE KIDS?"***
BY THE END OF TWO WEEKS I HAD CONVINCED MYSELF THAT ALL OF THE HABITS I HAD CULTIVATED TO AVOID CONFLICT WITH THE GANG WERE UNNECESSARILY CONCILIATORY.

MY BEHAVIOR WHEN I WENT OUTSIDE BEGAN TO CHANGE. I STOPPED GOING OUT OF MY WAY, OR CROSSING THE STREET, OR AVOIDING EYE CONTACT WHEN I PASSED THE GANG. IN FACT I BEGAN TO DO THE OPPOSITE.

I WOULD CHOOSE TO GO TO THE GROCERY STORE ON THE SIDE OF THE STREET WHERE THE GANGS GATHERED. I WOULD WALK THROUGH THEM, HEAD UP, EYES CHALLENGING, HAND IN MY COAT POCKET, FINGER ON THE TRIGGER.

I WAS PREPARED TO SHOOT TO KILL TO DEFEND MYSELF.

MY RATIONALE WAS THAT I WAS MINDING MY OWN BUSINESS, NOT BOTHERING ANYONE, BUT I WASN'T GOING TO TAKE ANY STUFF FROM ANYONE. IF THEY DECIDED TO JUMP ME, WELL, THEY WOULD GET WHAT THEY DESERVED.

I WAS LUCKY THAT WINTER BREAK.

TIME QUICKLY CAME FOR ME TO GO BACK TO COLLEGE AND NO MEMBER OF THE GANG HAD FELT THE NEED TO CHALLENGE THE STRANGE YOUNG MAN WITH FIRE IN HIS EYES AND HIS HAND ALWAYS IN HIS COAT POCKET.

AWAY FROM THE MADNESS OF THE SOUTH BRONX, THE GUN AGAIN BECAME JUST ANOTHER USELESS ARTICLE FROM HOME THAT I WOULDN'T NEED UNTIL IT WAS TIME TO GO BACK.

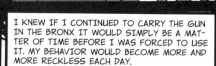

THE SERENITY OF MAINE HELPED ME THINK THROUGH THE TRANSFORMATION. THE SAME GUN, THE SAME PERSON, BUT A TOTALLY DIFFERENT RELATIONSHIP BETWEEN THE TWO DEPENDING ON THE ENVIRONMENT.

I KNEW IF I CONTINUED TO CARRY THE GUN IN THE BRONX IT WOULD SIMPLY BE A MATTER OF TIME BEFORE I WAS FORCED TO USE IT. MY BEHAVIOR WOULD BECOME MORE AND MORE RECKLESS EACH DAY.

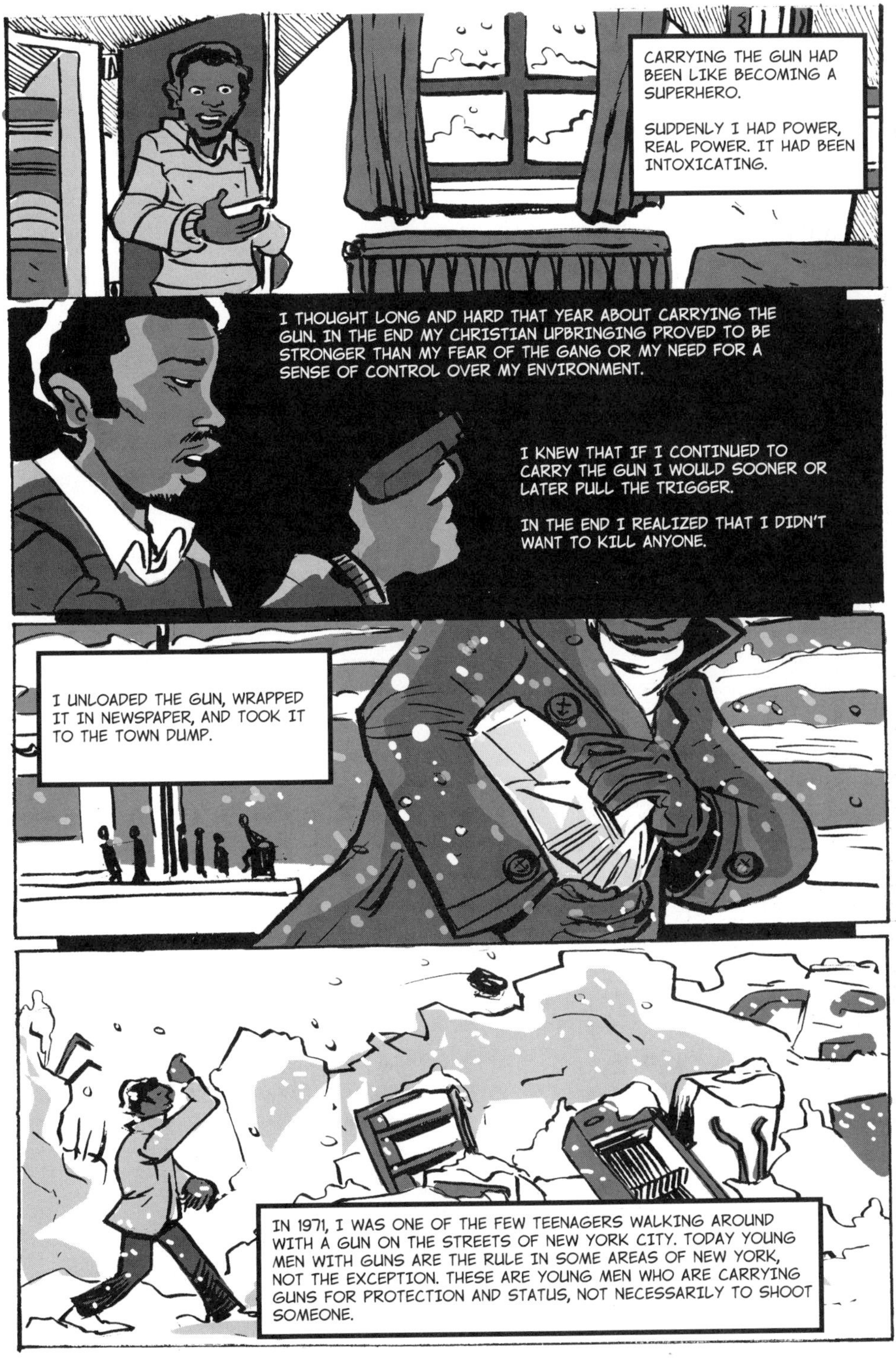
CARRYING THE GUN HAD BEEN LIKE BECOMING A SUPERHERO.
SUDDENLY I HAD POWER, REAL POWER. IT HAD BEEN INTOXICATING.
I THOUGHT LONG AND HARD THAT YEAR ABOUT CARRYING THE GUN. IN THE END MY CHRISTIAN UPBRINGING PROVED TO BE STRONGER THAN MY FEAR OF THE GANG OR MY NEED FOR A SENSE OF CONTROL OVER MY ENVIRONMENT.
I KNEW THAT IF I CONTINUED TO CARRY THE GUN I WOULD SOONER OR LATER PULL THE TRIGGER.
IN THE END I REALIZED THAT I DIDN'T WANT TO KILL ANYONE.
I UNLOADED THE GUN, WRAPPED IT IN NEWSPAPER, AND TOOK IT TO THE TOWN DUMP.
IN 1971, I WAS ONE OF THE FEW TEENAGERS WALKING AROUND WITH A GUN ON THE STREETS OF NEW YORK CITY. TODAY YOUNG MEN WITH GUNS ARE THE RULE IN SOME AREAS OF NEW YORK, NOT THE EXCEPTION. THESE ARE YOUNG MEN WHO ARE CARRYING GUNS FOR PROTECTION AND STATUS, NOT NECESSARILY TO SHOOT SOMEONE.

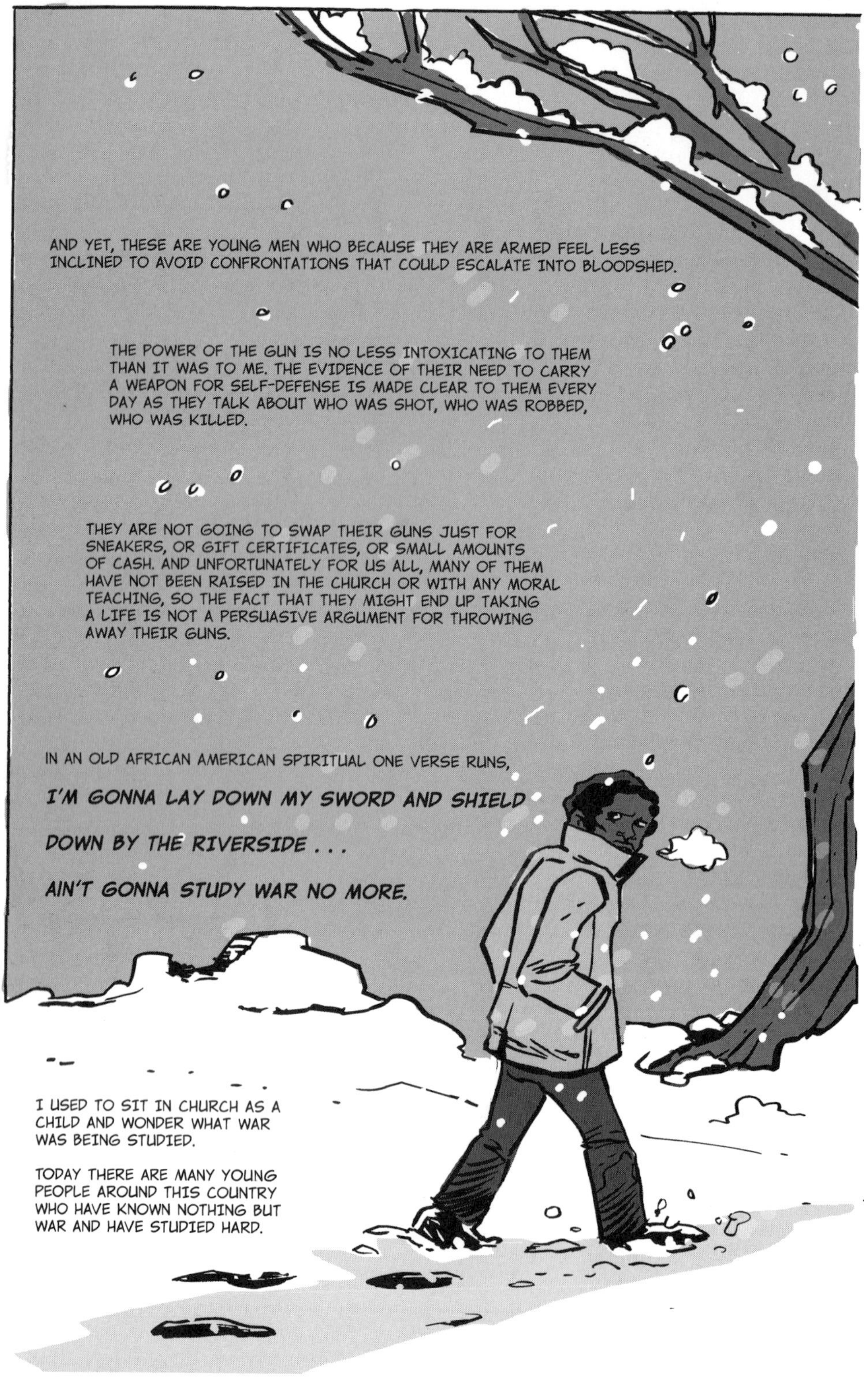
AND YET, THESE ARE YOUNG MEN WHO BECAUSE THEY ARE ARMED FEEL LESS INCLINED TO AVOID CONFRONTATIONS THAT COULD ESCALATE INTO BLOODSHED.
THE POWER OF THE GUN IS NO LESS INTOXICATING TO THEM THAN IT WAS TO ME. THE EVIDENCE OF THEIR NEED TO CARRY A WEAPON FOR SELF-DEFENSE IS MADE CLEAR TO THEM EVERY DAY AS THEY TALK ABOUT WHO WAS SHOT, WHO WAS ROBBED, WHO WAS KILLED.
THEY ARE NOT GOING TO SWAP THEIR GUNS JUST FOR SNEAKERS, OR GIFT CERTIFICATES, OR SMALL AMOUNTS OF CASH. AND UNFORTUNATELY FOR US ALL, MANY OF THEM HAVE NOT BEEN RAISED IN THE CHURCH OR WITH ANY MORAL TEACHING, SO THE FACT THAT THEY MIGHT END UP TAKING A LIFE IS NOT A PERSUASIVE ARGUMENT FOR THROWING AWAY THEIR GUNS.
IN AN OLD AFRICAN AMERICAN SPIRITUAL ONE VERSE RUNS,
I'M GONNA LAY DOWN MY SWORD AND SHIELD
DOWN BY THE RIVERSIDE . . .
AIN'T GONNA STUDY WAR NO MORE.
I USED TO SIT IN CHURCH AS A CHILD AND WONDER WHAT WAR WAS BEING STUDIED.
TODAY THERE ARE MANY YOUNG PEOPLE AROUND THIS COUNTRY WHO HAVE KNOWN NOTHING BUT WAR AND HAVE STUDIED HARD.

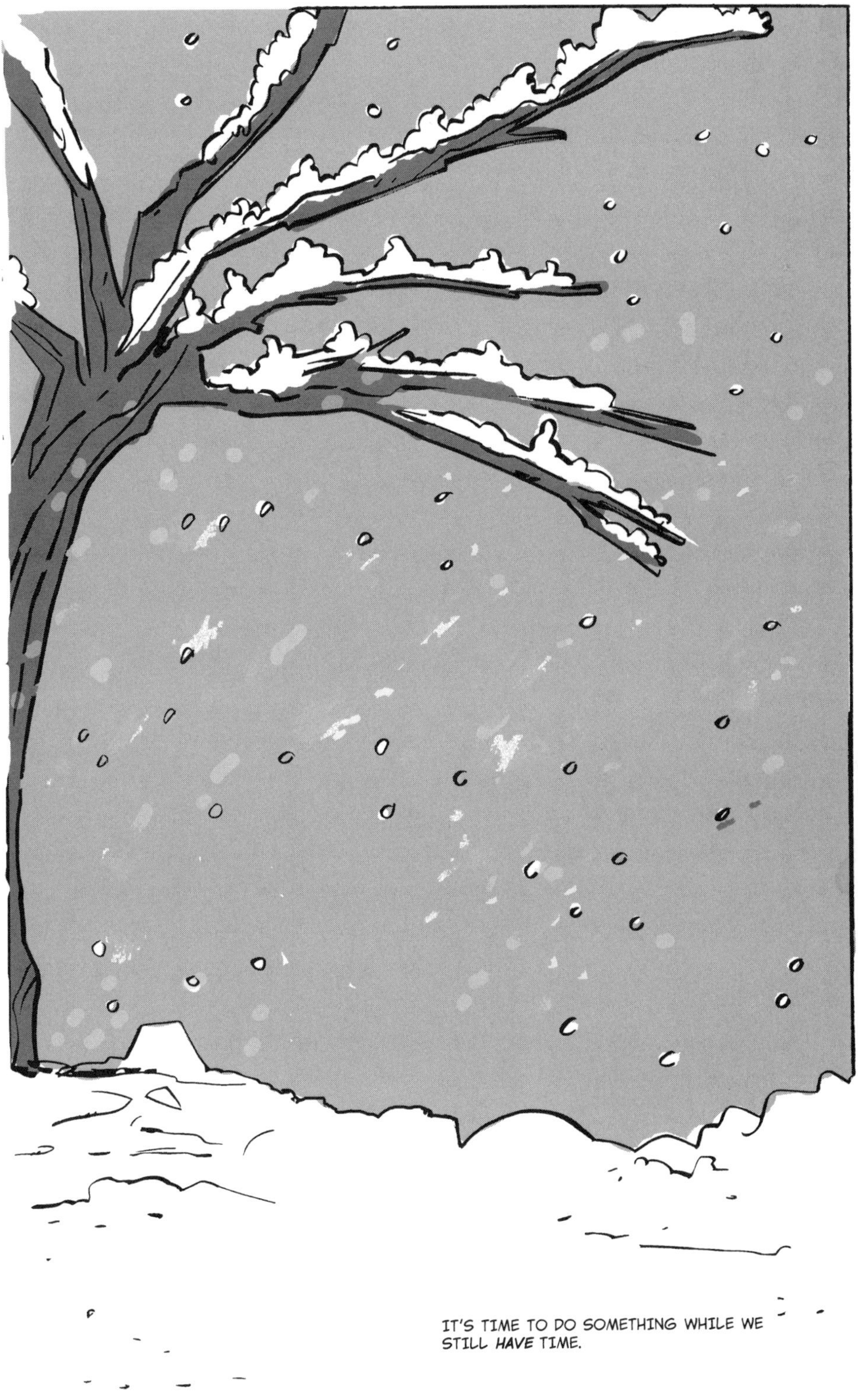
IT'S TIME TO DO SOMETHING WHILE WE STILL *HAVE* TIME.

EPILOGUE

America has long had a love affair with violence and guns. It's our history; we teach it to all of our young. The Revolution, the "taming of the West," the Civil War, the world wars, and on and on. Guns, justice, righteousness, freedom, liberty—all tied to violence. Even when we try to teach about nonviolence, we have to use the Reverend Dr. Martin Luther King Jr., killed by the violent. It is because most people in this country don't have to think about their personal safety every day that our society is still complacent about the violence that is engulfing our cities and towns.

While violence has been a factor in our slums and ghettos for decades, never has it been so deadly. I have spent the last twenty-six years working with poor, minority children from some of New York's most dangerous communities. Life is lived and lost on the streets. It really is getting worse. Too many guns, too much crack, too few jobs, so little hope. Some may think this violence is new, but it's not. Violence has always been around, usually concentrated amongst the poor. The difference is that when I was growing up, in the 1950s, '60s, and even '70s, we never had so many guns in our inner cities. The nature of the violent act has changed over these decades from the fist, stick, and knife to the gun.

Crack cocaine changed everything, seemingly overnight. As crack came on the scene in the very early eighties, no one seemed to be aware of the devastating influence it would have on our communities, especially on poor communities. As more and more children moved into drug sales, one of the first things they began to recognize was that they were in a dangerous business. And, slowly at first and then with more and more frequency, young people in and out of the drug trade began to arm themselves.

In 2009, the Children's Defense Fund reported that "almost nine children and teens die every day by gunfire—one every two hours and 45 minutes." The organization further noted, "Between 1979 and 2006, the yearly number of firearm deaths of White children and teens decreased by about 40 percent, but deaths of Black children and teens increased by 55 percent." And the gun manufacturers in their greed continue to pump more and more guns into our already saturated ghettos.

Young people in our inner cities know there is a war going on; millions have been accidentally or intentionally caught up in the many small battles that make up the war on America's streets. As the number of guns available to young people has increased, so have the odds that they will be shot in a confrontation. Most young people I know who carry guns do so for protection. Here you have tens of thousands of kids with guns, trying to protect themselves, but there are no clear rules to follow. I knew the codes of conduct were deteriorating when I heard young teenagers saying they'd "rather be judged by twelve than carried by six." The message on the street is clear: make a preemptive strike, shoot first. Odds are you'll live, and if you're arrested and then convicted at least you'll still be alive. We must come up with solutions that take into account that our children are armed for war, and that they will not put down their weapons until we can declare a cease-fire and bring an end to that war.

We will never convince them to give up their weapons with fancy television jingles or with marches alone. What these children need is a sense of safety, a certainty of surviving as they go to school or to the store. Schools in America are especially dangerous places. Intimidation, threats, and outright fights go on in classrooms, hallways, cafeterias, and schoolyards. Many children quickly learn that the teacher or principal might provide a sense of order when he or she is standing in front of you, but no one can really protect you in school except your fists and your friends. And this is one of the main problems with too many of our schools. When it comes to violence, school is too often the child's learning ground about the impotence of adult authority.

I returned to New York in 1983 with the experience of years of working with some of the toughest adolescents in Boston, degrees from Bowdoin and Harvard, and a recently earned black belt in tae kwon do. I was hired by the Rheedlen Center for Children and Families, founded by Richard L. Murphy in 1970 as a truancy prevention program for children. Over the years, Rheedlen's mission expanded with the expanding needs of poor children and their families, first to working with families, then to include an entire neighborhood. Known today as the Harlem Children's Zone, the organization I am now president and CEO of has grown to encompass almost 100 blocks and provides free programs that serve more than 10,000 children and more than 7,400 adults.

One of the answers to the plague of violence in America is the approach that the Harlem Children's Zone and other community-based organizations have taken. This problem cannot be solved from afar. The only way we are going to make a difference is by placing well-trained and caring adults in the middle of what can only be called a free-fire zone in our poorest communities. Children need to be able to look to adults for a sense of protection and security. Adults standing side by side with children in the war zones of America is the only way to turn this thing around.

When dealing with the issue of young people and violence in our country, it's clear that we can't separate violence from all of the other problems that plague our youth: educational failure, teenage pregnancy, drug and alcohol abuse, lack of employment, crime, HIV . . . The list goes on and on. We can't expect to make a difference unless we are willing to talk about comprehensive services for massive numbers of children and their families.

The Harlem Children's Zone is doing what it can. As I have traveled around this country, it has become clear to me that most communities don't offer even the inadequate range of services that we do. While nationally we have foolishly invested our precious resources in a criminal justice approach to solving our crime problem—including hiring more police and locking up more people for longer periods of time—we have nothing to show for it except poorer schools, poorer services for youth, and more people on the streets, unemployable because they have a criminal record.

The truth of the matter is that reducing the escalating violence in our country will be a complicated and costly endeavor. If we were fighting an outside enemy that was killing thousands of our children every year we would spare no expense in mounting the effort to subdue that enemy. What happens when the enemy is us? What happens when those American children are mostly black and brown? Do we still have the will to invest the time and resources in saving their lives? The answer must be yes, because the impact and fear of violence has overrun the boundaries of our ghettos and has both its hands firmly around the neck of our whole country. And while you may not yet have been visited by the spectre of death and fear of this new national cancer, just give it time. Sooner or later, unless we act, you will. We all will.

As an adult I have heard many times the argument about whether violence is part of the human makeup or a learned behavior. There is no way that I can buy the theory that humans have some genetic predisposition to violence. I know better. I remember clearly the time in my life when I knew nothing of violence and how hard I worked later to learn to become capable of it.

When I first found out that Superman wasn't real, I was about eight. I was talking to my mother who declared, "No, no, no. There's no Superman." I started crying because I really thought Superman was coming to rescue us from the chaos, the violence, the danger. No hero was coming.

Today, when the young people of the Harlem Children's Zone see me standing on the corner, watching out for them, they believe what children used to believe, what I used to believe as a child: that there are adults who can protect them. If we are to save our children, then we must become people they will look up to. Children need heroes now more than ever. Heroes give hope, and if these children have no hope they will have no future. We must stand up and be visible heroes, fighting for our children. I want people to understand the crisis that our children face, and I want people to act.

There are resources everywhere to help you become part of the solution, to take action. A good place to start would be on the Harlem Children's Zone Web site.

ACKNOWLEDGMENTS

GEOFFREY CANADA

When *Fist Stick Knife Gun* was first published as a book written with plain old words back in 1995, I dedicated it to my mother, Mary Canada, who worked tirelessly to provide for her children but still made time to pass on her love of reading and belief in the power of education. Reading and education saved my life. The debt of gratitude I owe my mother, plus the countless others who advanced my education—including the Harlem Children's Zone staff and community, Marian Wright Edelman, and my own children—can't be adequately expressed here. But I hope that their inspiration can be. I hope that the lifesaving power of education catches fire in your mind and that you do whatever you can, every day, to share that light with those who need it most: our nation's children. Their need couldn't be more desperate. And they have too few heroes.

JAMAR NICHOLAS

Thank you to Geoffrey Canada, for trusting me with your amazing story and for being a hero without the need of a cape. This project would not be possible if not for the love and support of the most important ladies in my life, Eula Nicholas and Darcy Russotto. Thanks also for the friendship and guidance of my family and friends, especially Michael Speranza, Kris Dresen, and Mike Manley, who have always helped me to hit higher notes using my creative voice. To Ben Harvey, for his assistance and eclectic iPod mixes. Special thanks to Beacon Press, in particular my editor Allison Trzop, who deserves a merit badge after directing me through this project. Also, P.J. Tierney, Bob Kosturko, Mandi Bleidorn, and the rest of Beacon's Production Department. I would like to dedicate this book to the memories of Lynn Gross, Jennifer Nicholas, and Mike Wieringo.

GEOFFREY CANADA

Patricia Lanza

In his many years with the Harlem Children's Zone, Geoffrey Canada has become nationally recognized for his pioneering work helping children and families in Harlem and as a passionate advocate for education reform. He is a graduate of Bowdoin College and the Harvard School of Education and the recipient of honorary degrees from Harvard University, Bowdoin College, Williams College, John Jay College, Bank Street College, and Meadville Lombard Theological Seminary. *U.S. News & World Report* named him one of "America's Best Leaders." The *New York Times Magazine* called the Harlem Children's Zone "one of the most ambitious social experiments of our time." Canada's work has been profiled on *60 Minutes*, *The Oprah Winfrey Show*, and *The Colbert Report*, as well as in the documentary *Waiting for "Superman"* and in articles for the *Wall Street Journal*, the *Washington Post*, and many other publications. A sixth-degree black belt, Canada is also the founder of the Chang Moo Kwan Martial Arts School, where he continues to teach violence-prevention methods and the principles of tae kwon do.

JAMAR NICHOLAS

Marc Manley

Jamar Nicholas is a Philadelphia-based artist and educator. He has dedicated his career to empowering young people, helping them to create their own comic books and cartoons, and has also taught and lectured on the topic of sequential art at several colleges, including Moore College of Art, Arcadia University, and the University of the Arts.